Inside the All Blacks

This edition is for the Consett Rugby Club in County Durham, maintaining traditional values with a progressive environment and, especially for Claire, John, and Vera O'Connor. It is also for John (rugby referee) and Mary in Texas, Gavin (Golden Oldie) in New South Wales and Jayne (All Black supporter) in Alberta. Special thanks to Penny McConnell.

Inside the All Blacks

Robin McConnell

CollinsWillow
An Imprint of HarperCollins*Publishers*

First published in 1998
by HarperCollins *Publishers (New Zealand)* Limited
PO Box 1, Auckland

This edition published in 1999
by CollinsWillow
an imprint of HarperCollins*Publishers*
London

A CIP catalogue record for this book
is available from the British Library

ISBN 0 00 218911 9

Printed and bound in Great Britain by
Clays Ltd, St Ives Plc

Contents

Foreword	7
Preface	10
1. Moving in with the men in black	11
2. Inside the black force (1):	
New Zealand v. Ireland, 6 June 1992	19
3. Inside the tradition: the All Black story	62
4. Life in the centre: the veteran All Black	96
5. The force of fifteen: forging a great team	103
6. Living with the legends: the All Black captains	119
7. Living with expectations: the All Black coach	144
8. Living with history: the Springbok rivalry	166
9. Up against the black jersey: the opposition speaks	189
10. Inside the black force (2):	
All Blacks v. Lions, 3 July 1993	201
11. Living with the All Blacks off the field	246
12. The tradition continues: a new All Black speaks	259
13. Living with the future: where to now in	
professional rugby?	268
14. The fourth World Cup era: the Hart-felt goal	275
Index	284

Foreword

I was All Black manager for the later period of Robin McConnell's research on rugby coaching and captaincy. One of my concerns was to ensure that the All Black team had its traditions respected and its privacy maintained. As a past All Black, I was aware of the need for public understanding of the high expectations the players place upon themselves and their commitment to playing in the black jersey, but I was also aware of the needs of the players to have their private lives and time-out from the intensity of test match preparation. Robin achieved that balance; he fitted well into the team environment, and at times his notes and ideas were utilised by team members. Being inside the All Blacks does give special understanding; after becoming the team's manager I gained new insights myself into Laurie's and Sean's leadership, and into their thoroughness and dedication to All Black rugby. As Robin found, and describes in this book, being alongside such players brings an appreciation of their abilities and their commitment to the mana of the black jersey.

The record of the two test weeks in this book conveys the focus and atmosphere of an All Black team build-up to a test match and clearly underlines the high standards that the team places upon itself and its awareness of the public expectations of the All Blacks. Past and present players will relate to these accounts.

Famous All Black captains have had an impact upon rugby and on New Zealand sport leadership (Wilson Whineray, for example, headed the Hillary Commission). Their views on All Black captaincy are clearly and frankly expressed, and make especially valuable reading for aspiring captains and coaches. This is the only time I have found the great captains' perspectives placed together like this for the rugby reader. While Wilson Whineray and Brian Lochore are completely different personalities — Whineray an academic and Lochore a down-to-earth farmer — their abilities to captain an All Black side at home and abroad were outstanding. They will always stand tall among the many renowned

All Black captains. Today's rugby followers will find many examples also of Sean Fitzpatrick's outstanding qualities and leadership in the test week chapters.

I have enormous regard for Fred Allen's coaching and am pleased to see him acknowledged in this book. Fred had a distinctive approach, and has continued to show in his later years an ability to analyse the game and provide relevant coaching points to players up to the present. Fred followed the coaching philosophy of Vic Cavanagh, the outstanding coach from Otago. While I never met Vic myself, over the years I heard Fred and many others speak of his exceptional ability. The qualities of good rugby coaching that Robin McConnell has drawn into his writing here, from his interviews and surveys, are of practical value to all coaches. Coaching is not easy, but coaches are so often the targets of a keen rugby public!

I have played in great All Black teams, and these have a special quality that players recognise but which are difficult to describe. Many factors make up a team, factors common both to the workplace and to the sports field. This book provides realistic insights into teams, such as the examples of Laurie Mains' detailed long-term planning, with Earle Kirton and Peter Thorburn, for the All Blacks' development through to the 1995 World Cup. Rugby today demands skilled management at the top levels.

I have always regarded the New Zealand–South Africa tests as the pinnacle of All Black rugby. I was particularly interested in the perspectives of Springbok opponents in this chapter, and rugby followers will enjoy the past players' insights into these tests. Selection for a test against South Africa is similar to being selected for the Olympics if you are an athlete. On the field there is no concession, but off the field the friendships have been lasting.

In 1994, while fulfilling my role as All Black manager — and with the help of the South African manager, Jannie Engelbrecht — I organised a get-together with both teams at the Springbok hotel after the game. It was a huge success, with many players saying they had never before had such an opportunity to meet with the opposition on a social basis, as was the case in the sixties when Jannie and I played.

Rugby in New Zealand today faces special challenges. Informed discussion and debate on our rugby is needed, and while I do not always agree with Robin's views, I am pleased to note that he raises the issue of club rugby. Club and rural rugby must be considered by the administrators as they provide a special dimension of the game in New Zealand, and we must protect our grassroots.

I am pleased to commend this book, as it provides new insights into All Black rugby. It gives the rugby reader a better understanding of the intensity and interaction that lead up to a test match, and is a valuable addition to the writing on rugby coaching and captaincy. The opponents' perspectives on All Black rugby and the overview of All Black–South Africa tests use players' voices to add interest and understanding. The real strength of the book is that it realistically increases understanding of the All Blacks' story, past and present, but avoids sensationalism.

The lasting impressions that I have from reading this book are not only the reinforcement of All Black rugby's special place in New Zealand life, and in world rugby, but the friendships and valued experiences that the sport can bring. I enjoyed the book and the memories and considerations it stimulates, and believe it offers a valuable picture of All Black rugby.

Colin Meads
April 1998

Preface

A book on the life of a great team draws sustenance from its subjects. I lived with some 240 New Zealand rugby players and coaches in their 1920s–1990s deeds and memories and 1992–95 test match realities. Their support was unique in the world of first-hand sport research. The acceptance of my presence by the Mains-Fitzpatrick All Blacks is warmly acknowledged. That team began the second 100 years of the New Zealand Rugby Football Union and reshaped international rugby. My gratitude to Laurie Mains and Sean Fitzpatrick (and Neil Gray and Colin Meads) is enduring.

The formal result of this experience is recorded in my University of Waikato doctoral thesis. In this book some informant All Black names, past and present, have been omitted at their request or because identification is not essential to the point they make. Similarly, some All Black codes or special moves have been renamed. Errors of interpretation of play or emphasis are the writer's.

The financial assistance of Steinlager and PSM Holdings for my doctoral research is acknowledged with appreciation. My personal thanks go to all those who gave of their time and knowledge — both All Blacks and opponents.

Robin McConnell

1

Moving in with the men in black

Dear Laurie,
I am undertaking research on élite team leadership for my doctor of phi-
losophy degree and have a particular focus upon rugby coaching and
captaincy at the highest levels. I have met with Neil and Sean and am
writing to ask if you would consider my observing the All Blacks' team
leadership in the actual environment of match week realities . . .

Love it, hate it or try to be indifferent to it, rugby union football shapes New Zealand social history and everyday life. It dominates the media, sets the mood of Monday's post-test workplace, and makes the All Blacks fifteen black-garbed icons for much of the country. Test match myths mutate into facts 'known' to the populace and Grizz, Pinetree, JK, Fitzy and Jonah are spoken of with never a surname required. Life and death still run second to major All Black happenings.

I grew up on a small farm with its own home-made manuka and gumtree goal posts. School mates biked out from Feilding on rural roads to play footy in our paddock. In school assembly we listened to a touring match on contraband radios and relayed the unfolding score along the sixth form rows. Every club had a provincial representative. Every rep team had an All Black. And every one of my rugby minded friends dreamed of being an All Black. Cricket called me in such a way until a knee injury stopped my progress. In both team sports the role and decisions of coach and captain have long held a special fascination for me. Eventually, as an adult academic working in sport and leadership, I developed the doctoral study goal of observing leadership in New Zealand's ultimate team — the All Blacks.

Consequently, the 1993 All Blacks changing room at Eden Park was a good place to be. The Lions had finally been decisively defeated in the third test, Australia had been put away at Carisbrook, the mercurial Western Samoans had been stretched beyond their resources, and I was an integral part of it all. The year before, it had been Ireland and, a year later, it would be the South African series win, then the glitch of Gregan's tackle in Sydney. However, for the present, I was content to grin with Dowdy, play a little guitar at Zinny's command, and share the team's relief that the series task was done. Players wearily packed ice onto injuries, the concrete floor was splattered with remnants of tape, the All Black coach was moving around his players, guys sat slumped on the wall seats with their heads between their knees, Michael was already moving slowly to the showers, Doc Bowen was checking a forward's head cut, the manager was having a word with the liaison officer, cans were being opened . . . and I was still taking notes.

Until 1992 and the new era of All Black coach Laurie Mains and captain Sean Fitzpatrick no outsider had been accepted into this national team to share their zealously guarded environment. In the 100 years of the New Zealand Rugby Football Union, and almost 90 years of its iconic national team bearing the All Blacks name, there had been no extended first-hand research carried out observing them, or any other international sport team for that matter. My presence provided inside-the-team understandings of leadership roles, team development and related fields such as goal setting, motivation and team culture. To my friends, to my students, and to acquaintances encountered in the rugby world, I had somehow ended up in the dream realm for sport researchers and rugby fans, studying the All Blacks from the inside.

The All Blacks had long been held up as a model of success. Their leaders — coaches and captains — had been recognised with public awards and favourable career prospects. We recognise the impact of the All Blacks team upon rugby at all lower levels, and also their linkages with the corporate world. I wondered why we didn't learn more about how that élite team is led, coached and trained in all aspects of its test match week realities. How does the team come together for such a critical game? Does the game plan work? Is the All Black tradition a myth?

Other questions also niggled away at me, demanding answers. Did the All Black coach rant and rave, as in the world of fiction writers and some public minds? Was the captain a dour veteran, typical of sexist rugby stereotypes and New Zealand male stolidity? Were the All Blacks an élite and self-contained group full of their own importance? What did their team leaders really *do*?

A warm reception

The early stages of my work included interviews with past All Blacks to establish a background picture of coaching and captaincy. These were to continue for much of the six-year study: talks with great players and those of fleeting fame alike, with present-day household rugby names and those from unfamiliar and bygone years. No request for an interview was ever declined. Typical of the past players I was to meet were such diverse characters as: Craig McKenzie, who described playing with Bert Cooke and Mark Nicholls and later wrote a biography of Walter Nash; Jack Griffiths, who brought the intensity and escape of wartime rugby into focus; the olde world courtesy of the gentlemanly Alf Waterman, who recounted Cliff Porter's team talks, and the experience of touring with George Nepia; Kevin Skinner and Ian Clarke, who were unfailingly helpful; and the irrepressible Bill Hadley. I also listened to the traumatic experiences of some recent short-term All Blacks, observations and reflections from the acknowledged great skippers, and experienced warm hospitality from Invercargill to Kaitaia. I encountered All Blacks in tears as a result of emotive recollections and repressed feelings, and wives who, upon hearing their once black-jerseyed husbands reveal past happenings, said, 'You never told me that!'

From Ron Ward in the far south, through a privileged lunch with the Saxtons, West Coast warmth from the Mumms and on to Guy Bowers and Bill Clark in the Nelson area, there was unfailing hospitality by South Island All Blacks of the 1930s, 1940s, and all later decades. The 1935–36 All Blacks and 1945–46 Kiwis became special teams as the bulk of their players unfolded their interwoven stories. In the North Island there was a barbecue and paua gathering with Graham Mourie; ongoing support from the inimitable Fred Allen; the prison ministering of Nev MacEwan; and the incomparable Hughie McLean's room at the Ranfurly War Veterans' Home. A number of 1990s All Blacks became more than acquaintances. I carry a rare debt of gratitude — not because these men were All Blacks but because they were unfailingly welcoming, responsive and good to be with. Many of their stories are still retained in the privacy of their sharing and my notebook. Their deeds, however, are inscribed in memories and on varied fields of New Zealand, and foreign winters.

The state of play in 1992

The interview of a past All Black captain, Andy Leslie, led to an invitation to observe the Wellington team he coached. This helped establish my credibility and acceptance within the élite rugby world. Interviews with Sean Fitzpatrick and the 1992 All Black team manager, Neil Gray, led to their tentative support for my observing the All Black captain and coach — 'But it's all up to Laurie.' Interviews with Peter Thorburn and Earle Kirton, the All Black selectors, followed and then came the pivotal first meeting in Dunedin with the All Black coach. As with each interview I prepared thoroughly, becoming completely familiar with the interviewee's rugby tenure and later career. The portents were not promising. At his Profile Buildings business office Mains tersely informed me, 'I've got twenty minutes.' Great! Thanks Laurie, given my travel expenses, that's costing me over twenty bucks a minute! Mains saw more depth in my questions than he expected and I quickly appreciated his thoughtful responses. We established a rapport and I consequently wrote formally asking if I could observe him and Sean Fitzpatrick in the team context. Mains' agreement opened the prospects of a unique research environment. He was to reflect later:

> We wanted to present a new face for the All Blacks. Too often they had become an enclosed group and forgot that, in a real sense, they belonged to New Zealand. If the guys intimated at any time, however, that they did not want the researcher's presence, I would have knocked the study on the head. I also thought there might be some value in having a relatively objective perspective on what we were doing, which might give us some things to think about. It seemed to me that top-level coaching could gain from a study which examined the realities of coaching. Sean's acceptance was critical. I don't think Neil really thought I would agree to having you around!

Mains had moved through club coaching ranks to be a successful coach with the provincial Otago team, before his All Black coaching appointment.

> With the Otago team I had gone through a learning process as a coach. In 1988 we played the Australian Barbarians and ACT in the wet. I recall making the statement, 'I've just seen the way rugby should be played.' It was the turning point in my coaching career. I developed this vision of rugby. The loose forwards were the key to this vision, the joiners, the creators of the unity. It all suddenly happened in Sydney and I had this

vision of where rugby should be going. It was a marvellous year's rugby. We didn't have a pack that could give us dominance in the tight five. I'd always been a believer that loose forwards were the key to the game and I always studied loose forward formations. In Otago we had a really distinctive loose forward pattern . . . we had to be 100 per cent technically correct, play the game at pace, and have continuity. It was critical to have the loose forwards linking with the backs, have very specific lines in the defensive pattern, to run the ball and to create opportunities by using the loose ball or creating a blindside where you break ground and feed the loosies . . . I think I changed my approach quite dramatically, selecting players with athletic skills to make rugby faster and more attractive. In 1989 we were devastated by injuries, we came second in 1990 and then won the national championship in 1991. In that last year I reckoned you could play all-out attacking rugby without compromising defence. Apart from creating lines, with the resultant tackles and turnover for attack, or creating an overlap, the players are using their natural abilities and creating an attitude in their minds. Earle Kirton had basically formed the same ideas on loose forward play.

When I looked at the All Black selectors in 1991, I developed more self-belief. Otago were playing well, I got informal comments from senior All Blacks and it suddenly dawned on me that I could do an All Black selector's job well. I thought that would be good, a couple of days here and a couple of days there . . . !

A couple of days here and there in the All Black selector role? Hey Laurie, get real in the rugby world! Over my three years of participant observation with All Blacks, through test match weeks, selection committee meetings, successive interviews of Mains and Fitzpatrick, and the analysis of documents provided by administrators and teams, I was to observe a virtual full-time commitment by the national coach. This was mirrored in the demands upon the time of Thorburn and Kirton, Mains' fellow selectors and associated coaches, who also suffered severe losses of occupational income when involved in their rugby duties. Along with Lyn Colling they were the final group of selectors in New Zealand's amateur rugby era. Thorburn, who had been a committed player as a provincial No. 8, brought a particular objectivity and range of perspectives to the selection team, often reflecting his innovative coaching with the North Harbour team and his business world acumen. The mercurial Kirton, known for his expansive play as an All Black first-five eighth for 48 matches in the 1963–70 period, was forever marked in the public's collective mind by his voluminous scarf and ever-present cigar. Earle's appearance belied an incisive and inventive rugby mind which had been illustrated in his coaching of London and Wellington teams. For the later part of the Mains era, the NZRFU replaced Thorburn with a past All Black, Lyn Colling. Lyn had a skilled and analytical eye, on halfbacks particularly, and gained a different perspective on New Zealand rugby administration during his term. Technically, the Mains-Kirton-Colling trio worked assiduously, but the personal chemistry and rugby philosophy was different from that of the original selectorial group.

Following this era the brief Mains-Kirton-Cooper selectorial trio preceded the Hart-Cooper-Hunter trio who took Mains' team to a new level of consistency. This latter regime of professional rugby kept Mains' 1995 Innovators virtually intact, drew upon a small number of new All Blacks selected or foreshadowed by the 1995 selectors, and utilised greater levels of support from the NZRFU. This support for John Hart included an increased number of players in a touring team, full-time coach and manager appointments, and more insightful appointments of support staff.

At the start of my All Black research in 1992, the new selectors were faced with picking a national team to play a World XV in a series of 'tests' to mark the centenary of the New Zealand Rugby Football Union. Never noted in their respective playing and coaching careers for blind acquiescence to the expectations of others, the trio drew up their new vision for All Black rugby through to the New Zealand team requirements for the 1995 World Cup. From this vision they outlined their requirements for the players who would produce the goods. Big name players were discarded if they were not seen as fitting the new ethos, and national reputations had to be won back by others. The most prominent casualty of the former was the previous season's All Black captain, Gary Whetton; Grant Fox was to prove an example, par excellence, of the latter. Other players, such as John Kirwan, were to prove valuable in the transition but not see out the new era. Some, once seen as Auckland All Blacks, a rather derogatory tag, were to reveal new dimensions of playing greatness. Significantly triumphant in this group was to be Zinzan Brooke.

The challenge of acceptance

At speaking engagements, the first questions I am asked about being inside the All Black camp are invariably, 'What did you expect?' or 'What were they like?' The day the All Black coaches agreed to my participant observation suddenly brought home the challenge of acceptance. Jeez! Will the team accept me being there? How will they treat me? To be accepted by the subjects in participant observation research is critical. The only All Black I had known previously was an old friend, Neil Thimbleby, who had toured South Africa with Brian Lochore's 1970 team. There were also practicalities of leave and travel to sort out. Thank God for a university's mid-semester breaks! If I was unable to observe virtually all of the coach and captain roles in action then would it all be worth it? Ideally, I would want to observe behaviour in the dressing room, attend team talks, suss out the game plan, talk with players, obtain Sean's and Laurie's views and be with the players whenever their coach and/or captain was interacting with them, plus learn how players saw the roles of All Black coach and captain.

It was asking a lot! I was conscious of the need to dress and behave so as to fit in with the team environment inconspicuously, and also the importance of taking full notes. I could not escape the reality that these were All Blacks — the ultimate group in the country. I expected a polite reception from the guys but a clear space between them and myself, and perhaps some indication of players putting up with my presence simply because the team bosses had approved my being there. My fears were unfounded. From the first encounter with the team I was made welcome. The players were pleasant, task-focused, aware of the unique mana of the All Blacks and concerned to meet individual and team standards. Each one was friendly and accepting of my presence. Over eight test match weeks and three years, I was in the All Black team room, sat in on team talks, blended in at training, participated in 'court sessions', travelled on the bus to the test ground, was present in the team changing room, attended test match dinners and parliamentary receptions, and participated in the team's social occasions. I was also fortunate to be part of certain aspects of All Black team life in which not all team members could participate. The captain, for example, has traditionally held a 'player only' meeting on the night before a test match, which usually takes place in the Team Room or his motel room. The coach, manager and team officials have traditionally been excluded. I was included in these occasions. Similarly, when the national selectors met to consider test or touring teams they made me welcome as an observer and recorder. In the periods between tests, and over the summer, I would press on with other parts of the research, meet with players and team leaders for interviews, and keep in touch by telephone with the coach and captain.

The basic test week has not changed. The build up is as in previous years, with some inevitable changes, but the test-match day, with its pattern and rituals, still continues. There is still a sustaining All Black tradition and pride, although it is tinged at times with sponsors' demands, NZRFU expectations for a cash-flow and the players' shift of focus under professionalism.

What did I record? Wherever I was I would make notes on the coach or captain. Take a team meeting: Whom do the guys sit with? To whom does the coach speak? Who asks this question? What is the pattern here? Who emerge as team leaders? What is the input of the veteran players? Is the game plan clear? How is it built up? How do players contribute? Which players will I later interview to see how they saw the session? What does Fitzpatrick say in the meeting? Who seeks clarification of any points? How are new players included? Who volunteers comments? How does the meeting link with training and the test on Saturday? What do the guys do in any spare time?

The openness of Mains and Fitzpatrick was the key to my being inside the All Blacks. Nothing was ever provided with reservations — the judgement of what to record was mine. The players completed revealing questionnaires, which had code numbers on so I could identify each individual, and their honest disclosure and trust was deeply appreciated. Similarly, the hours of discussion with John Hart in 1996, which drew upon my time inside the team, saw the new All Black coach's openness in discussions on such matters as individual players, media liaison, the captaincy (present and future) and team management.

Those years of my test match weeks, observations, and close interaction with past and present players would become the envy of every rugby fan who dreams of such opportunities. For some six years of my life, as no other person has done, I was inside some nine decades of the All Blacks — their memories, memorabilia, insights, anxieties, achievements and friendship.

2

Inside the black force (1)

New Zealand v. Ireland, 6 June 1992

On the bus I can see Grant Fox speaking to John Kirwan and gesturing towards me. It doesn't take too much imagination to decipher the words, 'Who the hell's this guy? What's he bloody doing here?'

Researcher's Notebook, 2 June 1992

New Zealand: Matthew Cooper, John Timu, Frank Bunce, John Kirwan, Eroni Clarke, Walter Little, Ant Strachan, Arran Pene, Michael Jones, Robin Brooke, Ian Jones, Mike Brewer, Steve McDowell, Sean Fitzpatrick (captain), Olo Brown. Reserves: Jon Preston, Grant Fox, Va'aiga Tuigamala, Graham Dowd, Blair Larsen, Paul Henderson.

Ireland: Jim Staples, Ron Carey, Mark McCall, Neville Furlong, Vincent Cunningham, Peter Russell, Michael Bradley (captain), Brian Robinson, Mick Fitzgibbon, Brian Rigney, Pat Johns, Mick Galwey, Paul McCarthy, Steve Smith, Nick Popplewell. Reserves: Ken Murphy, Jack Clarke, Paddy Kenny, Fergus Aherne, Garrett Halpin, Terry Kingston.

Half-time score: New Zealand 15 — Ireland 6
Full-time score: New Zealand 59 — Ireland 6

One in every eight New Zealanders regularly plays some form of rugby. In this southern hemisphere country some 250,000 men, women, and children run on to winter rugby fields, which illustrates the diversity and strength of their major game. In the South Island in 1992 the Leeston air was crisp in June, as club players' knees were dry scraped on the iced turf. In the North Island, the stubble of freshly chopped rushes scratched the ten-year-old ball carrier tackled short of the line in Te Araroa. The professional eye of the Auckland executive cast a calculating sweep over a Ranfurly Shield crowd at Eden Park, and the country tuned in to laud, condemn, or draw sustenance from fifteen men in black jerseys who ran on to Athletic Park at 2.26 p.m. on Saturday, 6 June 1992, to challenge the best of Ireland's visiting rugby players.

In that NZRFU centenary year Ireland was the only national team to tour New Zealand. Lacking big, strong, mobile forwards, the players also found their absence of fitness stranding them in the wake of most New Zealand teams. Although the coaching in Ireland has gained both momentum and an increased New Zealand input over recent years, in 1992 rugby in the land of the orange and green was coloured most prominently by Gaelic football (a variant relation of Australian Rules football) and it even — shudder, shudder for red-blooded Kiwis — ranked behind soccer in Irish sport allegiance.

On their 1992 tour the Irish beat South Canterbury, Poverty Bay-East Coast and Bay of Plenty, but lost to Canterbury, Auckland and Manawatu. The team lifted themselves in the first test to go into half-time at 18–18 and then lost valiantly, 24–21. The public reaction to New Zealand's narrow first test win brought Mains and Co up with a jolt, as the All Blacks had been expected to engulf the Irish rabbits like a rampant black calicivirus.

Media reports stressed the need for All Black improvements in line-outs, rucks and ball retention in this match. 'All Black side has no ex-cuses in this second test' declared a Wellington newspaper, and noted the difficult task faced by the All Black selectors in building a team.

The All Black team for the second test was not only selected to beat the Irish, but to establish Mains' expansive style of play and, maybe, show the critics that Auckland's eleven-try victory over the tourists did not justify suggestions that the northerners should be selected as the whole national test side. The media knives were sharpened. The changes from the first test were: Matthew Cooper as fullback, in his first test, replacing his brother Greg; John (JT) Timu recalled to the wing; Michael (Iceman) Jones and Mike (Bruiser) Brewer recalled as flankers; Robin Brooke brought in for his first test to partner Ian (Kamo) Jones at lock, and thus launch one of the great combinations in international rugby; and the inclusion of the indomitable Olo Brown, now deemed fit enough by Mains to join his Auckland front-row mates in his first test. In effect, a new All Black team had four days to gel and a fifth day to prevail.

Inside the All Blacks there was a distinct air of determination and purpose, heightened by impending selection of the team to tour Aus-tralia and South Africa.

Diary: Inside the All Blacks

Tuesday 2 June 1992

The 1992 All Blacks arrive in a large disparate group with the unifying sponsor's presence of the green Steinlager casual jersey . . . 'G'day mate!' as they greet each other in the foyer of the motel, drop their bags and wait to register. Most are in jeans. The office staff inform players that there is to be a team meeting in the bar area today. Players check out the arrangements for their rooms and head off to the various floors. Laurie greets me at the manager's door with a smile. The team meeting does not eventuate. Some players check with team mates to find out the arrangements. They are not sure of what is going on. The players are now told that their bus to training is to be brought in at the front entrance. Only Michael Jones, reserve back Va'aiga (Inga) Tuigamala and the liaison officer are aboard the bus waiting at the front. The big vehicle then cautiously and circuitously navigates the city block, taking a short cut through a big bus yard to the rear of the motel, where it picks up the rest of the team.

On the team bus Sean introduces me to the players. It doesn't take too much imagination to decipher their concerns. I can see Grant Fox speaking to John Kirwan and gesturing towards me: 'Who the hell's this guy? What's he bloody doing here?' I briefly explain my study and the participant observation. Laurie chats to me, as we drive off, about the media coverage of the previous test.

The bus arrives at Kilbirnie. The players carry their bags to the changing rooms of the suburban ground. They're discussing today's assembly, a day early, and didn't know it was for a training video. That explains the presence of Lee Smith, coaching director for the NZRFU. I had assumed — like a number of the team — that they were assembling to practise and train for the test one day early. John Kirwan and Grant Fox voice player concerns to the management — the use being made of them, and criticism of the perceived lack of official communication with the players. There are a few adverse comments but the players want to get on with test preparation.

The team now turn to Laurie who leads an open discussion on the last test and its implications for the forthcoming Saturday. The players are serious, intent upon their coach as they sit in the anonymous changing room. I am the only additional person present. A week ago this national team had 20,000 spectators. This day, in the cold concrete changing room of a suburban rugby club, they attend to Laurie's words.

'We need to get into the mental frame of mind that there are certain areas of the ground where we don't muck around . . . we thought we could go on the way we did in the last of the centenary tests, and that affected our mental view.' He pauses . . .

Matt Cooper, the new fullback, looks intently at his coach as lessons are drawn out from the last test. Matt is in his Waikato tracksuit and the thought is inescapable — why couldn't simple planning have had this All Black's new tracksuit ready for him today?

The coach goes on, noting that cold winds last week affected the preparatory times spent together on the field. He is self-critical. 'We didn't have a really effective strategy in place against the Irish. In the games they've played on tour we hadn't seen enough to fully base a policy on, and I take responsibility for that.' Players share their views on lessons to be taken from the first Irish test. John Kirwan has his head in his hands, his wedding band catching the light as he speaks, 'We got a fright . . . they got stuck into us . . . we seemed to work out things later . . . we should have put the ball through the backs straight away . . . ' John Timu adds the suggestion that more time needed to be spent on the backs' alignment. This triggers off the belief from JK that the team spent too much time apart in the previous test week training and 'We need to look at that.'

Kirwan further suggests that, 'All Blacks have always used the high kick as an attacking weapon, and we didn't do enough.' 'Absolutely,' agrees his coach. 'We didn't do enough work on punting. You cannot play test match rugby without bloody good kicking skills.' JK goes on, 'We reacted like Frenchmen, not All Blacks under pressure.' He notes the All Black first-five throwing the ball to second-five and a pass from the halfback to left wing as examples of poor play. He explains his directness by saying that 'We've all been a little nice to each other over the last five or six days . . . You know if you are in trouble get the bloody ball out, who cares? Let's keep control.' (The team discuss Jim Staples, the Irish fullback, in the context of kicking as they rate his play, and move on to various points on kicking strategies and poorly implemented first test tactics.)

The room is quiet. The coach addresses individual players . . . The halfback is leaning forward as he is addressed. 'Some balls you got from the end of the line-out Ant, you passed to Walter at first-five, but a dive pass straight to Eroni at second would have gone boom, and been more effective!' Mains smacks his hands across each other as Ant Strachan looks at him. Eroni gazes at the floor. Mains then points to one of the backs, and makes a tactical point: 'That was basically your fault, you let the guys down. You've got to think as a team member.'

The All Blacks' most experienced winger comes back into the discussion. 'It might take 60 minutes to crash a test side. If we think we can do it in ten we can easily get dinged by a team. No matter how it's going in the first twenty minutes I'd kick the bloody ball out.' He smiles with an acknowledgement of reality, 'Okay, if we're up by twenty points I might have a go. But on the 25, kick it out, on the 60 use the wipers.' There is a mix of smiles at the improbable prospect of JK not attacking if the All Blacks were quickly up by twenty points, but the air of intentness is not dissipated.

The team sit, momentarily reflecting on what they have shared. The analytical Fox breaks the silence. 'Don't go out and think Ireland can't play any better. We thought that about Scotland two years ago, and they nearly dorked us. They'll be thinking about what they can do differently.' JK reinforces Foxy's latter point. 'I had two Irish come up to me asking about fitness and moves and so on, and in the end I hedged a bit. They are obviously here to learn.' Mains doesn't pace up and down or rant and rave. 'We are going to spend a lot of time as a team this week, now let's go out and practise.'

10.55 a.m.
Laurie is with an official clarifying requirements for the coaching video of the All Blacks. The All Blacks are on the field in two lines opposite each other for moves and training exercises. Around two sides of the open ground the buses and busy traffic circulate in a background flurry of noise. A flock of seagulls wheels raucously out of the pale sun. Two cameramen in red jackets set up their video cameras. The Mizuno Company representative has a word with the new All Black fullback.

The backs move into their test formation, with Laurie checking on their perception of alignment, 'Would we not start a little wider in a game? I think we might be cramping in a bit.' Players respond with their comments and adjust the line as a result. They are in the middle of the field. Ant Strachan kicks the ball high, but his kick is slightly misdirected. Foxy, standing behind him, advises Ant on kicking more effectively with this wind. The practice has been going for 45 minutes. Pairs of backs have worked their way to different parts of the field, but the seagulls on the far touch line are undisturbed. JK talks with John

Timu and Bunce in midfield about kicking from their positions.

Another red bus passes, with the driver this time waving to the All Blacks and honking his horn. Fox comes up to explain the play when an in-field scrum can readily lead to a kick back into an opposing corner.

While the inside backs practise their moves, the coach checks that Matt, as the new fullback, is satisfied with his own understanding of moves. He is. He talks with his wings and coach about lines and moves. JK explains to Matt a call he uses, with its resultant move on the open side, 'although it was confused a bit last Saturday.' The major line-out moves 'Pen' and 'Bishop' are explained to the new fullback, along with moves from scrums. One such intricate move is detailed, 'But we don't call it that often. If you're not happy enough about that, Matt, we can look at changing it.' The discussion moves on to evaluating the success of man-on-man defence.

12.00 p.m.
The backs stop briefly for a break and are approached for autographs by the bolder onlookers among the 35 spectators. The forwards have completed their video work.

The team's bus driver comes over to tell Laurie that lunch has been obtained and is in the spare changing room. (I wondered why there'd been such a long period with no water, other drinks or sustenance.)

Players are eating lunch now in the small concrete block changing room. Michael Jones stands outside signing autographs before he moves to the other changing room with the physiotherapist. Lunch is varied, with lots of fruit available. It is set out on a large low table, and players sit around with plastic plates piled with food. (I'm struck by the size of the meal that Ian Jones has, which he is steadily demolishing with his stainless steel knife and fork.)

There is very little talk amongst the active eating! The first helping completed, some of the team take a refill. They can choose from fruit, cheese, rolls, hot food, orange juice, yoghurt and soup. Sprigs scrape on the floor as they settle down again for further eating. Buncey and John Timu sit together, as do Inga, Walter, Olo, Eroni and Michael Jones. Mike Brewer, Sean and JK discuss sports psychology. Three of the 'newer boys' (Robin Brooke, reserve Jon Preston and Ant Strachan) sit together. Laurie sits apart a little, at one end.

At the doorway of the changing shed, out of direct sight from the interior of the room, schoolboys push each other and jostle as they wait impatiently to ambush players. They shove some boys into the room and start to sing 'Why are we waiting?' A forward calls out 'How come you kids aren't at school?' (I wonder if this will lead to even more rowdy behaviour and the boys responding more volubly at the door!)

Inga gets up and walks around to the door. The boys cheer, but this changes to annoyance as he closes the door on them and they're all outside!

12.50 p.m.
After lunch, coach and captain discuss whether to do line-outs today.

Grant Fox calls to the liaison officer, appointed by the Wellington Rugby Union, 'Can we get any drink around here?' The reply is hardly an indicator of foresight and planning, as Fox is informed that the liaison officer will get something back at the motel for them. I go around the back of the building, across the road to a dairy for containers of fruit juice. They are quickly passed around and consumed by the dehydrated backs.

The video filming concludes, and the players are confronted by a throng of kids, all shapes and sizes, seeking their autographs. The boys and girls press around their heroes as JK tells them, 'Okay, let's get organised here.' They shuffle into an animated line and he signs their papers, autograph books and sweatshirts. A female teacher emerges from the rear of the group, as the boys and girls eventually disperse, and speaks to the All Blacks who have been signing autographs. 'Thank you very much, you've made their day.' The All Blacks board their bus to return to the motel, and JK and Grant wave to the kids who are watching the bus leave.

The team has a quiet period in the later afternoon and evening. In the Team Room, which already has faxes and letters building up on a table, I talk with the assistant coach over coffee to get Earle's expectations for the All Blacks in the forthcoming test, as he is their back coach. 'I want the cerebral part, I want to see Walter Little getting back under pressure and clearing the ball effectively. We're not yet playing to a pattern because of the dominance of individual skills. We can't wipe a ball across to their wings and we haven't used the blind. We'll be working better to get the ball faster through to JK. We would like to see the tight five driving and not standing off so much and watching the other poor bastards working, but giving Strachan a decent ball. Walter, I expect, will take more right options. Part of the difficulty is having had him at second-five for two years, but he can open up guys at the national level and when away he goes, he can't be stopped!'

After a quiet evening meal together it is soon 9.00 p.m. Mike Brewer is still trying to get some fruit in his room. Peter Thorburn, the third selector, has arrived and discusses with Mains and Kirton the Ireland-Manawatu game, lost by the visitors 24–58. They are agreed on the need not to underestimate the Irish. They talk about player fitness in the light of Saturday's test. The All Blacks have now virtually disappeared to their rooms, although two of them chat quietly over a drink in the bar.

Wednesday 3 June 1992

Breakfast is healthy and hearty for the All Blacks. There is a clear effort by the motel staff to meet requests for particular meals of milkshakes or health foods. Players do not appear to sit in particular groups or cliques, but fill up spaces next to each other as they arrive for their morning meal.

At the team meeting, Mains and Neil Gray, the team manager, sit in the front facing the team, who are in four rows. Senior players (Sean Fitzpatrick, Mike Brewer, and Steve McDowell) are in the front row, with Strachan, Ian Jones, and Olo Brown. Grant Fox sits directly behind them. A couple of 'old hands', Iceman and JK, are in the back row with reserves Inga and Paul (Ginge) Henderson. The other players sit quietly among their team mates. I sit in a back corner.

Neil starts by congratulating Matthew Cooper and Robin Brooke on their selection and asks if there are any queries. There are critical comments on the lack of fruit juice and the lifts not working. The lift that is working takes only a few players at a time and is slow. The manager assures the team that he'd looked at different hotels before deciding on this one. 'I went around and saw what there was . . . ' Foxy asks about getting gear washed. The players' committee is named as Sean, Mike Brewer and Ian Jones. Neil checks on sponsorship gear for training and asks if there are any other requests. Then, 'All yours Laurie.' The players now edge forward a little on their chairs. The test match is only three days away.

The coach explains that the video tape of the last test has not yet become available, and moves directly into continuing discussion on the previous test, linking this with individual players and specific needs for improvement. 'Let's be honest, nobody rated the Irish except one or two senior players, who warned you that when it came to a test they would be different. Talking about attitudes, we coaches were as much to blame as you were. On that Saturday morning some of you were involved in a fair bit of hilarity in the physio's room. You're only fooling yourself if you think you had a good attitude, you didn't fool us.' He goes on to criticise the forwards who were too high and invites them 'to ask yourselves how many times you were guilty of taking someone around the top — you went in as individuals and wrestled. It's a different story if you go in with numbers so you can split them and blow them back — that's fine.' (Later, after today's training, a small group in the Team Room would comment that the episode in the physio's room had been a simple good-natured release from stress of the imminent first test, and not a slip in focus.)

Ian Jones comments that when the Irish were going back through the line-out it was difficult to tell how many actually were in the line-out. A selector adds an observation to this. 'We'll go in with Iceman, Bruiser, Kamo, and Robin Brooke and perhaps one other — perhaps you Steve, go up front.' Mains notes the plan for an Irish call of a short line-out and tells his No. 8, 'Arran, I want the second five-eighth creamed as he takes the ball.'

A selector raises another point on the illegality of the Irish team being within the 10-metre mark, and Laurie pauses to consider this and passes it on to his captain for checking during the course of play. 'A two-man line-out will be Jonesy and Robin.' Kamo and Sean respond to this, to get absolutely clear who goes into short line-outs and details for that. There is a checking of play, positions and the players involved. Kamo notes, 'Regardless of who I'm marking, I'll go through.' Brewer, in response to a player comment on a line-out play, advises, 'Let's be careful, if we're watching them we're not watching the ball.' He looks across the row of players, 'Where do you stand, Fitz?' His captain responds to this, and they talk across the room on his possible role. Ian Jones adds his viewpoint. Sean wraps it up. 'The big thing is to be alert, ready to go, and have the urgency to get there.' Laurie has been closely following this exchange. 'Anything else to check about that? So we're all clear on the line-out variations? Okay, let's move on.' He turns to his halfback, 'Every time they kicked off there was no one covering the long box and that's where it's got to go. Even if the wing hangs back, what can they do about it?' Fox and Kirwan make points to which players respond.

The coach raises further points about tackling and aspects of back play. His captain asks Walter Little, then Inga, to discuss points of clarification. 'This is test match rugby, we don't muck around in our own 25.'

Laurie Mains turns to the centre, Frank Bunce, and explains how there were opportunities in the previous test to whack the ball off his left foot. He smiles and says to Frank, 'Maybe you weren't confident with that, that's why we're going to practise it more this week.' Frank explains that he thought he had time for this in the test, but it didn't turn out that he actually did! As discussion moves on to the back play, the coach points out that with the first Irish try Paul Henderson was there, but there were no midfield backs present. Fox adds to this, making a point that Eroni had been caught in the ruck and that when he counted the numbers the All Blacks were clearly outnumbered in the scoring movement by the Irish. The coach checks Fox's observation with the playing first-five, 'Walter, when their first-five made a move, did you count the players outside?' There is a palpable air of concentration threaded through the players.

Earle Kirton, the past All Black first-five and now selector, adds his view for the first time in the meeting. 'It's absolutely imperative you follow your man across. I didn't hear you yelling for your man on defence. Go for the man, not the numbers. Learn their bloody names, it makes a difference. When they stand the guy wide, bring a loosie in, give them that man to mark.' He used Michael Jones on Ofahengaue, of Australia, as an example. 'You've got to practise your defence in this way and practise it at pace. Today we need to go through defensive moves on the field.' Then he pauses, and adds as an afterthought, 'We never hit the pill in the last test, we went at half pace.' 'Yes,' adds the coach, 'and that makes us easier to tackle.' Then he asks for the main points that the team learnt from the centenary tests. They discuss these briefly.

They continue to discuss tackling. 'If you're going into a guy and he's clearing the ball you tackle him, and that takes him out . . . Just after half-time, Walter, you had a ping up the side line and you were run out over the line. It was a waste, you've got to get back into the forwards,' Mains asserts.

(At the door, the video tape of the first test is handed to the team.) Laurie goes on with his comments. 'Cover for the wipers kicks wasn't good. You weren't good on the high kicks either. We would look at it and grab their guy high. One of the things All Black teams have always done is really drill the guy who takes the high ball. If the ball gets spilt it goes off at an angle and they can't really use it. It's an opportunity for us to use it. When a guy takes a high ball, take him around the legs when he lands, drill him.'

Grant Fox now talks about the technique of running and knowing how to go for the ball and the man. 'Time your run. The rule is clear, first person competes in the air for the ball, second person drills the opponent going for it.' Laurie: 'Foxy's right, time your run, communicate, and look. Don't hesitate to call out, "You've got him, you've got him." That puts a doubt in the catcher's mind. You're too nice out there Eroni, you're too nice Walter.' Paul Henderson then puts his hand up. Laurie notices it. 'Ginge?' 'I've found that when the No. 8 was having a go that the back five take a step or half-step off at scrum time.' They talk about that as an advantage that the Irish take and the veteran front rower, Steve McDowell, joins the discussion. 'The referee was trying to get them around but he never penalised them. We need to go crab-wise.' Laurie: 'Yes, but can they do that if we're really putting pressure on them?' Sean, 'We've got to sort that out.' The discussion moves on. Mains comments, 'We just didn't have the variation in midfield, the commitment to put the ball and player in the right place wasn't there. Our whole aggression factor was missing, except for Sean, and perhaps that's unkind to Ginge. We just didn't commit ourselves to the ball on the ground.' (For this test, Henderson is a reserve. I notice quite clearly the coach's use of the inclusive terms 'we' and 'our' in the points that he makes, assuming responsibility with his team for their actions.)

Laurie makes a point about tackling, about position. He points out that with one tactical move, 'If they'd done an Aussie-One we'd have been in trouble. We seem to be having some trouble coming to grips with it. Sean was probably the only one making five or ten yards over the advantage line. I don't think we need another runner. We need to use that opportunity and get the ball out to the backs.'

Laurie suggests for this test they will use two runners, and everyone else goes up the guts of the ruck or maul, as he wants everyone getting in together and driving. This is endorsed by his past provincial captain, Brewer, who declares, 'We're too predictable. I think they're reading our game plan.' As an example of the need for difference, he outlines JK's move that led to the try they scored in the first test. Points are made that the biggest thing the team needs on the field is communication.

Earle Kirton adds the point about the Irish number four player being a dangerous player, at times appearing to exceed the law. An All Black veteran's reply is succinct, 'Why don't we whack him? Drill him and deal with him.' Another veteran adds, 'It's urgency we need in some of those situations that we didn't get last time.'

The All Black coach addresses the illegal play issues. 'We cannot go through a test match with the line-out not being refereed. You've got to do something if the ref hasn't done anything. And with the rucks, we don't want anything dirty. It's all in the rules of the game, so you ruck as aggressively as the rules allow. We can't have every side in the world making their own rules. We deal to cheats. I tell you, we're going to deal with some of these guys with legal ferocity. No way does any rugby team take the All Blacks cheaply.'

They discuss the need to ruck strongly. The assistant coach, Kirton, makes the point. 'Once you've got the ball from the ruck it's one-on-one, three-on-two, two-on-one . . . Inga, on your side are you running for glory, or what? You've got to be clear in your mind how you're playing.' He goes on, 'We've got to get into a kicking game for variation. It's called football. You've got to get into the kicking mode where you can drill, you can drill yourself to saturation point by practising your chip kicks, grubbers, wipers. The old timers are right, you guys must work on that and get it right in your time so you're good kickers.' Earle makes the point about being more creative. Inga and Ginge lean forward to listen to him as Vivaldi's 'Four Seasons' floats in from another room.

The coach now summarises and notes, 'We'll go to training, we'll warm up for the doc first. We'll take everyone through the exercises, and we'll go through the strategy of some whole team runs. We'll work to create better positions. Anything else, Pete?' Thorburn has a focus upon the Irish team. 'I've watched them three or four times, and outside they're weak. One-on-one they're okay, but if we create confusion in defence we can break through their line.' Thorburn is critical of the lack of tackling skills. 'We have the two biggest wingers in the world. When you tackle, look at their hips and thighs, don't look at their faces or the ball or that's where you'll tackle. You look at their hips or thighs and go strongly for them. We need to use the practice bags. We're wrestling too much instead of hard tackling.' The coach indicates his agreement.

10.30 a.m.
The team have come by bus to a school ground in Lower Hutt, having changed in a wooden-panelled room off the gymnasium. The manager

checks with the sponsors on gear for the larger players. The players throw a ball around while they wait for their team mates.

Earle Kirton walks past and asks for three extra balls. There is the smell of liniment in the air. 'Right, let's go, guys', calls Laurie at 10.37 a.m. A veteran forward pokes a football into my genitals with a grin and bawdy comment. (Jeez mate, remember your strength. This research project could be a tricky mode of interaction . . .)

The sponsor's representative comments to me that his firm likes to think the All Blacks are brand ambassadors for them. As he is talking, the team warm up and jog the line with the team doctor in the front. They lie down at one end of the field and exercise. Kids are lined up on the sidelines of the field. Now the team sprint to the 22-metre mark from the goal line, and back. They repeat this, and again. Then they move into their grids. (I wonder how often they use these skills in the game. Are these still the most relevant skills to be worked upon in such intensity? Do coaches use this as a warm-up time, or for the reinforcement of skills? Has the time come for a critical re-evaluation of these?)

They run to the half-way line and then run back. Now they are doing it competitively, in groups, although they haven't got quite enough footballs for each group. JK is speaking to his jogging group, urging them along. Now they're kneeling, stretching. Now they run to the other end of the field where the tackle bags are ready.

The forwards are in one group, the backs move off into another. Sean Fitzpatrick is laying down the law to his forwards, shouldering a cold wind with murky grey clouds in the distance. The forwards group is with Laurie Mains, while the backs are with Earle Kirton.

Earle wants a couple of small runs to double-check moves with his backs. 'Doc, you might have to run on the wing.' They practise kick-offs. The kids laugh as the principal of the college takes the ball from over the line and kicks it back onto the field of play. A teacher comments to me that there are as many of the public here as there normally would be for a local representative game.

11.15 a.m.
Earle and Peter Thorburn check through a point together on the way the backs are moving. Ant is practising his dive pass along the lines that he and Laurie had discussed yesterday. The kids crowd Sean at a throw-in on the side line. Laurie moves across to them, 'Come on you kids, could you give them five yards of room please?' Sean also speaks to them.

Laurie goes through a move with the forwards, a runner off the Willie Away movement. Now they bring the forwards and backs together, with Earle reinforcing the moves that start to flow out through the backs.

Today, Matthew Cooper has been given new boots, which are causing him some pain. Matthew's foot is checked and Jon Preston is moved to fullback. Mike Brewer also has his leg checked.

Onlookers hear the comment from the coach, 'Good play, Foxy,' as Foxy puts the ball into the corner for the All Black defence to counter. It is exactly what the coach has asked him to do and a distinctly realistic challenge for the All Black back three. Now there is a sweeping, low, long and fast pass from Ant to his backs. Walter Little drills it out on the left-hand side of the field with a right-foot kick.

The team moves to the 10-metre line. Walter Little, this time on his other foot, drills it right up the line. Now the All Blacks are practising attack in the opposition 22. Their coach stands, hands on hips, on the open side as they run through a blindside 'sixty-six move'. There is another break as Laurie has a word with his forwards, and Frank Bunce and Eroni Clarke clear up a point together.

On the open wing, John Kirwan stands with hands on hips, wearing a black and yellow jersey and tracksuit pants tucked into his All Black socks. Laurie commends his forwards, 'Good work, forwards. Now a couple of attacking scrums and we'll try a Coleman move.' He checks with JK on the move's optimum use. Arran Pene gets the ball to Eroni Clarke as JK cuts past in a dummy run into centre field. They try a defensive scrum. Laurie calls, 'Okay, back here for another one,' and stands with his left arm extended out like a ref playing advantage. John Kirwan acts as Michael Brewer's eyes, 'Listen for me, Bruiser,' he calls.

Laurie and Peter are with the forwards, checking on how they will cover a blindside move by the opposition. They are not satisfied with the way the forwards go through this . . . Now it's scrum time! 'Break it up. Opposition ball.' This time the All Black pack do it more urgently, scrumming with an intense accord of power. They've only got three days to get it all together.

Mike Brewer tackles Jon Preston. It's the second time he's stopped a blindside move and the coaches appear satisfied. The All Black power switch has been turned up a notch.

12.10 p.m.

The forwards are at the scrum machine. The backs are with Earle who has them chip-kicking and following through. The backs move over to get their tracksuit tops. One boy gives cheek to Grant Fox who tells him not to be rude. Eroni Clarke still has his beanie on.

There's a big crowd around the forwards now, as the backs practise out on the field taking kicks from the 'opposition'. (I'm standing guard over the players' gear now, as the boys move in closer with covetous eyes and comments.) An old brown leather ball bounces past me and a kid runs to get it as it bounces off Jock Hobbs. The boy is unaware of the presence of this past All Black captain, grabs the ball, and runs off with it, happy to be absorbed in his own action and not an observer of others.

Jon Preston is kicking well in the back practice, but I find myself noting Fox's special gift as the ball flows from his foot, soaring with rare physical aesthetics to land in the exact spot he has delineated. Now Walter Little does the same. John Kirwan tries a left-foot kick, wryly observing the skewed result. Now there is a change around and Matthew Cooper is taking the kicks, wearing someone else's boots. Walter Little miscues a kick. (I wonder how much time he spends practising. Fox drills the ball with well-honed artistry, the air is sculptured with precision and an individual exactitude of flight that none of the other players has matched. I imagine Laurie and Earle would happily settle for Walter to develop expert forgery of such art.)

The backs now move into a circle. They run, pass, stretch and warm down as the practice ends. JK is rushed by fans. Foxy's on the field surrounded by boys. He has a string bag of eight rugby balls cutting into his shoulder. I take them off him and walk to the changing rooms. I have deposits of tracksuit gear from different players on my arms and give this out to them as they sign autographs. (I muse on the spectacle of Grant Fox out on the field. Here he is virtually submerged as the boys push around. They are quite clearly rude and inconsiderate. They jump up and slap his back, they call out to him, they thrust bits of dirty paper under his nose for him to sign, and they pretend to take the balls out of the bag before I reach his side. They push on him, and all the time he stands quietly signing autographs with friendly words to those polite enough to ask for his signature. It is a different picture that I'm getting now, inside the All Blacks, to that which I had formed from the media and people's comments when I was outside this team. I can't help but think that few people would put up with such rudeness and physical attention without some sort of retaliatory comments.) Public relations concluded, the guys shower at the training ground clubroom.

Back at the hotel the players drift in and out at lunch time. Tonight will be the parliamentary reception. The closing part of the afternoon is free for the players. Some are going to go down town and others are going to stay at the motel. Some have family and friends visiting them. They are quieter than yesterday.

We board the early evening bus for Parliament Buildings. It parks in the ground between the old and new and we file into the Beehive. The reception has a preponderance of men in dark suits — rugby administrators and politicians — and only a scattering of women. There is red and white wine, beer and fruit juice. (It seems obvious to me that the Maori and Island players tend to stay in a group towards the entrance end of the foyer: Michael Jones, Inga, Robin Brooke, Eroni Clarke, Olo Brown.) The team is dressed for the parliamentary visit in their 'number ones' of black jacket, tie, white shirt, grey trousers and black shoes. Prime Minister Jim Bolger welcomes the team and guests. (This welcoming speech is quite banal. It timewarps the listener back to the 1950s — a completely monocultural and monolingual welcome. In sharp contrast to the Irish manager's bilingual opening, the Prime Minister's speech does not reflect our bicultural country or the multicultural All Blacks.) He notes that 'It is good to have the Irish team because of the empathy between the two countries. We're playing that great sport of rugby — it's well known that I am a supporter.' He comments upon the way the NZRFU 'do a great job of reaching out into the community with this great game of ours.'

Peter Tapsell, of the Opposition Labour Party, assures the Irish that in the first test 'You were morally the victors,' which brings almost inaudible comments from some All Blacks advising the speaker to recall the score, or suggesting he provide support for his country. Michael Jones and Inga are literally grabbed by their local MP who flaunts them as constituent trophies from his electorate to other MPs, some of whom do the same with other players.

A mixed group around me discusses the speech by Noel Murphy, the avuncular Ireland team manager, who had toured New Zealand twice as a memorable Lions player. There is approving comment on Murphy's Gaelic welcome, and Irish players comment on their team manager's great playing record. Murphy is an example, like Meads and Lochore, of a special class of rugby person..

Matt Cooper, first time test All Black, is now commandeered by his MP as the politicians continue to display their electoral trophies to each other. The players endure this with dignity and appropriate small talk. One of the players grins as he hears a relatively new MP, who does not introduce himself, bombastically address two All Blacks nearby, stating 'One thing that has surprised me is how many people recognise you as a Member of Parliament.' He pauses for breath, and one of the duo asks politely, 'Yes, but who are you?' The MP looks disconcerted, mutters a word or two, and moves away quickly as his audience of two retreat further to the back of the room.

Dinner back at the motel finds a novice All Black and me together. He makes the point that a significant part of All Black pride comes from the traditions of all the All Blacks who have been in previous teams. He is keen to play South Africa. He knows it will be hard but believes in the New Zealand team and its ability to win. Through his life he has had playing ambitions shaped by public expectations. Now he is part of the élite team that has to deliver. I ask him if he understands the changes in play made since the previous test. Has he assimilated these? Thinking of the team talk this morning he pauses, and responds that he hasn't completely understood what is required. 'What do you think I should do?' he asks. I try to be uninvolved and reply, 'What do you think you should do?' He decides that he should go and talk with Laurie, and get a clear idea of what the coach means and wants. (Now that seems a pretty good idea!)

Eroni Clarke and John Timu are enjoying giant hamburgers and milk shakes at lunch. JT considers another bite along with a response to my question on expectations of a coach. He wants a coach who sets things out clearly and explains the player's role. 'Then it's over to me, and if I don't perform I expect, and accept, that I will have my butt kicked in front of my team mates.'

9.45 p.m.
We gradually gather in the Team Room to watch the Australian State of Origin rugby league match. Laurie, Earle and Sean are discussing possible selections for the forthcoming tour. They consider one particular player from a range of perspectives. How would he relate to other guys

on tour? Can he learn and develop? He has skills that demand consideration — have we looked at the skills of the other players for this position as closely as we're looking at him? What is he like as a guy to have in a team for three months of touring? (I ask them if they would prefer me to move away. They don't. For all of Earle's public extroversion and Laurie's apparent conservatism, their trust in an observer's confidentiality is warming and appreciated.) The room divides in support of the reds and blues.

Thursday, 4 June 1992

9:29 a.m.

The Team Room. The team assembles. The individual greetings are becoming familiar as they gather. Laurie warns JT, the duty boy, to 'make sure that the bus doesn't take off without Neil as he's got different lots of business to get done.' Neil arrives, 'First of all, I've got to say Happy Birthday, Skip.' The manager checks on dinner and the distribution of vests. 'Anything you want, you see the liaison officers. Anything else?' JK points out, 'We're missing some laundry.' Neil asks if anyone has seen a player's envelope missing since yesterday with sizeable expenses money.

Laurie talks directly about aerobic levels. He names the players who are down on the fitness figures that Marty Toomey, of Otago University, has kept in individual records. Two bulky players are down 10 per cent in their test results, as is one player who had bad injuries in recent months. Four players are down 5 per cent. 'You guys have to do some definite work. You've got to keep it going fellas, until two weeks into practice on tour.' He then moves to training plans for today. 'We'll work through the skills of line-outs, okay?' His controlled gaze covers the forwards in the room, and fastens on one of the great All Black flankers, 'What's our policy on short line-outs?' The player, holding two university degrees and blessed with a munificence of rugby intelligence, shrugs a little and asks for clarity. Laurie goes through his plans for the line-out again, concluding with the reminder that, 'If we pick up one of their line-outs, then Arran [goes] straight out to second-five.'

The coach now addresses the backs. 'I've chatted through a couple of things with Earle, moves we'll use today and on Saturday.' He indicates he is thinking of using the blindside more: calling the runners up and going blindside on the wing. Sometimes a Willie Away move will be actioned, and then Sean will be in the play with the ball going to Walter for the blindside. He explains to his new fullback not to run the blind if it is less than 20 yards to the Irish goal line, as it would crowd the play, and reminds the backs 'Walter will just call two if he is going blind.' The planning continues . . .

JK looks up from his clasped hands and seeks more clarity on a specific move. Mike Brewer supports him. (This is interesting. Is it that two of the most senior and experienced players don't understand, or are there others who are not clear about what is to be done but don't want to ask? The player who had mentioned his uncertainty to me yesterday hasn't raised this yet, with Laurie or Earle.) Laurie: 'Okay, thanks JK and Bruiser,' and works the ground over again. He explains that they will practise these moves today. 'It has to happen in the match, so it has to happen at practice today.' He is direct and unambiguous.

Laurie discusses the wing cutting in outside the first-five and the resultant phase of play. 'Where will the ball be, Eroni?' The player responds. 'If Matthew comes up on the outside, then he's seen the real chance of his position and I just want to make the point, Eroni and Frank, that when that happens the ball goes to Matthew. I want you to call out "Matthew" because you'll be able to support him, Frank. Clear with that, Eroni?' He speculates on possible Irish developments in play from the last test. Today at practice the All Blacks will do kick-offs to ensure their control from that piece of play. Other situations are outlined. 'They'll try a little more of what they've done, and then introduce something different. Now, if we get the ball in this part of the field, Walter, what do you do?' he asks, pointing to the board. Laurie attempts to reassure any uncertain player and stresses that anyone not fully understanding a move should ask. 'If anybody's got any confusion it must come out today.' (This is a double bind for a coach with a short timespan before a test — he wants complete understanding but time places an onus on honest player responses. From what I saw of the apparently disjointed aspects of the game plan earlier in the week — probably due to my own inexperience at this level — there is now a clearer fusion of the purpose and tactics of the test play.)

Brewer raises a point about broken play and the loosies driving from Buncey. He notes three possible developments. To the first move his coach is directly responsive, 'That's out, Bruiser, that's 50:50 stuff.' 'Okay,' responds Mains' former provincial captain, 'so the call is "feed" or "on me" and we provide complete support.' Earle cocks his head on the side and makes a point. 'Hang on Bruiser, "on Buncey, on Buncey"

should be the call. Too many guys call out "on me" — who the hell is "me" in the heat of a test . . . Give the name, give your name if it's on you.' Laurie adds, 'Good point, Earle. Anyone else got anything?' He moves on to clearly reiterate the role of runners.

Their co-selector adds his first observation. 'We must face the ball all the time. The old head-in-the-sand thing is no good! They can't pull these things if we keep our eyes on the ball all of the time.' As Peter concludes, Sean takes his eyes off him and glances around the room. Thorburn reinforces points made by Laurie about running back, and directions that he's to give to the forwards, by emphasising that, 'It all comes back to urgency and mental hardness.' Matthew Cooper has hardly taken his eyes off the speakers. He asks about options for penalty clearances. Laurie relates his explanations to the previous game and Matthew checks on one option with his captain, 'Is that your option Fitzy, or mine?'

The talk moves to more fluid options. Laurie tells them that the ball between the 22 and 10-metre marks goes right into the corner. Sean adds, 'If we do that, it's vital we have the chasers.' He gazes at John Timu, 'JT?' 'And JK and Frankie,' adds his coach. 'The first guy forces the Irish player to the touchline and the second guy finishes him off.' (There are a couple of anticipatory smiles.) John Timu stops plucking idly at his jacket and makes his point about the same situation but, 'With them having numbers up there we need to steady up and keep our formation.'

The need for clarity and moves is revisited. 'Let's hear you calling today with scrums, etc.' says the coach. 'I don't want to call them.' His halfback responds to this with a question, to clarify the caller of scrum moves, 'Me, Walter or Bruiser?' Grant Fox, for game after game the director, script writer, lead actor and designer, acts as prompt here and says, 'Walter, usually.' Laurie qualifies this. 'Walter calls the moves assuming he will get the ball, but if Bruiser or Arran sees that a move is on they will call it.' A succinct Brewer joins in. 'Too many callers.' They discuss this and clarify it. (Forward reserve Blair Larsen moves his attention from one speaker to the other — it reminds me of a table tennis fan watching the ball in play.)

The bus to today's training is the one used yesterday — same bus, same driver, all week. Ant and Walter, halfback and first-five, sit together. (I wonder if this is deliberate, their choice, or the coach's suggestion.)

Strachany keeps his eyes on Walter's face and talks animatedly through moves that he 'draws' on his arm and on his thigh with his fingers.

Buncey and reserve forward Mark Cooksley sit by themselves. The sponsor's representative sits with the captain. Inga sits by himself and Olo is with Robin Brooke. JT is with his Otago mate, Pene. Up front are Laurie and Earle. The physiotherapist, Gary Sye, sits with Doc Mayhew who catches up on the morning newspaper. As we drive along the waterfront, on the early stage of the motorway, Walter is more voluble, and now looks at Ant more frequently as he discusses his options at first-five. Inga has fallen asleep. Eroni leans over the aisle to check a move with Walter, on a tactic involving skip passes. Ant, in the opposite aisle seat, explains. Eroni, slowly affirms, 'Oh, I see,' and ends with a confident assurance, 'Yep.'

Another field, another training. Peter Thorburn and I discuss learning styles and the apparent contradiction of diverse learning styles with the need for 'getting as much about the game into them as possible in a relatively short time.' We discuss Walter Little, whom Thorbs has had as a player since Walter was eighteen years old, 'And I still don't know what his best position is.'

We watch closely as the forwards move into a line-out formation. The onlookers crowd the perimeter of the ground as Sean prepares to throw the ball to the line-out: Steve McDowell in the front, Robin Brooke, Olo Brown, Ian Jones, Arran Pene, Mike Brewer, Michael Jones. We hear the familiar calls of 'AKPO orange, LYSO, PYMO'. Laurie walks a line parallel to the forwards, watching his players. 'PIKO,' and Ice is off the back and passing to a fellow loose forward.

The session lacks impact. Mains stops the players. 'Let's have it harder, a bit more aggro. We're playing in a test in two days.' They repeat the move, with greater application, and some onlooking boys break into spontaneous applause in recognition of the heightened intensity. Sean, in his short-sleeved jersey, throws in again, leaning forward with weight on his left foot as the ball arcs from his overhead throwing hand. They try a move now with Mike Brewer and Steve McDowell around the end of the line-out. Another throw-in, and their captain urges them, 'Drive it.'

Ant and Foxy have a quick word. The line-out call is 'GKCO' and then Foxy calls 'Frame' — the ball goes to Kamo, out to Ant, on to Fox and then back into the forwards. The captain and coach have quick words and then revise the practice move. They move into a defensive line-out, 'MKYD'. The forwards drive. 'Straight back,' calls Fox and drills a defensive kick with precision. There is a distinct cohesion today. The plan is coming together.

Laurie has a quick word with the grouped forwards. The onlookers hear his final words, 'We want red hot ball.' The pack moves into action. Jones to Jones, to Ant, to Arran, and then regroup for the next move. 'Rob drive, Jonesy runner, Ant out to the backs.' Exactly as discussed in the team session, and Captain Demanding now grins his approval. Earle, meanwhile, is with the backs as he sees Matthew Cooper coming into the backline, with JT on his left, and passes to Walter. Earle gesticulates to Matt as they walk back to their positions. He then chats with JK, concerned that the winger is changing Eroni's understanding of a certain move. They sort it out and discuss the next moves . . .

The All Black forwards huddle. Sean is in his bright red shorts and shirt replete with sponsors' logos. He observes his team mates in a two-man line-out, calling out to check with players as the coach confirms the 10-metre law with the halfback. Satisfied, they decide on a drop-out practice after the forwards' briefing. Grant drop-kicks out but the forwards' reaction lacks urgency. The coach is not satisfied. 'Too slow,' he criticises, 'too slow. If it goes over your head you've got to get around and face it.' An elderly woman in a black and white coat jabs her bulky companion and points to the forwards repeating the taking of the kick-off. 'See, they mean business, Ava.'

The onlookers can pick up the All Black coach's satisfaction at a better effort. 'Good work, Robin, that's the way. Good kick, Ant. Good nudge.' The forwards stop for a drink. Michael Jones is the only one in his tracksuit top. The backs are swinging into another movement as JT takes the ball, on to Matt coming outside him, and then Eroni Clarke scores the try. They take a break also.

Earle and Laurie talk over the next stage of the practice. Beside them, their locks, Robin and Kamo, chat to each other. (This will be Robin's first test and Ian's twenty-second. Two years younger, at 26, than his locking mate, Kamo is a senior member of the team and a possible New Zealand captain. It's difficult to believe that his deceptive frame fills out 120 kg.)

The team lines up for a kick-off. Jon Preston kicks down the short side and Inga takes the ball, along with the oncoming tacklers. JP has another kick, drilling it down the middle this time. Walter takes the ball, and finds touch well down from his position inside the All Black 22. 'Good nudge, good nudge,' comes the vocal encouragement from JK, his team mate of some fifteen or sixteen tests. Now, Eroni uses a wipers kick.

The forwards feature in the next move as Arran (Rewi) Pene gathers the ball going forward, and the halfback verbally whips the other seven with such commands as, 'Get on Arran, get on Arran.' (It brings to mind the team talk, with coaches making the point about calling the name of the team mate to support.) Ant is not so certain with the next move at a line-out, and seeks clarification. From the line-out JT cuts through the midfield. A ruck ensues. There is a flurry on the short side. Try!

Earle Kirton, the back coach, stands out among the backline. He watches the second-five on the ball with six pairs of All Blacks' feet flying over him, and smiles a little as Eroni leaps to his feet, bouncing up with an irrepressible India rubber immediacy. The hard drive culminates in a try to Sean. Their coach smiles, no southern reservation apparent, 'Well done, that's the idea, hit those blokes, good stuff.' Another move, another try by Matt Cooper coming into the backline. The coach's, 'Good call, good call,' is supportive and specific to a key player in the move.

The coach drops out for the 'Irish team' in a left foot kick, redolent of his own All Black custodianship. The ball hangs high and drops just over the line. Arran gets it, out to JK and back into the ubiquitous Iceman. The move lacks urgency and Mains calls to his captain, 'Sean you've *gotta* call Red Hot,' to reinforce the need for speedy distribution from forwards to backs. Earle is complimenting his backs, his pleasure more evident in their role.

Matt Cooper's turn now. He place-kicks from the half-way line. The trajectory is similar to that of his coach's earlier kick, and Ian Jones is up to take the ball on the full. The ball flows from forwards to backs in an orthodox move and JK scores under the bar. The team breaks for a minute, Laurie with the forwards, Earle with the backs. Now, together again, they scrum and Walter Little on the right hand side, midway between the 22 and halfway, kicks to the far 'Irish' corner. JT races up on the ball . . .

The forwards move to the scrum machine. Sean is not at all pleased with their setting. The pack readjusts. 'Kamo five, for real, up to you Olo, take it up, Olo . . . in the knees . . . in the knees, Olo.' The eight bodies heave concertedly and taped heads strain. The Vaselined ears are wedged and the legs of the No. 8 quiver with the pressure of anchoring seven conjoint bodies. The effort is prolonged. The coach is at the front of the machine. Now, down on his hands and knees, Laurie is virtually in the space of the front row as he watches them intently. Sean directs the next scrummage on the machine. 'On their ball, Bruiser, we call "coming, weight". Okay guys, let's bloody do it.' They do. 'It's coming right guys.'

The verbal demands and self-setting expectations of the pack are clear. With their own perpetuation of All Black standards the front row resets, 'In the knees, in the knees . . . and . . . weight.' The captain's head is down in the front of the scrum. He has 'Fitz' inscribed on his collar. The flankers' legs are bent, with their knees almost down on the sawdust-sprinkled mat. 'Good call, Stevie,' comes a voice from out of the eight forwards. From Brewer, 'I'll say "coming, coming".' Kamo adds, 'And "weight".' They apply the scrum pressure again, and Arran Pene's boot, sharply angled against the alignment of his leg, slips on the mat. Every grip, every tortuous hold, is critical. Mains checks on the calls. 'That repetition's not confusing is it?' The forwards seem to find no difficulty with it . . .

Morning tea in the clubroom. There's abundant food, with a proliferation of chunky sandwiches and plentiful cups of coffee and tea. Some of the team drink orange juice. Sean comments to me that the scrum is feeling stronger for this test.

A sign of the commercial era is evident as JK puts on his Steinlager hat preparatory to a television interview in the corner of the clubroom. The players appear to enjoy the fresh sandwiches and appreciate not being pestered as they eat. A player makes the speech of thanks. An onlooker might consider that his words range from the considerate to the commonplace as he mentions how good it is to get out into the smaller centres, and concludes by asking the team to 'show their appreciation in the usual way'. (Perhaps it is not rugby players alone, but many New Zealanders placed in this situation, who would gain from some training or guidance in speaking.) Laurie and Earle have been conscripted by two local rugby administrators and are patiently and pleasantly talking with them.

Players file out to the bus, calling out their thanks to the tea ladies. (John Kirwan always does this.)

The bus arrives back at the motel for 1.00 p.m. lunch. Laurie asks Doc to say something to the team about the type of food they should be eating, but Doc is unsure what Laurie wants. The coach's response is brusque.

'Okay, I'll tell them then,' and proceeds to point out that some players were eating too much, more than they would normally consume. They should eat much as they do at home. (Over lunch, the doctor discusses this with me. His view is that he doesn't think the players are overeating. One of the experienced players disagrees with the doc.)

3.30 p.m.
Back at the team motel Sean Fitzpatrick pops his head around the door of the Team Room and asks if I want to go with him to TV3 as he is being interviewed. (*I'm seeing Laurie at 4.00 p.m. and Sean won't be back by then. Bugger! I ring 8205 for Laurie but there's no answer. Very reluctantly I say that I'd better stay behind and keep faith with my appointment with Laurie — knowing that Laurie may well be late or not available! Off Sean goes by himself — a different life now from being one of the boys with communal command of the test bus back seat. I get through to Laurie. 'No, Robin, it's not convenient, can we meet tomorrow?' Ruefully I check with Neil Gray, the manager, to see if he has time to meet with me. Neil is in and we arrange to meet in an hour.*)

5.00 p.m.
Room 201. Talking with the All Black manager. His room has All Black jerseys, socks and shorts laid out. Neil has found the 'old hands' to be cooperative and stable — JK, Kamo, Bruiser. He has a high opinion of Sean, and of Mike Brewer whom he finds to be 'a great lieutenant, has great organisational skills.' The manager will 'be extremely disappointed if they don't play well on Saturday.' He has a belief that the All Blacks are extremely well aware of their obligations to the press and public. Neil explains the manager's report written after each home test or tour. This includes the team sheets, statistics of the games, and comments on the assembly, food and accommodation. The organisation of All Black gear allows each test player to have one set of gear per test to keep, and one to exchange with an opposing player.

In the bar of the motel I chat with the two liaison officers about their roles, rugby issues and today's programme. I can't reconcile the manager's praise for the excellence of these two officers with the actual events of the day. Eddy, the liaison officer, is self-congratulatory at getting Grant Fox to do a bit of coaching at a college in town. There had been a verbal request for Eddy to ask Grant if he would do it. The bus driver points out that because of the unscheduled demand upon the player there were other players not picked up by him as a result, and they were annoyed at this because they didn't know what was happening. A player, critical of this shift of events, had mentioned the unscheduled change to me before I met with Neil, but I did not want to ask the manager about this with the liaison officer present.

After this Saturday's test match dinner the players will be able to go their own ways. There is no set team dispersal time. Liaison officers will organise the players' transport to the airport as required. (I wonder if there's any point served by having the team meet on the morning after the match, even with wives and partners present, before dispersal. That could build up the social interaction and enable coach, manager, and others to speak to them. Perhaps key points from the previous day's test could be then noted for later action? Or do the players want their full freedom to follow from the test-match dinner?)

Later, I meet with Sean in his hotel room. A schoolboy has come in seeking an autograph. There is less than 48 hours to the critical test against Ireland, when the All Blacks must lift their game, but the All Black captain has made time available for a researcher and a rugby-keen schoolboy. A micro-second incident from the test, in the heat of the game, will receive more public attention than the private half-hour now currently being spent. The balance of rugby reporting could be improved with more adequate public relations from élite teams. This PR failure was exemplified by the irate message from a college principal who had expected the All Blacks to train at her school. As they hadn't turned up she wanted a visit from two All Blacks. (This situation apparently arose because a liaison officer had contrarily decided to switch training to a venue he had favoured!)

6.15 p.m.

The team assembles in the Team Room for another ball and autograph signing session. Pamphlets on drugs are given to the players, along with a guide on nutrition from a provincial union. The signing is followed by the team photograph. Neil brings in the team's playing gear. The floor is quickly littered with pamphlets and rugby gear, as changing begins. Chairs are moved forward and team seating organised. Some players keep an eye on the television screen. JK: 'Let's go guys. Get changed while you're watching it.' Matthew is in his All Black playing gear, and now pulls on his socks. I ask him 'Do you just pull on any gear that fits for the photo?' Matt grins, 'I suppose so — this is my first test photo!' Graham Dowd, front-row reserve, gives out test tickets. 'Hey guys listen to this. The tickets for your wives or partners aren't in those envelopes. They'll be here at the hotel for them.'

7.57 p.m.
The guys are now sitting on chairs for the official photograph of the New Zealand Representative Team v. Ireland, Second Test, Wellington, 6 June 1992. There are throw-away comments and some signs of slightly nervous pleasure. Some jibes are directed at JT for his allegedly dirty boots. Only the front row wear their boots. JK has football shorts on over his black jeans. As an old hand he minimises the extent of changing clothes and stands in the second row. The six players in the back row of the photograph are all new 1992 test caps. The photographer makes some adjustments, moving the Iceman into the front row. Michael now needs to pull on his boots and quickly slips his watch into a sock. He blushes as he grins, 'This is the first time I've been in the front row.'

There are now drawstrings on footy shorts to be tucked in. Earle points out that he can see JK's sneakers as Foxy and Walter look at each other and grin. They've been through this a few times now. Grant stretches and rubs his neck. Suddenly, 'Thank you' from the photographer, and the players' reactions. 'Is that it?' 'Was that it?'

Neil reminds them: 'Don't forget it's Skip's birthday, let's have dinner together,' and is interrupted with a player's assertion that, 'Hey, it's Fitz's shout.' Dinner then follows an already familiar pattern. The players fill up tables as they arrive, in no obvious cliques or groupings.

Long training sessions this week sought an establishment and reinforcement of game plan patterns. The coach now expressed to the media the need for players to understand the team tactics and move towards thinking two or three movements ahead. The use of 'opposition players' at training has introduced a different sense of onfield reality and compelled some adjustment of backline organisation. Set pieces had been emphasised to re-establish a traditional All Black dominance in these phases.

After the narrow first test win the coach is on trial as much as his team.

Friday, 5 June 1992: test day minus one
Breakfast. Sean pauses over his sliced, raw tomatoes, as Bruiser sits next to him and they go over a set move for Saturday. They are two contradictory physical figures — the stocky hooker with the bustling gait and the leaner flanker bursting into athleticism when free from injury. One

has trade experience, the other has a university degree. Pakeha and Maori provide distinct blood lines. Sean is an inspiring leader from the front, Mike a visionary inspiring his teams with deed and will. Catholic and Protestant, captain and lieutenant. Yet, Brewer also has a streak of hardness just as Fitzpatrick has a revealing compassion. But they share commitment, integrity, skills, and true leadership. JK drops next to them. He eats quietly. Listens to what they have to say — Captain Steadfast and Captain Athletic, Captain Reality and Captain Intended. A formidable trio of rugby accomplishment. I wonder why they're not used more gainfully by administrators for rugby and for themselves.

Team Room. Manager's messages first. Neil comments on the confusion last night over the rubber (masseur) and when he was available. 'He'll be here today at 1.00 p.m. in Gary's room. At 11.00 there's the players' committee meeting, and from 2.30 to 4.30 I'll be at the NZRFU matches committee meeting. At 4.30 the team will watch the video tape of the last test in the Team Room.'

The focus moves to the test. Laurie concentrates on Athletic Park and its features. He notes the need for goal kickers to critically consider the ground and factors of wind strength and direction, location of stands, and place and effect of the sun. He and Earle will take the decision-makers — Sean, Walter and Ant — around the ground and talk through the main considerations. 'There's a bit of edge coming into this game that I'm not happy about. The opposition are sure they can win this. There's only one thing — to concentrate.' His captain adds to this. 'We're going into this test hard-nosed. I want to see them put away in the first ten minutes.' Laurie continues. 'The key to this game is to be physically aggressive inside the law — hard and fair.' The atmosphere now has an air of tension and singular purpose.

The All Black coach resumes. 'What they have said is that we're going to go outside the law and fix it and influence the referee. That's gamesmanship, and we're not getting into bullshit like that.' There is no public relations mileage for Laurie in making such statements, as there is only the team here. To an observer there is little of the macho 'kill the bastards' scenario often sketched by rugby's social antagonists. Indeed, the inescapable observation — given the risk of this observer having lost some objectivity — is of a team who play to the edge of the law with personal commitment and fulfilment.

9.55 a.m.

Athletic Park, Friday morning, the day before the test. The players are on the bus. I sit with Rewi Pene who observes the rule already that, 'Younger guys in front of the bus with no special seats, except for the manager, etc. and captain, and the backseat boys rule at the back.'

Onlookers glance at the bus, and then look back again as they recognise the All Blacks. We pull up Rugby Street to the park. The ground is freshly marked with cut strips where the lines are set. A pleasant smell of freshly baked bread drifts in from the nearby bakery. Players quickly and quietly sketch the ground with their eyes, and glance over to the virtually bare stand where a band rehearses. The team moves into silent stretching exercises on the test ground 22-metre line, before Doc takes them to the far posts. One of their coaches tells them to look at the goal line, suck in the atmosphere of the ground and to visualise. 'The first five-eighth should sense the touchline and the crowd. The fullback is to get the feel of the middle and make sure he's hitting the touch,' advises Earle.

He leaves his backs for a few minutes, as they familiarise themselves with the ground. He discusses with me the need for players to replenish their glycogen stores. (Even five years ago I suspect few coaches would have been concerned with the links between storage for carbohydrates, high-intensity exercise and fatigue, and the depletion of their fuel source resulting in exhaustion . . . Now it's part of the knowledge base.)

Earle moves to check a point with JK, and Eroni asks him to clarify a short-side move. Laurie also runs through a short-side move with Ant, JK and Sean. Laurie and Earle pass a couple of comments to each other about their social outing the previous night, then move back to the business at hand. Earle stresses that loud, clear, calling is required from the backs. The voices give thoughts, diagrams and audible planning their physical shaping today. 'Coleman move coming up,' from Laurie. 'On the run Strachany, on the run,' from Eroni. 'If you want to play two you have to call early,' from Ant to Walter . . . A line-out call and Sean rocks forward on to his left foot to release the ball from the throw-in. His halfback kicks the ball precisely and smiles as team mates call 'Good kick, Strachany.' Another one. 'CMPO Coleman' . . . 'BAYD' and Arran Pene takes the ball, which moves to Walter who drills it over the 22-metre line. On the call LKXD, Sean has his first poor throw-in of the week. The next line-out call has an added code informing the forwards of the type of throw coming in. The letters in another line-out call indicate to Mike Brewer he has to move forward in the line, and he leaps for the ball successfully. 'Well done, Brew, good work,' acclaim his mates.

The forwards move through a range of calls. Laurie straightens up JT's position. 'Just a half or three-quarters of a yard JT, nothing desperate.' A five-man line-out group is addressed by Sean, earnestly discussing their drive, and Kamo clears a point with Ant.

The halfback and the captain observe Michael and Robin coming around the end of the line-out. Now it's Stevie and then Bruiser. The point is made to look and see who is up on the flat advantage line, and what to do to capitalise on this. 'Also, with these guys, have a look and see who's hanging off.' A comment floats in, that JK 'never had the opportunity to go straight at the man — let's give him that chance tomorrow.' They discuss this.

Laurie asks the team for their views: 'If it's a windy day tomorrow what do you want for the first half?' (I imagine in the old days the coach simply made an autocratic decision.) The general accord is to take the wind. JK talks it through with Earle, who is very familiar with the ground. Kirton reckons, 'It could drop about 4 o'clock, but it hardly ever does.' They discuss this. JK is 'inclined to take the wind and have a good go.'

Earle will check with the meteorological office. The players listen now to Laurie. 'It's a matter of condition if we have to play into the wind. The runners must hit and get on into a wall. We don't use wipers to give them the ball, we kick along the sideline. We use our wingers on the blindside — it's simple, they're going to run it at us to score a try. As Earle's been telling you all week, they'll set up rucks midfield to attack.'

Earle digs his heel into the turf. 'If it's a scrum here and the wind is coming from the south you could find the ball blown anywhere. It might be the creating of another blind.' (I wonder if the players really know where north and south are on this ground.) Laurie speaks to Earle, pointing to a corner, 'Gram One would be a good ploy over there, they can work it infield.' The players listen intently. JK has a cap on, a short-sleeved jersey, collar up, and stands with his arms folded. Eroni also has a cap on and is still in his black tracksuit trousers. Earle takes Walter and Eroni around the ground. Earle confirms with Walter the timing of Ant's pass on attack. Walter: 'I sort of like to receive the ball here, so by the time I get the ball I've almost beaten him,' referring to his opponent. They discuss the breeze. Eroni wants to be absolutely clear in his understanding of what is required of him in the optional moves. Earle takes them through the action for a kick to the corner, and avoidance of 'crashing for the sake of crashing.' He stresses the need for Walter, 'when he takes it up Eroni, to have you as the foil for him.' (Eroni appears more confident after Earle's calm, assured, directions and support. He starts to ask about positions beyond such planned moves, such as when Walter is caught in a ruck, or action to be taken in certain penalty situations 'in that area' or 'that area' as he points.) Walter appears more assured also, and goes through situations from the first Irish test that he thinks can be better handled this time. Earle draws him into describing these, and then asks Walter what action he will take in such situations in tomorrow's game. Kirton assures his first-five that 'their No. 8 is big, but what's he going to do? He's not going to catch you.' He talks similarly to Eroni. 'If you look and see whichever side it's really on, then go for it wholeheartedly, really take off.'

Laurie has the team together now. Ant is asked to develop a point he's made about the scrums in the preceding test. 'Once we're down, bang. In, out. It just didn't happen like that last time.' Laurie asks Sean how he saw this, and revisits the Irish technique of going down to scrum. Stepping across before the ball was in they secured an advantage. 'Okay, once it led to a great tackle by Walter, but that shouldn't have been needed. How do you see it?' Laurie points out to Sean that, as captain, 'You can stand up and say to the referee at a stoppage, in a responsible way, something like, "Can you keep the scrum straight?"'

The team check other phases and move back to the bus.

12.30 p.m.
Back at the hotel, the press conference is set up by the sponsors, who arrange large advertising placards and indicators of their product. The All Black captain wears a cap with the sponsor's name. His coach sits next to him in a light blue shirt, and the manager watches in his sponsor's shirt. I tape the conference.

Two hours later, 24 hours before the critical test match of 1992, Fitz and his forwards gather in the car park of the motel. A ritual of first class football, the car park practice cements line-out calls and, I suspect, a little more team interdependence. The call is 'AROI', and a planned move with Iceman results, to be followed by 'GJKJ' with a drive off Kamo.

There is a late afternoon chill as two boys stop to watch. The practice becomes a little more insistent. Paul Henderson pulls out a comb and

$5 from his pockets and hands them to me to hold. The young passersby who pause to watch comment on some of the moves that unfold. One observes with a smile that they have no youth grade rugby tomorrow 'because of these blokes'. A small group of Islanders in red and brown jackets stand watching. I wonder at the risks of All Blacks leaping on this rough surface. Is it too fanciful to have one of the fans, an All Black group person, motel staff member or liaison officer check the area first or even sweep the ground? At some stage a test result will be affected by a leaping lock's withdrawal through twisting an ankle in a car park . . .

4.33 p.m.
The team are signing rugby balls in the Team Room before watching the video of the preceding test. The balls have not been inflated as they will be retained by team members as a souvenir of this second Irish test. To avoid an easy check on any missing signatures a team wag calls, 'Don't number them Stevie.' Players are getting a little tense now. There is not as much joking around today as there was at yesterday's ball signing session. Foxy tells Steve just to get them around and get it done. I am given one of the signed balls. It is a gesture I deeply appreciate. The team finishes this duty and settles in to watch the video of the last test. Their coach has made written notes from his Dictaphone comments recorded during observation of the previous test. He has recorded reminders at the top of his two pages, of 'Team Spirit' and 'Attitude'. (His notes go on explicitly to list major points for the video discussion, referring to the Irish as 'they.')

1. *They hit and feed well, they must be hit low and be driven back.*
2. *Too often the forwards went high and they set up a maul — must go around the legs.*
3. *They upset us in the first five minutes. Quick line-outs etc. we didn't react well. Get more numbers to the line-out — all tall timber, then pull out. It also slows them down.*
4. *After we scored our first try, Ant you kicked 2 metre — their line-out. They had no one in the long box. It should have gone there.*
5. *Appeared to be no more communication for the defence in the backs when they won mid-field rucks. 'Pick your man up. Tackle someone.'*
6. *Walter you ran one up straight after half-time and ran out. Should have fed into a forward. Look for forward support. We just gave them the ball.*
7. *Cover the wipers.*

8. *Chasing the high kicks. Going forward ball.*
9. *Eroni improve making contact, pull ball into chest.*
10. *Big kicks to corners.*
11. *We took on up touch — when we are unsettled, go for ground.*
12. *Up after high kicks turn back so we don't knock on.*
13. *Wings outside one or two.*
14. *Aggression factor.*
15. *Commit body to ball on ground and in air.*
16. *Runners.*
17. *Arran late to scrums.*

Into wind — five-man line-out. Arran up.

22-metre kick-offs for us and them.

The team watch the video. There is silence, with little jocularity or comment. Mains, Fitzpatrick and Brewer sit near each other. As the backs fumble the ball on-screen their coach mutters, 'Go down.' He follows with an immediate point to his team. 'Now as soon as that ball goes to ground we've just got to put a body on it.'

Staples scores against the All Blacks. A passage of play follows and leads to another comment from Mains, 'Look guys, there's a ball sitting on the ground there for us to claim.'

There is no expression on the coach's face as the on-screen commentator describes him as 'looking pensive'. 'No,' rejoins Mains, 'pissed off!' There is a ripple of tense laughter. There is no humour as he next points out 'how high we were in the tackle.' Stopping to show a passage of play in replay he checks that, 'Tomorrow we want to suck that in, and drive.' Russell attempts a drop-kick at goal for Ireland and JK makes a point about the lead-up play that allowed their opponent time and space.

A player's voice, 'Too flat fellas' as the backline spreads out. 'After making the advantage line by five or six yards, get it out,' comes the voice of the coach, who follows with another admonition, 'We're too high there, front row.'

Frank Bunce scores a try on-screen. 'Good stuff, Buncey' comes a team mate's voice. Another claps his hands. There is a brief ripple of laughter at the announcer calling Bunce 'The Quiet Terminator'. They see Cunningham score for Ireland. An All Black states quietly, 'I should have had him. I came across too quickly.' Foxy points out to Ant, 'Don't kick with your back to the forwards, Strachany.' Fitz supports the comment, as the ball had been taken off Strachan's boot. Ant replies, 'Yeah, I realised that as soon as I kicked it!'

Commenting quietly on play towards the end of the first half, one experienced All Black suggests to his long-term team mate, 'This is where we started to crack them, but we let them off the hook with silly mistakes.'

An All Black is considered by the television commentator to be disadvantaged by illegal Irish play but this is not accepted by the intent players who are self-critical of their efforts. Inga then knocks on, to a low groan from the observers. Now Ireland break away. It is foiled by the All Black centre. 'Well tackled Buncey,' approves a fellow back. The test ends with a lacklustre win for New Zealand.

The team management move out, leaving only the test match All Blacks and myself in the Team Room. This is now the traditional captain's test-eve session with his team. Outsiders are never present . . . The guys are focused on their onfield leader. Fitzpatrick, an All Black captain in stature and peer recognition, points out that it was good to watch the video. 'Now is the time to get focused. Collectively, as a team, we can't be happy with what we've seen.' He pinpoints the team approach. 'Attitudes have to change. If we don't harden up, they'll have it over us. How much did it mean to each of us to pull on that jersey? What did it mean to you, what did you feel?' An Auckland and All Black player replies briefly, almost inaudibly. (This is up-front interaction. Just as the old hands have more to say during the week and a more prominent role in the game plan, so they are used more as the lightning rods and focus in the team talks.)

The sage Fox stresses the importance of attitude. Brewer is asked, 'How do you see tomorrow's game, Bruiser?' Brewer indicates that the team this week is better prepared. He talks about the use of runners tomorrow at the appropriate times. 'We've addressed where we were lacking urgency and attitude.' Stevie McDowell listens, sitting back, more relaxed, with his head up. Jon Preston and Ant Strachan — the reserve and test halfbacks — are intent upon the experienced flanker's comments as they sit still, in their team tracksuits. Brewer continues fluently. 'We've got to take control. The training runs on into tomorrow. When you pull on an All Black jersey . . . ' He pauses with emotion in the silent room. 'An All Black never thinks "I shouldn't be here." You've got to be prepared to piss blood to wear an All Black jersey.' It is an effective and direct message.

The captain eases the intensity. 'Be confident to have a run, Eroni. Let's play well. Go through the moves tonight, Rob. The number one job is to hit the rucks. We owe it to ourselves. Anyone else want to say anything? JK? Foxy? Go over it tonight. Write the moves down. Write the calls down.'

Dinner time. The team eat in an area separated off from the hotel restaurant. Eating with Graham Dowd, JK, Michael Jones and Gary Sye, we discuss memorable tests. JK recalls his first test, when he didn't feel any physical sensation of weariness as he played the whole game in a buzz. In the second test, his legs felt so numb he thought he would have to go off . . . 'like with the Australians last year.' Michael Jones' biggest test was the World Cup final in 1987. Dowd grins at his own additional contribution to these great players. He recalls the 10 minutes he was on the field in the test the previous week against Ireland!

A female chef come out to the team seeking autographs. A group of All Blacks discuss violence in rugby. They name violent players, including those who are blind to everything but 'team loyalty' or are 'simply thug-like.' JK has just finished describing a frightening incident in which a player's head was ripped open, when a brother and sister approach, with an air of trepidation. The girl, eleven or twelve years of age, has her hair piled high on her head. They quietly, tremulously, ask for the players' autographs. 'We are on our way to the airport to pick up someone, but Mum saw you here yesterday and we left home early today hoping we could see some of you for autographs.' Dowd chats to them briefly, JK asks how they are and Michael asks what school they go to. It is 8.12 p.m. and kick-off is only eighteen hours away. As they leave, the girl gulps, glances at her brother for reassurance, and looks a little surprised at her own boldness as she blurts out, 'Good luck for tomorrow.'

8.25 p.m.
Players head to their rooms where they will watch club rugby on television, and then a league match. One of the longest serving Auckland All Blacks, John Kirwan, leaves for his room, 'Well, Robin, off to bed to watch the boys play rugby and the boys play league — and then everyone can watch us.'

Saturday, 6 June 1992
Second test match: New Zealand v. Ireland

It is breakfast time on the final home test day of the year. Tomorrow the touring All Blacks are finalised. Laurie and I eat and talk. He is, understandably, a little preoccupied. What is he considering? His immediate concern is to have a word to Mike Brewer about his watching brief on the field, which is to provide leadership and support for Sean's changing of play if necessary. The captain is often locked in the depths of the forwards and Brewer's experienced and insightful eyes serve the leader well. In addition, Laurie wants a quiet word with Ant and Walter, but overall he feels the players should be ready for the game.

10:00 a.m.

The forwards are practising their line-outs. The reserves are also practising, often interchanging with test players in the line-out, to ensure they are familiar with the calls and responses . . .

Half an hour later, as the backs have their meeting, the forwards gather in the dining room for a light brunch. The intensity has geared up a notch. Stevie is urging, 'Let's get into them early.' His captain is direct. 'Head down, arse up. Let's do the hard work at scrum time.' The two flankers talk quietly about running off each other. I'm struck by the warm interaction. Michael Jones reflects on the loose forwards' interdependence and trust. 'Yes . . . the knowledge that you have a bond beyond the physical one of place, of space and time, of putting your trust as a person, your body, in your friend's hands . . . if he doesn't appear or do what he has said then you're at risk — and so is that trust. Yes, there is that dimension.'

1.03 p.m.

Kick-off for the test is 90 minutes away. A player, who has spoken to me of his pride in being an All Black, sits silently. He bites his nails. The Team Room fills slowly, silently. Piped music filters in. Even as a reserve Ginge Henderson sighs and blows audibly. It reminds me of my observations of a first division team before their Ranfurly Shield game. Tense. Keenly nervous. JK moves around the room with a cup of coffee. There is a diagram on the whiteboard. The chairs are in a circle. There are seats in front for the coaches and manager. Sean Fitzpatrick coughs, blows, muffles another cough. He sits still. He gazes ahead and then downwards. The air is tense.

The All Black coach speaks. 'I'm looking for aggression . . . use the blind into the wind . . . use the blind side, and we scrum, and we repeat it 40 times if we have to. Be prepared to graft it out for 40 minutes . . . We hang onto the ball. The most important thing today is to hang on to the ball in the tackle. No 50:50 passes.' He pauses and deliberately repeats the point in the stilled room.

'Blocks, get quickly around the ball carrier. Think, forwards, "I've got to be part of the platform". There are two runners only — Sean and Jonesy, otherwise Arran sometimes — but he will be called. Otherwise, all the time, Arran, it's up the middle. Use five men in the first line-out. Aim to put pressure on that ball so they have to scramble it out. If they have the ball, they get drilled. First man there, get around the legs. Attack — discipline — thinking. With the wind, first of all we get it down there, high down the middle, around half-way drill it into the others . . . *Concentrate.* You're getting there, Robin, Olo, Stevie. We're alert to their quick 22-metre drop-out. Eroni, you're starting around there. Go for it. If they're silly enough to do it — and you run for it — use your support, Buncey, JK. It's your day, Olo. Take our yard at every line-out. You don't come off and grizzle about being distracted — you do something about it as a team. You drill them in the tackles. They can't do anything if they're drilled to the ground. Hit everything at pace. Be very positive this time. We show them from the start, fellas, that you've got a Black jersey on. You have concentration and thinking.'

The All Blacks then file silently out to their team bus. Nobody speaks on the bus trip to the test ground except Mains and Kirton, in the front, who share whispered points.

The dressing room rituals for an All Black team take place in a zealously guarded setting. The players head up through the concrete catacomb of Athletic Park to look at the ground. The curtain-raiser participants are soaked. Sean makes the point that possession will be vital.

Laurie speaks to Walter, who is busy rubbing liniment onto his leg. Little does not reply. Mains brushes back his forelock as he speaks quietly to Rewi, recently only a provincial player. Foxy and Lamby Larsen sort out the reserves' pegs on which they want to hang their clothes. JK appears from the shower area in his tracksuit. 'Ball?' He receives one and heads back into the shower area.

This rugby changing room is small for big men. It is a concrete-floored dungeon, reached by going down concrete steps from its entrance door outside. That door opens to a corridor which leads to a panelled lounge with bar and carpet. The reserves area is essentially a one-bench seat in the shower area, which players push past to get to the sole lavatory. Cobwebs above have the same familiar location as when I was here last year with the provincial team.

I crouch in a corner of the reserves area, which is not easy as there is little room. The changing room is unexpectedly reminiscent of the men's urinal at a major London train station — grubby, off-white colour with a host of unappealing smells. Ginge Henderson comes in. JT works on his sprigs. Earle stands, bulky, in the doorway. He has been in this test setting thirteen times, in years when far fewer test opportunities arose. Players strip. Foxy is resplendent in his purple underwear. The atmosphere is organised and professional.

JT appears at my side. It is his ninth test. He asks if I am writing notes. I say 'no' as I see he wants me to help change his studs. Thorbs and I start to unscrew the sprigs rather unskilfully. Foxy leans over me and takes the boots as I try to use the pliers JT has given me. The quick, efficient, considerate professional, Fox, has a small tool kit which he unrolls and then deftly switches JT's sprigs. I am impressed by the action and thoroughness.

Sean has won the toss and New Zealand is playing into the Wellington wind. Laurie has a word with JT about his defence partnership with Matthew. 'You have to get back and support Matt, JT,' he says quietly to his wing. Peter Thorburn, once an Auckland player and later North Harbour coach, shakes John Kirwan's hand, 'Have a big fiftieth, JK.' 'I will,' replies the 49-test veteran.

The coach has a quiet word with his captain as Sean stands at the mirror, cream on his face. His lock and fellow Aucklander, Robin Brooke, jogs on the spot, tossing a ball high in the air. Laurie now moves to Arran in the corner. He eyes his No. 8 and gesticulates as he talks.

Kamo emerges from the lavatory. This is his twenty-second test. 'Good luck fellas.' 'Plenty of communication,' adds Laurie as he puts a supportive arm around the shoulder of his first-five . . . Here, inside the All Blacks, the atmosphere is one of cohesion . . . communal nods at team leaders' comments, no jostling for the loo, brief verbal exchanges which do not cut into individual focus on the task, personal routines, the shared use of limited space . . .

It is time. The New Zealand men in black move up the concrete steps with an uneven clatter of boots. Laurie tells Doc to remind Sean he's playing into the wind! The strains of the haka are echoed in the stand with some spectators joining in. Neil squeezes in next to Laurie. It is cold. Rain speckles the pages of my notebook.

2.30 p.m.
Kick off. The Irish score quickly but a dominant blanket of black is soon spread out over the green of Ireland and the forwards are rampant . . . Kamo comes to the sideline but is soon back in the contest. Dowd, a front-row reserve, comes back into the stand to tell Laurie that Sean has some broken teeth. A punch from the Irish hooker, Steve Smith, has chipped three or four of Fitz's teeth. The coach is clearly concerned that his captain might be in pain or have a nerve exposed. Doc Mayhew has a role as conveyor of messages. Laurie asks him to tell Sean that 'they don't change tactics in the second half.' It is now 3.13 p.m. 'They drive right up the middle.'

Sean checks out his mouthguard as Staples moves off the field, and is replaced by Murphy. Laurie has a tactical message for Sean: 'Say to the boys to get onto the ball carrier early.' From a 15–6 lead at half-time the guys press the team turbo button for the next 40 minutes. In ten tests, through almost 90 years from 1905, New Zealand has not scored more than 24 points against Ireland. Today, the deluge. Every leprechaun on every Irish shoulder is swept aside, crushed and emasculated. Typical of this savage tide were John Kirwan's try in this, his fiftieth test, Bunce's two tries, and the sustained force of the forwards.

The second test ends at 59–6 to the All Blacks. The players move from the cold and showery field into the dressing room sanctuary . . . An Irish player clatters down the concrete steps into the All Black room asking for Michael Jones, but 'He's not in yet mate.' Guys grin, arrive in by ones and twos, and sit. Sean comes in to check his teeth, and places his arm around Laurie's shoulder with a bloodied smile. His coach grins at him, 'Good stuff, eh?'

4.10 p.m.
Photographers enter. Laurie is out of the room for the press interviews. The manager brings a boy into the changing room. Steve McDowell, still in his soaked jersey, crouches with the boy for a photo. The All Black captain cuts plaster off his foot. He turns to the photographers, 'Okay guys,' and they leave the room. It is now 4.18 p.m. The steam

from the showers drifts through from the reserves area. To my surprise, three of the players light up cigarettes and draw contentedly upon them. One of them smiles as exclamations and squawks come from the showers. There are sandwiches and drinks on the physio's table, which virtually fills the centre of the room. The special position of the All Blacks in world rugby is illustrated by the Irish player who approaches the naked All Black captain standing at the steam-coated mirror. 'Sorry to ask you now, but could you sign my programme?' 'No trouble.' The All Black captain signs and resumes his shaving.

Robin Brooke, some 30 minutes after the end of his first test, still sits on the bench. He is still silent. He is still unsmiling. His hands are clenched on the inside of his knees. Sean turns to dry himself, a red welt scored across his buttock. He glances up at a visiting Irishman, who has a bruise over one eye and the other one reddened.

The captain gingerly feels his mouth and asks his forwards, 'Who hit me?' To their reply of 'the hooker', he responds, 'But he wasn't even the guy I tangled with!'

It is this weekend that the All Black selectors pick their team for the tour. That is clearly on the All Blacks' minds. A team mate turns to Ian Jones, now a veteran of almost 40 matches for New Zealand. 'Well done Jonesy, you're in my team to go to Australia and South Africa.'

Another Irish player descends to ask, 'Anyone want to swap a tracksuit?' 'Yes,' responds Kamo, before turning to look. The size difference is extreme! JP agrees to swap. Ant, clad in a towel, combs his hair. Arran still sits, water bottle in his hand. The representative from Steinlager asks Ant, Eroni and Buncey if they want to ring anyone — and produces his cellular phone. This is the modern age guys! The players grin and take up the offer.

The All Black coach is in his shirt sleeves. He opens a can of drink and shakes hands with Eroni, 'Well done, Eroni.' JK's father, Pat Kirwan, comes in to be with his son on this fiftieth test occasion. It adds a special touch to the scene. A couple of players kid their coach that, with the test match lead well in hand, he wanted to pull on his playing gear hoping Matt Cooper would go off! (It is sixteen years since their coach was an All Black fullback.) In private conversation they comment on Matt's hard running, 'He added some punch,' 'Yeah, a really good bloke.' I had asked Matt earlier in the week about his preparation for this test. He felt confident and understood the back move calls. 'A lot are like our provincial team moves.' He had confided that with the way the team was training, and with his own confidence, he was aiming to 'score twenty points in the test.' (I thought that was markedly excessive and did not share Matt's target expectations with anyone. However, he was to score 23 points today — the record for a first test player!)

Laurie compliments his experienced lock. 'Well played, Kamo.' 'Good game, eh?' responds Ian, who clasps hands with JT and Inga in turn.

I am standing on the reserves' side of the door between the two rooms. Laurie comes over to me. 'As a psychologist what would you do . . . let those who're going to tour know about it?' (I am unprepared for such a question from the All Black coach. He is certainly more open than I expected!) My response is that if even one player is not in the touring side for Australia and South Africa, then nothing should be said. If they are all selected to tour, I would tell them and discuss the confidentiality and trust implicit in this. Laurie: 'They're all going to tour.'

A caterer re-enters with more food on a tray. 'King of the Road' fills the changing room, tunefully enough, but Roger Miller is not threatened. On the floor, the scattering of beer can tabs mingle with turf clumps that have fallen off boots. All players are now sitting beside their All Black bags on the bench seats. The physio's table has gone. There is a companionable silence . . . The setting moves to a team focus. The room is cleared of non-team persons. Pat Kirwan and myself are the only outsiders inside the All Black changing room.

Neil Gray congratulates JK on his fiftieth test. The 28-year-old has built an acknowledged record as one of the game's great wingers since his debut in 1984. The manager then congratulates Matt on his record number of points for a test debutante. Olo ('my-talk-is-in-my-deeds') Brown is the Most Valued Player for the test. Then comes the special occasion that will only occur for the first test in any All Black's career. Kamo presents a test tie to his fellow lock, Robin Brooke, whose debut has been a singular success. Olo's All Black status has been fully justified and his experienced propping partner, with some 48 tests, presents him with a test tie. Stevie tells him that 'it gives me a hell of a lot of pleasure to present this tie to you, Olo. We go back a long way and you've come through . . . '

The presentation of the third tie, for the tyro fullback, is done by the test veteran of the team. 'Well, Matt,' begins JK, 'I might not be the tidiest of room mates . . . but I'm very proud to present you with this first test tie.' Sharing a motel room this week, there is only two years'

difference in age between the two backs, plus one's accumulation of 49 more All Black tests and half a million kilometres of rugby.

It is now JK's turn to be acknowledged by his team mates. Grant Fox, his fellow Auckland player for the best part of a decade, speaks warmly in congratulating Kirwan on his fiftieth test. Foxy asks everyone to stand to recognise the achievement . . .

Neil says that Laurie wants to speak to the team. The All Black coach moves to a vantage point in the restricted space. 'Thanks very much, fellas.' He pauses and smiles slightly, 'I hope you enjoy tonight. You can *all* let your hair down and not worry about tomorrow . . . ' (Twenty-one players are aware of the impending touring team announcement and ponder on their coach's words.) 'And if you can't read between the lines, you're bloody thicker than I thought!' Some players appear to immediately relax, while others seem to replay Laurie's words in their minds to confirm the clear implication of their impending selection. I reflect upon the message Mains has given and wonder how many national team coaches would have done this, with its attendant risk of a player speaking, even unwittingly, to the media. It is gratifying to see such a gesture by the selectors.

In the changing room, Inga has his arm around JT. Pat Kirwan sits quietly in a corner, his pride both evident and fully justified. An All Black voice in my ear asks, 'How's that for ultimate Yuppiedom?' and gesticulates to the open lavatory door where a player is urinating while simultaneously talking on a mobile phone! The image of remote and insular All Blacks hardly seems valid in this context. Foxy, gear nearly packed away, chats with me about joining the team for dinner. Laurie has a final dressing room word with the team. 'Enjoy yourselves tonight . . . but there's no going over the top like last week . . . and look after your mates.'

At the formal test match dinner, Stevie and Frank discuss their appreciation of Mains telling them about the touring selection. Brewer has been primed by Fitzy to be prepared to deliver the captain's speech if the skipper has not returned from the emergency dentist in time. (Sean had commented on his smashed teeth, 'At half-time I said, "You're going to have to speak to the TV, Bruiser" because my mouth was mangled a bit.') However, thanks to Earle's assistance and one of his helpful dentists, the captain arrived at an appropriate time of the dinner programme..

Later, three of the All Blacks and their girlfriends are in the hotel lobby waiting for the bus that does not appear. A couple of the guys banter with a duty player about the absent bus . . . It is a pleasant unwinding and eventually those in the lobby take taxis and private cars back to the team hotel where small groups sit and stand chatting in the bar area. Laurie, Earle and myself chat about touring policy, the considerations of resting players from midweek matches before tests on tour, and about Laurie's coaching style. And so the final stages of the test night roll on. Some people retire early, some move off to spend the night with partners, and some assuage their thirsts and retell the victory. It has been an intense week for a researcher living inside the All Blacks . . .

3

Inside the tradition: the All Black story

*It was appropriate that the first players from overseas should have been
New Zealanders, for the All Blacks, as they have been called since 1905,
have been probably the greatest rugby players of the twentieth century.*
The Illustrated History of Ball Games, Viney and Grant

Early nineteenth century: informal rules rule

The first reported football games played in the Australasian colonies
took place in Australia in 1829. A number of variant forms of football
quickly emerged in the young European settlements in New Zealand.
Influential in this process were visiting warships, English public school
teachers, migrants and visitors. Many of these games were hybrids, noted
by historians as featuring elements of the three main forms of football
played in the colonies — soccer, Gaelic football and Australian or Victorian Rules. The flexibility of football rules was a necessity, as the
number of players in a team ranged from ten to 50 and the period of
play varied according to mutual agreement. The form of football now
developed as Victorian Rules was very popular in New Zealand's
goldmining areas, and was suggested by its proponents as being most
suitable to become New Zealand's national game. Some games were
still played in the 1870s with Victorian Rules in one half and ball-carry-
ing football in the other. Understandably, Victorian Rules was especially
dominant in Otago (where 64,000 Australian migrants arrived in the
1861–63 period), on the West Coast of the South Island, and in the
Thames districts. It was to these regions that the Australian and Irish
miners had come, complete with their footballs.

An early form of rugby had been played by pupils of Christ's College, Christchurch, in the 1850s. Their game featured a huge paddock, an unlimited number of players, and an inflated bullock bladder which could be picked up and run with if caught on the full. This exercise reflected closely the game being played at the same time in public schools throughout the Mother Country, England. The pattern of elemental rugby experience was to continue into the twentieth century. Ray Dalton, 1949 All Black vice-captain, later described his rural boyhood days of playing rugby with a bladder ball, and 'when that wasn't available we used to fill up an old ball or bladder with packed grass'.

In 1870, Charles John Munro (1851–1933), son of Sir Charles Munro, the Speaker of the New Zealand House of Parliament, returned from his public school education at Christ College, Finchley, in London. Munro introduced the sport of rugby football to Nelson College, which led to the historic match between the College and the Town (18 a side) at the Botanical Reserve in Nelson, on 14 May 1870. The score of two goals (Town) to nil has long since paled in significance compared with the occasion, which is now acknowledged as the first organised game of rugby in New Zealand in its modern form. The College team later travelled by steamer to Wellington, on 12 September 1870, then overland by coach to the Hutt Valley, where they played a Wellington team.

Late nineteenth century: rugby's rapid growth

The relatively standardised version of rugby, although not always played with fifteen men a side, spread quickly. Historical commentators suggest the major appeal of the sport at this stage lay in its limited need for sophisticated equipment and grounds, which required little preparation, unlike cricket. Rugby was not unduly affected by mud, as was soccer. The clear objectives of the game, the influence of schools which played it, the limited rules, and the dominant characteristics of physical contestation, were also significant. The spread of the game was aided by the rapid development of a comprehensive railway and telegraph network, national government, and a reduction in work hours, which allowed more time for leisure pursuits and competitions.

The appeal of rugby broached racial divisions in the colony. By the mid-1890s, European settlers and the indigenous Maori were engaged in playing rugby in most regions of the country. While New Zealand society was not as defined as the social hierarchy apparent in England, social classes were identifiable. The colonial rugby field, however, was seeded with a comparatively egalitarian tradition.

Sociologists suggest that the male-oriented pioneer culture was prey to the appeals of a visibly aggressive sport and its related male socialising. Historians and sociologists describe a culture of drink, mateship, utter commitment to the team, camaraderie and ascribed masculine values as dominating the rugby game in New Zealand at this time. Elements of these aspects are still evident in the rugby culture of today. Prior to the 1995 World Cup, campaign manager Brian Lochore demanded that 'anyone not willing to die for the cause better get off the [All Black] bus now'. A respected rugby journalist, T.P. McLean, has also reflected, in 1995, values traditionally ascribed to rugby, by asserting that 'Rugby by its nature is only incidentally classifiable as "entertainment". Primarily it is a manly contest challenging the skills and courage of its players.' As the twentieth century runs into the professional era, McLean's view may become, sadly for many, outdated.

The emergent rugby culture of late nineteenth century New Zealand emphasised physical aggression, not showing pain, and a tacit acceptance of illegal play within an unofficial, but universally understood, code of conduct. The exclusion of women from most of rugby's social rituals swiftly became a deeply rooted phenomenon, especially at the 'after-match' function, where women were largely confined to a role of making tea and sandwiches for the men. This phenomenon still characterises some occasions related to the game, as the exclusion of females from a 1995 All Black trial match dinner in Auckland illustrates.

Emerging in the 1870s as New Zealand's dominant popular sport, rugby was very important at school level. English public schools had a significant influence upon secondary education in the colony, particularly in the provision of teachers in private, and some state, schools. In Dunedin, rugby had been introduced by a teacher who was the son of a Rugby schoolmaster, and former English school pupils became colonial schoolmasters and headmasters of influence. In Auckland, such teachers influenced the change of popularity from association football, or soccer, and Victorian Rules football to the rugby code.

While the sometimes brutal nature of the game may have been attributed as a primary cause of rugby's rapid growth and appeal, that same quality also engendered a degree of public condemnation. Mild criticism centred on the opinion that rugby had none of cricket's discipline and etiquette. As hacking (kicking of opponents' shins) and tripping were legal elements of rugby until the 1880s, more severe critics of rugby complained that the sport tended to develop 'the worst impulses of man's nature'.

In July 1879, the Canterbury Rugby Football Union was established, the first provincial rugby union in New Zealand, followed by the Wellington Union three months later. The emergence of provincial unions became the dominant factor in New Zealand rugby of the 1880s. In March 1881, the Otago RFU was formed, and Auckland founded the fourth union in April 1883. The process continued throughout the colony, with the formation of eighteen unions in the fifteen-year period to 1894.

The game itself was played by businessmen and miners, Pakeha and Maori, urban clerical workers and farmers. Rugby players came from all walks of life, and could not be defined by one simple profile. Administration of the game developed one early but lasting characteristic. By the 1880s there was a predominance of middle-class men engaged in rugby's control.

In 1882, the Southern Rugby Union of New South Wales toured as the first overseas representative rugby team to play in New Zealand. This visit was reciprocated in May 1884 by the first team from New Zealand to play overseas. It won all eight matches. 1886 saw another New South Wales tour of New Zealand. The first British rugby team to visit New Zealand shores arrived in 1888. Hints of controversy followed the tourists, who introduced the concept of heeling the ball back from the scrum, allowing backs to handle the ball behind the forwards, a practice previously believed by New Zealanders to constitute offside play.

The first major international tour by a team from New Zealand occurred in 1888–89, when a 'Natives' team toured Britain, being the first overseas rugby team to do so. The squad was predominantly comprised of Maori, with five Pakeha team mates, and attracted substantial media attention in the Home Country. A coach went with them, primarily to teach the players Victorian Rules football as a demonstration sport. The Natives underlined the superior development of the New Zealand game through winning 49 of the 74 games they played in the British Isles between 3 October 1888 and 27 March 1889. Their exhausting world trip took fourteen months. A British comment of the time, from the 28 August 1888 *Daily Telegraph*, reflects prevailing attitudes on imperialism and sport:

The spectacle of the noble Maori, coming from different parts of the earth to play an English game, is a phenomenon that is of the very essence of peace. It is one of our proud boasts that wherever we go, whatever lands we conquer, we found the great national instinct of playing games. Plant a dozen Englishmen anywhere . . . and in a wonderfully short time . . . the level sward is turned into a cricket field in summer and a football arena in winter.

The Natives, who played 107 or 108 games on their odyssey, were met on arrival by the British press. One of the first questioners asked the captain, Joe Warbrick, if New Zealand had any criminal like England's Whitechapel murderer Jack the Ripper. This was the first of some 110 years of British media questions seeking a response on subjects other than rugby from international teams. The tour attracted considerable press attention and germinated its own historical stories, such as that of Davy Gage's love affair with the grand-daughter of an earl and the music hall contract offered to Gage and Tabby Wynyard.

The importance of this tour went far beyond the team's playing record. Historians have come to see its sporting exchanges as a starting point in the boosting of national confidence in an attempt to shape New Zealand's national identity.

By 1890 there were nearly 700 rugby clubs and eighteen provincial unions in New Zealand. However, the continuing growth of the national game was not a totally smooth progression. The number of clubs rose and fell with the vagaries of a population exhibiting a high degree of geographic mobility. In 1891, the public announcement of a representative women's rugby team for a national tour was met with widespread condemnation, reinforcing images of the sexist culture which was operating within rugby and the wider New Zealand society. However, there is evidence that, in 1897, a predominantly male team in the Bay of Plenty included four female players in at least one game.

The need for a national governing body was voiced by representatives of the Wellington and Canterbury Unions as early as 1879 and supported by the Auckland RFU in the 1880s. Despite the increasing regulation of rugby in New Zealand, regional disagreements remained over fixtures, scoring values and interpretations of the rules, and a body was needed to organise and coordinate tours. The need for such a centralised authority to be nearer than the control exercised by England was now beyond question.

E.D. Hobden, an administrator of the Hawke's Bay Union, spent

1891 travelling the colony discussing the proposal for the formation of a national body with existing unions. Hobden called a meeting in Wellington, on 7 November 1891, to discuss the possibility of forming a New Zealand rugby union. The unions of Wellington, Auckland, Otago, Wairarapa, Hawke's Bay, Taranaki and Manawatu were all represented. The meeting set out the essential functions of the New Zealand Rugby Football Union in a draft constitution. They were to foster and control rugby football at a national level, to manage international matches, to arbitrate on the rules, to foster inter-union matches and generally to govern all matters relevant to the game's wellbeing and growth.

In 1892 the New Zealand Rugby Football Union (NZRFU) was formed at a meeting on 16 April, although the South Island unions of Southland, Canterbury and Otago did not join until 1893–94. The chairman of the meeting, G.F.C. Campbell of the Wellington Union, articulated the 'need for a supreme football Court of Appeal in the Colony'. The famous black jersey with its silver fern emblem was adopted as the national representative team's playing uniform at the annual meeting of the NZRFU in 1893, upon the motion of Tom Ellison. A black cap with silver monogram, white knickerbocker shorts and black stockings were agreed upon also. Ellison, a seminal figure in New Zealand rugby, played in the Natives 1888–89 team, captained the first New Zealand team to play under the patronage of the NZRFU, in 1893, and produced New Zealand's first influential rugby coaching book.

A new century of rugby

Even on foreign soil in the Anglo-Boer War, the New Zealanders' rugby world overlapped the combat environment. Victoria Crosses were won by Thomas Crean and Robert Johnson, who both played for Ireland, British Isles and Transvaal, and by Major William Hardham, who played 54 games for Wellington. Some New Zealanders engaged in informal matches, and two post-war Kiwi clubs were formed — the NZRFC in Johannesburg, and Durban New Zealanders Club. Past and future New Zealand players were volunteers for the war. Bunny Abbott and Dave Gallaher were but two of 6,500 New Zealanders on the continent. Perceived by some as a martinet with rigorous training methods, Gallaher was later said to train 'by running through the back country in heavy boots and concluding the run with a bout of two-man pit sawing!' His letters reveal a little more of the man. In Charleston Hospital, 18 October 1901, his thoughts were on his sport: 'Darling Old Sis . . . I suppose you have been at most of the football matches this year . . .'. Two months later he wrote again:

> We spent Xmas Day partly in marching. Halted about 3.00 p.m. and had a biscuit or two and a bit of fried mutton for dinner, and had to go up on outpost that night. Next day was on observation post all day with Joeys dodging about, had sundry shots at one another. Came into camp at dusk and received navy ration of pudding and a draft of beer. Turned in and dreamt it was Xmas. Trekked out again next day and had two great fights before New Year.

A more revealing personal insight into the first great New Zealand captain came with his account of a fight with Botha at Opperman. Gallaher, often described as a hard man, reveals a very human side in his letters at Wellington's Turnbull Library: 'I got a bullseye that day when they were doing a retreat but two of them came back and got him away between them and I did not have the heart to fire at them while doing so.'

Abroad, New Zealand was absent from the 1900, 1908, 1920 and 1924 Olympics rugby competition. Thus, the United States were the reigning Olympic champions! At home, the Ranfurly Shield, presented by Lord Ranfurly in 1901, swiftly grew in prestige as the most significant tangible symbol of provincial supremacy, even with the introduction of the National Provincial Championship (NPC) in 1976. The Shield is still contested in a 'one-off' challenge, generating a great deal of fervour and continuing public interest. Unlike the Ranfurly Shield matches, the NPC consists of a round-robin format followed by play-offs, which results in a build-up toward a climax.

In 1904, the desire for autonomy saw North Otago and Mid-Canterbury bring the number of unions to twenty. On the international scene, competition was becoming more regular. A representative team toured Australia in 1903, under Jimmy Duncan, winning all ten matches. The following year, the first fully representative British Isles team came to New Zealand, under D.R. Bedell-Sivright, who would next be encountered as a medical officer at Gallipoli. The development of New Zealand rugby then faced its most demanding challenge to date — the first official tour of the Home Unions.

In 1905 the national team set out on a tour encompassing Great Britain, France and North America. The team became labelled the 'Originals', and was captained by the famous Dave Gallaher, in whose memory the Auckland club competition trophy is still named. The team, with Jimmy Duncan as coach, played 35 games, losing only one, the very controversial test match against Wales in which the Welsh victory rested on denial of a much discussed New Zealand try. The success of that 1905 tour lay in two broad areas — those of the players' personal and positional skills and the team's skilful game plans. For the first time in international rugby, positions in the team had specialist players and the forwards played with pace in support roles for the backs. These New Zealand initiatives shaped new perspectives of rugby in its land of origin, the British Isles. The silver fern genealogy of rugby is further illustrated by the line of influence from Jimmy Duncan (1903 New Zealand captain and 1905 'Originals' coach), who coached young Charlie Saxton, the 1938 All Black and post-war Kiwis captain. Saxton became the All Blacks manager in 1967, with Brian Lochore as captain. Lochore was a marked influence as 1987 All Black coach and 1995 World Cup campaign manager, with a clear impact upon his young charges.

The patriotic emphasis placed on the tour and the establishment of New Zealand as, arguably, the world's foremost rugby playing nation, provided a lasting link between rugby and the national ethos of a young country. By providing a specific focus for national pride, the 1905 tour was central to assuring rugby's premier position in New Zealand sport. The importance of the national team's achievement was reinforced by the fact that the results had been achieved in rugby. In demonstrating their mastery of an upper-class English game, the colony marked out its own sporting identity and renewed linkages with the Mother Country. The tour elevated rugby to an importance beyond that of sport itself.

In the course of that 1905–6 tour the team was dubbed the 'All Blacks', a name which has been indelibly linked with the national rugby team of New Zealand ever since. The precise origin of the term is still debated, with some, such as Gallaher and Stead, arguing that it came from the dominant and sombre colour of the players' uniforms, and others claiming a report of the team playing like 'all backs' was misquoted as 'all blacks'. The former is the more credible explanation.

Strong links between rugby and politics in New Zealand were established during the 1905–6 tour. Prime Minister Richard John Seddon followed the results of the team closely, having the results cabled to him as government messages. In 1905 the New Zealand government advertised in for immigrants in British papers when important matches were about to be played. Seddon obtained parliamentary approval to finance the team's return via the United States as a reward for a successful tour. This recognition was reinforced on the team's arrival back in New Zealand, with a reception from the prime minister in Wellington and praise from the leader of the opposition.

The professional rugby league code split from the amateur code over the question of compensating players for rugby time taken away from employment, this separation being formalised in 1895. League was not initially perceived as a realistic threat to the strength of rugby union. In 1907, a New Zealand professional rugby league team left to tour England. The team was labelled the 'All Golds' and included some 1905 All Blacks.

Reactions in New Zealand to that tour portrayed social attitudes ascribed to followers of both league and union. One newspaper letter characterised the union player as a 'clean cut thoroughbred', in contrast to the 'ungamely draught horse' of the league player. Since the splitting of the codes, the relationship has often been bitter, dominated by the moralistic attitudes amateur rugby administrators have shown toward the professional code. The relationship remained strained until 1995, with rugby administrators resenting league clubs 'poaching' élite union players, and descriptions in the media of union players 'defecting' to league. Historically there have been severe restrictions upon rugby union players re-entering the rugby code after playing league.

Prior to 1914, the Waikato and Bay of Plenty Rugby Football Unions were formed. This brought the number of provincial unions to 22, of the total of 27 in 1998. Of the 127 matches which New Zealand's national representative teams played prior to the First World War, 117 were victories, three were draws, and seven were losses. New Zealand teams scored 3,110 points, and had 439 scored against them. By the time war, on an unparalleled level, was untangling national alliances on the European side of the globe, the running game had become interwoven in the fabric of New Zealand society.

The First World War era

Gus Hart, a First World War veteran, in 1991 recalled the early days of the century.

> It took all of our time to get a shilling from the old man for a football. We had an old school football and often rode bareback to other schools

to play. Those were still pioneering days. I grew up in the Ngaruawahia–Huntly area. After matches we travelled by horse-drawn bus. Once the game finished we changed into our clothes (there were no showers or baths). We would get as far as the Huntly pub for a round of beers, then on to Taupiri where we would have a few more beers . . . and so on . . . When I got into the Army and was off to Ypres and other places we were in those bloody trenches, in all the mud. You were always wet or lousy, or both. We were loaded down with ammo so we threw a lot of it away, and the officers knew we did that. We never read of bloody Services rugby teams. It was easier to play that sort of rugby if you weren't really a soldier, if you were safe at Headquarters and eating well. We were just the poor bloody infantry. Never saw a football. The farther you got from the line the better off you were. We went into the line, rain, hail or shine, at night-time — and wet through. Jerry used to put up these flares and they were beauties. They used to have a stroll around at night-time and so did we . . . You wouldn't be thinking about rugby then, unless it was to wish you were back on a footy field at Ngaruawahia . . .

A fellow Ranfurly War Veteran's Home resident was the Gallipoli soldier Charlie Harrigan.

We had a very flash team in the old Taumarunui sub-union, and would catch the train at different stops, so we didn't know who was who until we got on the field! The train home usually didn't leave Ohakune or Owhanga, or wherever, until 10.00 p.m. . . . God, Gallipoli was a bit different from that! After Gallipoli they sent us down to the Suez Canal for a while and we had to 'stand to' at dusk and at daylight . . . at day-time we played football. I still remember, after Gallipoli, this soldier pulled a football out of his kit and said, 'You know the first thing I'm doing when I get away from here is kicking this ball up and down the Suez Canal!', and the ball was deflated anyway! We had fun games there, practically all kicking, something to do I suppose . . . Then I went on to France. In France the ones who were good at it played rugby, I'm told.

The New Zealand Combined Services team, representative of the country's Armed Forces, won the King's Cup international tournament in wartime Britain. It went on to play in South Africa, though some excellent Services players were omitted because of their colour. Thirteen All Blacks died in the First World War, their young lives symbolic of the 16,697 New Zealanders killed in that foreign inferno.

An unusual account of one All Black's death of wounds on the Somme is found in the Storey's family history. Frank Wilson had been an All Black wing in 1910, choir singer and skilled rose grower. His mother, who was believed to have a psychic sense, told her family how she was lying in bed at 5.00 a.m. when her thoughts were drawn strongly to her son in France. Suddenly she saw Frank's form in the doorway, and he moved to her bedside, where he said, 'I'm not coming home Mother,' and disappeared. Two days later, Mrs Wilson was advised of her son's death at the time of the vision. Eight cousins in the Storey family sailed overseas and four returned. Three of Frank's cousins met up in Heliopolis, Egypt, to watch an ANZAC rugby football match. Another cousin is buried in Nine Elms Cemetery, Poperinghe, Belgium, near Dave Gallaher.

Sergeant Albert Downing was killed on Chunuk Bair, on 8 August 1915, and Sergeant Norky Dewar lost his life one day later, his regiment having taken over from the Wellington Regiment the day before. The CO of the Wellington Mounted Rifles on Gallipoli, Brigadier General William Meldrum, was another top rugby player, having been a wing forward for Auckland in 1884–86. A 1905 All Black, 'Jum' Turtill, played against Australia, then joined the 'All Golds' and played league in England. Joining the West Lancashire Division he was killed in the war. Ironically, his sister became nanny to another soldier and Lincoln College First XV rugby player — Charles Upham, New Zealand's double Victoria Cross winner.

Between the wars: the 1920s and 1930s

Following the Great War, rugby organisation spread at a rapid pace through rural New Zealand. By 1922, the number of provincial unions had risen to 26. This increased the formal national administration of the game and, arguably, facilitated an accompanying increase in the social importance of the game in these areas. The early development of the provincial unions has been a source of regional rugby pride and tradition, as 25 existing unions are at least 65 years old, including 16 which are at least 100 years old. Ironically, the sense of tradition which has become so deeply entrenched in these unions is now seen by many commentators as a barrier to needed change in provincial and national rugby administration and competition structures. In rural districts the school, rugby club, netball club, community hall and church were not only the focus of local society, they bore their own special inter-relationships, often with rugby as the linchpin. On the wider scale of world rugby, the values of the age are illustrated by J.M. Kerr, a 1930s Scottish fullback opponent of the All Blacks.

At Twickenham against England, a kick to the far corner just crossed the line. [The Scottish fullback] arrived with the English centre and we finished in a heap, and the ball shot onto the side stand like a rocket. The small Welsh referee was at the 25-yard line and on arrival asked me, the defender, 'Was it a score?' As the ball touched the ground over the line, the Englishman had got his hand to it. It was a score, and I said so and Scotland lost 9–8 (and one man short). A good loser? Not at all. You play the game by the rules, or not at all.

Post-war, Scotland was playing France in Paris and in a flurry of activity Scots and French finished in a heap over the line. The referee gave a 25-yard drop-out to Scotland but the Scottish fullback, Geddes, went after the referee and indicated that indeed France had scored. He gave a try, and the French were so impressed by Geddes' sportsmanship they presented him with a silver salver!

The guides for emergent All Blacks were few and coaching was not always available. A rugby coaching manual of the period provided advice for young players, suggesting they choose a tight pair of boots and sit with their feet in a bath of hot water for 'twenty minutes or so' and then 'let the boots dry on your feet'. This would be followed by a rub of good dubbin into the leather, 'and they will fit you like a glove'.

Representative New Zealand Universities and Maori teams made their first overseas tours in early post-war years and the seminal year of 1921 saw the first South African tour of New Zealand, captained by Theo Pienaar. The rivalry between the All Blacks and the South African side, the Springboks, swiftly developed into the most intense rivalry in international rugby. This first series between the two sides was drawn. The tour was keenly followed by the New Zealand public with nascent signs of the controversy which would increasingly envelop the sporting contact between the two teams over the ensuing decades. Jock Richardson, a 1921 All Black in the series against South Africa, recalls that South Africa's strengths were in their forwards, who had a very high level of play, which was especially hard.

They were a good team in the backs and forwards. In 1921 we had one week's training together in Dunedin. Two coaches were appointed. One was Alf Griffiths and the other was Donald Stuart, who had been selected for the 1905–6 All Blacks but failed the medical examination . . . the changing room was not unusual, it was like an ordinary representative team's. The coaching had been done out on the training ground during the week. Our captain at Dunedin, George Aitken, had worked in coordination with the coaches. As I remember we didn't do the haka against South Africa. We won 13–5.

Bill Hadley, All Black hard man, hooker and humorist, had his wonderful wife Mary as a key person in his rugby life. Bill recalled the boyhood days of the 1920s when, 'If you saw a pebble you'd kick it, you'd make up rag balls, anything you'd see as a kid you'd kick! I played for my school every Saturday on the Domain, there'd be about fourteen teams playing. We just could not afford anything in those Depression years — if we saw another boy with a ball we'd do anything to get into a game.'

International contact became more frequent in the years between the world wars, notably with the 1924–25 All Black tour of Britain, France and British Columbia. That team became known as 'The Invincibles' through winning every match of the tour, prompting *The Times* in London to issue a special supplement on the play of the All Blacks. This again underlined the strength and importance of the game in New Zealand, and reinforced the sport as a lodestar of nationalism. The captain of the 1924–25 All Blacks, Jock Richardson, recalled in 1992 that, 'The atmosphere was different against Wales as they were the only team that had beaten the first All Blacks team. We were determined that we would avenge that defeat.' Richardson, the longest survivor of the 1924 All Blacks, recalls another famous match on tour.

> I didn't see the incident, I was only told by the referee what had happened. He said that Cyril Brownlie had kicked someone. I asked Cyril if he had kicked him [the English player]. I appealed to the referee but he sent him off. I had to reconstruct the team . . . in the dressing room the team was mostly sympathising with Cyril Brownlie and believing him. The British didn't come up to our dressing room. Cyril's brother, Maurice, never spoke, never raised a protest about it. Maurice was inclined to be a little taciturn and kept to himself quite a deal — a very quiet natured fellow who had very sound and solid playing skills.

The two most acclaimed Maori players of that tour, Jimmy Mill and George Nepia, found themselves omitted from the 1928 tour of South Africa because of their colour, this being the first time the All Blacks ventured to that racially segregated rugby nation. The two countries have historically shared a passion for rugby, and a similar approach of intense physical commitment to the game. Richardson provides a very debatable perspective on a 1924 icon. 'George Nepia played in every game. We needed him. He had an easy tour because he had such good players in front of him. There was some discussion between myself and George about resting him . . . He was only 19 years old and his game had to be continually moulded.' Alf Waterman, the longest surviving All Black until his death in 1997, recalled Nepia.

> He was absolutely perfect in his play in the one game he played on the 1929 tour of Australia. I remember he would start off at practice with six or seven balls and old George would put his blazer down and kick for accuracy onto his blazer. He was also a real gentleman in every way. On the *Mahino* going over to Australia George sang 'Waiata Poi', after a lot of requests. He could sing beautifully . . .

New Zealand rugby continued to develop its international contacts. The first tour of New Zealand by the fully representative British Isles and Ireland team, known as the Lions, was seen in 1930 with the All Blacks playing in white jerseys to avoid the similarity between their normal jerseys and the visitors' dark blue jerseys. In the following year, the Bledisloe Cup was introduced for trans-Tasman rugby test competition, and remains one of the supreme prizes which New Zealand contests in international sport. In 1932 also, New Zealand moved from the traditional 2-3-2 scrum and wing forward position. For the 1934 tour of Australia, Alan Andrews played in two All Black trial matches and was then selected for the final trial. His subsequent experience is a reminder of the academic and social attitudes of the times, as his unpublished biography records.

> I developed influenza. I made little improvement during the week, but did not inform the selectors of my illness as I desperately wanted to play. I went to Auckland determined to play although I was in no fit state to do so.
>
> As the time neared 3.00 p.m. I was feeling pretty poorly but decided to do or die. I had a brilliant first half and at half time I was pulled off so someone else could have a go. It was just as well as by then I was virtually finished. The pulling off was a good omen as that night my name was among those selected for the tour. At long last my ambition was achieved.
>
> Alas, my elation was short-lived, as when my Engineering Professor heard about my selection he advised me that he would not allow me to sit my final examinations if I went to Australia, as he contended I would miss too much study time — this, despite the fact that three weeks of the tour took place during the August vacation. He completely overlooked the fact that, instead of being in Australia, I spent two weeks touring the North Island as captain of the Canterbury team . . .

The economic depression affected gate takings at rugby matches in the early 1930s as well as the financial security of amateur All Blacks selected for overseas tours. On the steps of the Grand Hotel at about midnight, the 1935–36 All Black touring team was announced by the Chairman of the NZRFU, Mr Deans. Bill Collins, one of the named All Blacks, recollected:

> We had to prove to the Rugby Union that we had six stiff shirts and boots and 40 pounds in our own personal bank balance! Then on tour we were given an allowance of three shillings per day in vouchers, with the book ruled off at midnight Saturday night. We were supplied with the All Black match kit, a pair of slacks and sand-shoes.

It was of one such announcement that Bill Hadley recalled, 'They said I was a hard man but when they announced the team I was like a kid and raced all the way home to Mum!'

In the 1920s and 1930s a major rugby tour had many facets which illuminated life for a young All Black. In the days of ship travel the All Blacks stopped at Panama, where they would encounter the notorious denizens of the red light district. 'We had a lecture about the dangers of Panama from the ship's doctor and he was right to the point; in fact, it was a very interesting half an hour . . . ', noted Merv Corner's 1935–36 tour diary.

Simple ethics hardly noticed off the field have always prevailed in the All Blacks —one example is that you don't pass to a team mate in a worse position than yours. This is not simply for tactical reasons, as an attack could be wasted, but because an All Black does not put his team mate at unnecessary risk of injury or in receipt of a 'hospital pass', when the player is compelled to catch the ball and is left relatively un-protected as the attackers hit him. Hugh McLean recalled a graphic example from 1936 in Australia. 'I saw one All Black bite the dust and as he did so he passed to Pat Caughey, who had two blokes just flying upon him. I said to the guy on the ground, when I saw what he'd done to Pat, "You'll never play for the All Blacks again." It was just bloody cowardly! And he didn't.'

The Springbok tour of 1937 again reinforced the All Blacks' high profile, despite their losing the series. Harold Milliken, 1938 All Black, was a strong lock, and a reserve for the 1937 team. Despite the revision-ist historians who suggest the elemental life of New Zealand males may not have been a reality so many decades into the twentieth century, Milliken recalls travelling by jigger fourteen miles to Springfield, on the railway line, to play rugby. 'And we used to go pig hunting to get fit.

We would go on long tramps and hunting trips, over the West Coast in the Haast area. We walked the Haast Pass and went through the Haast River . . . that certainly got us fit for rugby!' The final pre-war season, 1939, saw Fiji make its first tour, highlighting the international and South Pacific development of the game.

The Second World War to the 1950s: golden years

The Second World War saw rugby played by New Zealand troops in all theatres of war. Rugby and wartime have links forged by the need for recreation and fused by common qualities. You grew up in New Zealand before the South African war? You knew how to play rugby. You grew up in New Zealand before the First World War? You knew how to play rugby. You grew up . . . you knew . . . War became a metaphor and cliché in rugby match descriptions. It is easy to decry the absurdity of this analogy as lives in test rugby are not at stake, nor does the sheer terror of destruction hang over 80 minutes fraught with little more than the unexpected moment. And yet, for veterans of the most demanding of each of these fields, there are similarities — the intense task fusion and interdependence; the mateship so easily derided by social commentators; and the driving pride of proving oneself and meeting external demands for commitment and achievement. Examples of the link have come from sober-minded citizens. Neil McPhail, a Second World War veteran who coached the All Blacks, comments, 'Yes, there are similarities. What you might call interdependence and I might call mateship are essential when a group or team is under intense pressure from outside, whether it's war or top rugby. If you haven't been in there, it's hard to describe. What you value rests on your mates . . . '

The parallel is also drawn by rugby administrators, as seen in the immediate post-war Newport Rugby Football Club article which referred to the Kiwis team who would 'battle anew, this time on the pleasant pastures representing the Rugby fields of the Mother Country'. Jim Bolger, the New Zealand Prime Minister, in a speech to the All Black and Springbok teams at a small function in 1994, expressed satisfaction at the cessation of apartheid, stating that 'now the battles can take place on the rugby field'.

'I was over in Italy during the war and there was the same confidence and comradeship — going to the Returned Services Association is just like rugby players getting together,' Peter Johnstone, an All Black captain, observed to the author.

Immediately after the armistice in Europe, a representative army team, named the Kiwis, was selected from the 2nd New Zealand Expeditionary Force. The team toured the British Isles, France and Germany, then played matches on their return to New Zealand, being recognised for their free-flowing style of play. (The team's legacy was to resurface with the late 1960s appointment of the two senior Kiwis, Charlie Saxton and Fred Allen, as All Black manager and coach.) Following the Kiwis' tour, New Zealand was admitted to the International Rugby Board in 1948. The continued dominance of the international governing body by the northern hemisphere countries of England, Scotland, Ireland and Wales was not a reflection of playing strength, but of the voting strength originally assigned to them as founding IRB members.

Following a tour to Australia in 1947, the first major tour by post-war All Blacks to South Africa took place two years later. This new era started poorly for New Zealand, with the loss of all four internationals in the republic and a further two at home to Australia. In New Zealand society there were isolated voices seeking the recognition of non-white players in South African teams and, particularly, the inclusion of Maori in All Black teams to South Africa. The often discordant skeins of politics and sport were becoming more visibly interwoven. Louis Duffus, in the *Johannesburg Star*, asserted that even war had not generated the nationalistic feelings in South Africa that sport had, 'in a nation otherwise split by racism'. Accounts of the tour rarely note the embryonic protests that were forming. Sam Weller, in a topical publication, *Here and Now* (October, 1949), noted: 'I see no reason why we should have connived at such social discrimination. We falsified our own tradition in doing so.' The Wellington Communist Party distributed leaflets and displayed placards outside Athletic Park to protest at Maori exclusion from the 1949 tour. The All Blacks subsequently selected for the tour were overweight, albeit basically well skilled, and given a coach whose methods were behind the times. Recognised as formidable by their opponents, they were a potentially excellent side who drew large crowds. The *Johannesburg Star* in June reported that students were offering to stand in booking line-ups for fees of two guineas, and the South African parliament voted itself a holiday so that members could see the opening match. A South African writer recalls a different memory of the hardened All Black forwards.

I was working at the time in 1949 for a dentist and when the team arrived here to play Border, a couple of the chaps needed a dentist. One

Final Itinerary of All Blacks Visit to Salisbury

Friday, 29th July, to Sunday, 31st July, 1949

Friday, 29th July, 1949

Official.   8.0 a.m.   All Blacks and Rhodeian teams arrive
                          at Salisbury Railway Station – trans-
                          port to Meikles Hotel to be provided.

Official.   10.0 a.m.   All Blacks team to be taken to Old
                          Hararians ground for practice and
                          training.

Unofficial. 11.15 a.m.   Visit of All Blacks and Rhodeian teams
                          to Tobacco Producers' Floors to witness
                          tobacco sales and have tea.

Unofficial. 12.30 p.m.   United Services Club for refreshments
                          before lunch. Both teams.

Unofficial. 1.15 p.m.   Return to Meikles Hotel for lunch.

Unofficial. 3.15 p.m.   Visit to State +Lotteries. Both teams.
                          Note:– A small sweep will be run to
                          make the visit interesting.

Official.   6.15p.m.   Civic Sundowner party at Tea Kiosk,
                          Salisbury Park. At this function the
                          teams will be officially welcomed to
                          the capital of Rhodesia by His Worship,
                          the Mayor, Councillor Morton Jaffray.
                          The Manager of the All Blacks will
                          reply.

                          Rhodesian Rugby Football Union welcome
                          to the All Blacks by the President,
                          Mashonaland Rugby Football Board.
                          Reply by the Captain of the All Blacks.

                          Mr. Frank Roselli, Chairman, Rhodesia
                          Rugby Football Union, will propose the
                          health of the visitors. Mr. Bo. Wintle
                          South African Manager, will reply.

Unofficial. After dinner. Free

— a very large forward — was one of the most nervous patients I'd ever known. He prowled the verandah and couldn't sit in the waiting room and was in a complete cold sweat in the chair. I felt very sorry for him!

The impact of South Africa's inhuman social conditions upon the 1949 All Blacks was not insignificant. Members of that team, some 45 years later, have expressed the pent-up anger, even despair, of never having spoken out about their encounter with Afrikaans separatism. On one typical social occasion, the team was entertained at a barbecue at a beautiful farm, with quality winter quarters for the stock and immaculate surroundings. Jack McNab recalls:

Knowing we were country people the farmer said we might like to look around. We admired the buildings for the animals — far better than many of ours at home. Then we noticed smoke coming from pieces of corrugated iron standing up against each other. We went over and peered in the opening. Slowly we saw the whites of two people's eyes. Two native people were cooking something in the most terrible living space you can imagine. The animals had far better buildings. We were quite upset by this. As we turned away, Jack Elvidge [father of All Black Ron Elvidge] turned to me and declared, 'My God, there is a day of reckoning coming.'

To remain silent for years, as the players felt was demanded by the NZRFU, weighed heavily with certain All Blacks.

The year of 1950 returned the status of the national game to pre-war heights of popularity. The Lions tour of New Zealand was a huge success, with the tourists playing attractive rugby under the acclaimed captaincy of Ireland's Karl Mullen, although the home team won the test series 3–0, the first test having been drawn 9–9. The third test of the four-test series saw the All Blacks win despite having only six forwards; these men, supercharged by will, covering the deficit of two badly injured players. This was the era of no replacements. Ron Elvidge, the captain, returned to the field with torn chest muscles and a head injury. Although commended for his courage, the *Waikato Times* of 4 July 1950 declared that 'All talk in the strain of "the game's the thing" is mere humbug if the desire to win is to be satisfied by putting an injured man through the trial that Elvidge happily survived.' One of the 1924 Invincibles declared after the match that Pat Crowley's play in that All Black–Lions match had been reminiscent of Maurice Brownlie's in the test match at Twickenham in 1925, when England 'saw Brownlie at his very best'. It was the ultimate accolade across All Black generations.

Jean-Marie Brohm in his Marxist-oriented writing on rugby describes the game as 'a text book case of tolerated violence, and the deliberate cultivation of brutality. It reflects the torture mentality and the cult of physical force and confrontation typical of the goon squads of creepy fascism.' Mon Dieu, mate! The borderline may seem blurred at times to an unskilled spectator — and let's not gloss over the culpable actions of some All Blacks — but measured against the span of a match, or accumulated years of test play, players' shabby deeds are few. There is an unwritten boundary or code which defines, for All Blacks, the acceptable and the unacceptable levels of onfield confrontation, as the *Weekly News* of 12 July 1950 illustrates.

> Though the code of the game was rarely infringed, there seemed abroad a certain degree of ferocity which manifested itself in the deadly and devastating tackling which occurred when the packs clashed. The sight of big men being seized, tossed and hurled to the ground became commonplace. Both sets of forwards must have been as hard as nails and in perfect physical condition to have withstood and endured to the end this gruelling ordeal.

On the provincial score, the Ranfurly Shield generated large crowds throughout the post-war decade, with Otago dominating its possession for much of this period. A 1948 newspaper item noted of star Otago All Black Ron Elvidge, New Zealand captain 1949–50, that 'when he walks down the main street, he turns more heads than Bing Crosby would'.

The 1956 South African tour of New Zealand saw rugby reach the zenith of its popularity in New Zealand. A bitterly intense rivalry between the two countries had been building since 1919. With the losses sustained in the 1949 series the expectations of New Zealand rugby administrators now equalled those of the vocal public in demanding success from the All Blacks. This was the era when the whole nation tuned in their valve radios to the sombre broadcasts of the All Blacks. Don McIntosh, 1950s All Black, heard of his selection after a club match at Petone in Wellington. 'There were no portable or transistor radios in that year of Springbok fever, so somebody drove their car into the gymnasium and we gathered around and heard it from there!' The national team responded to national exhortations by winning the series 3–0, reaffirming the public appeal of rugby in this country.

The national game clearly dominated the New Zealand sports scene in the 1950s and 1960s. The public held a strong belief in the values of sport being transferred to life situations — and vice versa. Eric Boggs, an All Black and a provincial coach, believes, 'The rules and disciplines on the field are transferred to community life. Rugby is a stepping stone to self-esteem.' A typical perspective on this period comes from an outside observer, prolific writer and author of rugby books, J.B.G. Thomas, who noted that 'New Zealanders are crazy about the Rugby Union game . . . Rugby, to a normal New Zealander, is a way of life and far more than a mere sport. It is a national form of demonstration of the physical prowess of the youth in the country.' The ultimate demonstration of such capabilities was, however, unsuccessful in the next series in South Africa in 1960, despite the presence of such great players as Whineray, Meads and Graham.

1960s and 1970s: the winds of change

New Zealand participated in increased international competition through the early 1960s, including hosting tours by England and France. Male stoicism continued to be sorely tested by the practice of a touring team being announced to an assembly of hopefuls after the intensity of All Black trials! Ron Horsley, an All Black lock in 1960–64, went from being a youngster afraid of getting hurt, to running in the harriers, and then into rugby after his compulsory military training. Eventually he progressed through All Black trials to the stage where he had to wait under the Millard Stand at Athletic Park for the 1960 team to be announced. 'It was quite nerve-wracking and it must have been awfully difficult for players listening who did not have their names read out.' Some 30 years later the 1987 World Cup team was to be announced in the same unfeeling way.

The 1965 tour by the Springboks again generated strong public interest as it fused national pride and a focus for rugby ascendancy. The All Blacks won the series 3–1. Widespread national support for the All Blacks continued as they displayed an expansive playing style, and won 38 of the 43 tests contested, in the later 1960s. This playing style under Fred Allen's coaching, combined with the team's success, ensured the retention of rugby's place in the national psyche.

Tours of New Zealand by overseas teams in the 1960s and 1970s reflected the international expansion of the sport, with visits by Victoria, Romania, Western Samoa, Cook Islands, Argentina and Italy. International politics also affected New Zealand rugby as the pressure built on

New Zealand to cease contact with the apartheid state of South Africa. In 1965 the South African Prime Minister Dr Hendrik Verwoerd reiterated that Maori players would not be welcomed as touring All Blacks. The growing number of New Zealanders proclaiming 'No Maoris, No Tour' led to widespread debate on the extent to which rugby and politics interacted.

Verwoerd's successor, J.B. Vorster, shifted the official viewpoint, and the seminal 1970 All Black tour included three Maori and a Samoan, granted 'honorary white' status for the purpose of the rugby tour. Violent protests marked the Springbok tours of England in 1971 and Australia in 1972, yet the New Zealand government continued to deny links between politics and sport.

The 1976 All Black tour to South Africa was concurrent with student riots and police shootings in the republic. These events led to vigorous public condemnation in New Zealand of rugby's close contact with the racist state. Some prominent All Blacks, including the captain Graham Mourie, declined selection in teams to play the Springboks. Rugby faced a decline in schools, where teachers were withdrawing from their involvement in rugby coaching, influenced by a belief that the NZRFU was offering tacit support to the apartheid government of South Africa through maintaining rugby contacts.

The relationship between rugby and television developed rapidly in the early 1970s. Some 51 per cent of the available New Zealand audience viewed the third test between the All Blacks and the 1971 Lions, with 52 per cent seeing shots of the Apollo 15 moon exploration immediately afterwards. The difference in importance to New Zealanders was marginal. In 1972, the third test match against Australia was broadcast live and, later in the year, a direct satellite telecast was received in New Zealand of the All Blacks' test against Wales at Cardiff. The impact of this communication medium was immediate and lasting. Television was vital in increasing the visibility and profile of players, allowing more advanced marketing and advertising of the game. Rugby was being taken into households previously untouched by it. The game was now truly able to penetrate every part of the country in a direct way, and this was important in attracting the younger, more television-oriented generation. The introduction of television created conditions for changes to the existing market for rugby. For the first time, rugby had the means of becoming a form of global entertainment. In 1977 these conditions influenced the first attempt to introduce a professional competition.

This was to have been based around New Zealand and British players competing in a televised competition.

1980s: Boks and barbed wire

The debate on rugby contact with South Africa escalated with the imminent tour of New Zealand by the 1981 Springboks. Two hundred thousand New Zealanders signed a petition against the tour. Many former All Blacks, including such prominent players as Bill Meates, J.J. Burrows and the Maori fullback George Nepia, publicly voiced opposition to the tour. The New Zealand Prime Minister, Robert Muldoon, said the decision on the tour taking place was in the hands of the NZRFU. Rather than a decision being based on the beliefs of New Zealanders or the views of New Zealand society, the rugby union was seen as making its judgement calls purely in the interests of rugby. In the belief of rugby's national governing body, what benefited the rugby code was a tour by the Springboks.

After this decision was announced the arguments became more bitter and clearly delineated. Most who supported the tour clung to the belief that the tour was simply a series of rugby games, and seemed not to comprehend the potential for social unrest. Once the intensity of feeling against the tour became apparent, defenders of rugby adopted a siege mentality, according to their critics.

Rugby administrators had completely misread the mood of the populace and blindly stumbled into an intense confrontation with half of the country's adult population. Two matches of the traumatic 1981 South African tour of New Zealand were cancelled on police advice. The Springbok match against Waikato was one such cancellation, sparking clashes between rugby supporters and protesters. The tour culminated in the third test match, in Auckland. Protests were planned and negated in the manner of military operations, and the playing area was surrounded by barbed wire. A light plane buzzed the field throughout the game, dropping flour bombs.

The 1981 Springbok tour markedly damaged the sport of rugby in New Zealand. The country was ostensibly a bicultural society, experiencing the increasing visibility of Maori as a political force, and the tour became a focus of social and political protest. New patterns were emerging in the social culture of New Zealand, which were seen as being at odds with the traditional and entrenched culture associated with rugby. These new social patterns had the effect of marginalising the game. Rugby moved from its central position on sport's communion table, with a perceptible drift of youth away towards other activities and sports.

In the more diverse, multicultural, urban and sophisticated New Zealand society of the 1980s, rugby no longer served as a certainty of New Zealand society. Rugby may have remained the 'national game', but no longer reflected the fullness of New Zealand society. Rugby administrators faced a decade of rebuilding to restore the image and national acceptance of the game.

In 1983 the International Rugby Board rejected the idea of a World Cup for rugby, despite its obvious success in soccer and cricket, believing that the concept was not in the best interests of the game. Following this decision, an Australian businessman, David Lord, announced his plan for a professional rugby tournament involving the eight senior IRB nations (France, England, Ireland, Scotland, Wales, New Zealand, Australia and Argentina) to commence in 1984. The tournament had a budget of almost $11 million, with plans in place for seven competitions. The tournaments were to be played continuously, lasting two months each, with a similar break between tournaments. Despite having 208 players signed up for the competition, Lord's deal ultimately failed, primarily because he was unable to acquire the necessary revenue of pay-TV backing.

The NZRFU allowed the rebuilding process following the experiences of 1981 to be interrupted by a renewed debate over an impending All Black tour of South Africa. Just four years after the 1981 tour had unleashed a massive force of public feeling, national rugby administrators were advocating another series against South Africa, this time in the Springboks' own country. The NZRFU still espoused their policy of maintaining sporting links while being opposed to apartheid. Again, they misread the mood of the nation.

As in 1981, the two sides to the argument were broadly delineated along political and socio-economic lines. A *New Zealand Herald* poll of the populace, on 22 December 1984, indicated 42 per cent opposed a tour and 42 per cent favoured it. National Party supporters were largely in favour, while Labour Party supporters largely condemned it, reflecting party policies on the issue.

On 9 July, two Auckland lawyers sought an interim injunction to prevent the departure of the All Black team to South Africa. On 17 July, the NZRFU abandoned the proposed tour after a legal battle, a decision which All Black and entrepreneur, Andy Haden, attributed to a disorganised defence rather than a weakness in the union's legal position. The NZRFU then organised a brief French tour of New Zealand, comprising a match against North Auckland and a test, which resulted in a financial loss.

A private tour of South Africa was organised by many of the then current All Blacks, the team being known as the 'Cavaliers'. Rumours surfaced immediately about the size of the team fund, which led to suggestions that the tour was the initial step in professional rugby. This assertion appeared to be supported by a belief that the Springbok players threatened to strike over their pay for the series. The Broadcasting Corporation of New Zealand decided Television New Zealand and Radio New Zealand would not broadcast the Cavaliers' games. The players were suspended by the NZRFU for two test matches on their return, and their coach, Colin Meads, was dropped from the All Black selection panel. This limited punitive action was widely viewed as an ineffectual response by the NZRFU.

In 1987, New Zealand was the primary host of the inaugural Rugby World Cup, with Australia also hosting several games. Under the coaching of the highly respected Brian Lochore the All Blacks initiated a new era of international dominance as they swept through the tournament unbeaten. They exhibited all the qualities of a top professional sports team. No side came within twenty points of beating New Zealand as they became the first winners of the William Webb Ellis Trophy. The team was a singular entity. It marked the entry into world rugby of Zinzan Brooke and Michael Jones, and contained the incandescent qualities of players such as John Kirwan, John Gallagher and Wayne Shelford. 'It was the team of the decade. I will never forget the special feeling that team had — every player was especially skilled,' reflects Michael Jones.

Exposure was assured as one and a half million viewers, half of New Zealand's population, watched on television, and 100 million viewers watched worldwide, as New Zealand beat France in the final. The team's many young players, and their expansive style of play, attracted supporters nationally. The win was vital in rebuilding the public's faith in the national game after the débâcles of 1981 and 1985. Central to this achievement were the leadership roles of David Kirk and Andy Dalton.

For the next four years New Zealand completely dominated international rugby, not losing a test until 1990. Rugby again enjoyed a positive relationship with the public of New Zealand. There were 100 per cent increases in playing numbers in some areas. The biggest increases came in the lower grades, with the wave of popularity overriding concerns about injuries to young players, particularly at schoolboy level. The number of eight and nine year olds involved grew 80 per cent from 1987 to 1988!

In 1989 the NZRFU announced a record profit of $1.5 million. This commercially successful result included Lion Nathan signing a major sponsorship deal linking its Steinlager beer brand to the All Blacks, and an apparent million dollar deal from Canterbury International clothing manufacturers for the rights to the Silver Fern, which the NZRFU had protected as a registered trademark. The importance of television revenue was underlined when TVNZ paid an estimated $1 million for a three year contract, and Japanese television rights generated another $1 million.

1990s: into the professional era

As New Zealand rugby entered the 1990s, it found a multitude of new issues facing it. Professional training and playing sacrifices were not being rewarded by open payments, sparking calls for an increasingly professional approach to player payments. Bans on players for drug-taking and onfield violence, debates on World Cup locations and organisation, controversy over the selection of national coaches and administrators, and intense media debates within New Zealand and on the international stage all impacted on rugby and its administration. Young people were being drawn to alternative leisure pursuits, from individual recreation such as surfing, to team sports such as rugby league, although rugby remained at the top of the public sporting interest. The *New Zealand Herald* of 23 August 1991 noted a Member of Parliament 'demanding the resignation of the All Black selectors if they do not bring back Wayne Shelford for the World Cup'.

The All Blacks were eliminated from the 1991 World Cup by Australia in the semi-finals, and much criticism of their having an undue focus on money and commercialism was noted. One player saw the team as 'divided into groups; there was the absurd co-coach situation; selections were not always strong; we were too concerned with ourselves and making money; and the team was not well led.' Despite the viewing time of 3.00 a.m., 25 per cent of the New Zealand population watched the match against Australia. The success of the Cup as a vehicle to promote rugby internationally was readily apparent. An audience of 1.8

billion people in over 100 countries watched the competition, compared with 300 million in 17 countries in 1987. The international growth of rugby continued in part because of the increased visibility of its élite level through the globalised television coverage of the first two World Cups. This growth was evidenced by such events as the establishment, in October 1995, of the first rugby competition in China.

After matches against international selections celebrating the centenary of the NZRFU, the All Blacks lost the Bledisloe Cup in a tight 1992 series. At the end of the 1992 season the New Zealand team played a test match against South Africa in Johannesburg, the first test for the Springboks on their return to international rugby after the dismantling of apartheid. The All Blacks won narrowly, 27–24. Under coach Laurie Mains, the All Blacks won only thirteen of the 22 tests played from 1992 to 1994. This caused much concern about the standards of New Zealand rugby in the international arena, as seen by the degree of debate surrounding the retention of Mains as coach in October 1994. Interest in the fortunes of the national game remained intense, with the largest television viewing audience in 1994 being that for the Bledisloe Cup test, with 41 per cent of the nation's homes watching the encounter!

In 1992, semi-finals and a final were added to all three divisions of the National Provincial Championship, which engendered a marked increase of interest in the end of season provincial games and added another notch of inexorable pressure on 'amateur' players' time. This move was an unqualified success, with interest and media coverage of the competition growing annually. In 1994, North Harbour and Auckland made the first division final. Respective captains Richard Turner and Zinzan Brooke were estimated to have committed five hours a day in the week leading to the final responding to media and promotional requests related to the event. The success of the NPC was concurrent with the interest in the 1994 visit by the Springboks. The seven-week, fourteen-match tour generated $23.7 million worth of economic activity for the New Zealand economy.

In 1993, the touring Lions were defeated, and the NZRFU commissioned the Boston Consulting Group to detail strategic options for the sport in New Zealand. The Melbourne branch of the American organisation was contracted at a cost suggested by a national rugby administrator to be approximately $40,000. The organisation had completed, in similar circumstances, a highly successful report for the Australian

Football League in the mid 1980s. In addition to the personnel of the Boston Group, an NZRFU steering committee was formed.

The NZRFU attached a strict caveat to the brief for the review: 'Paramount to the above brief was the need to recognise the important part rugby has played in the heritage of New Zealand and to ensure that so far as practicable the traditions of the game were preserved.' It is commonly felt by critics of the report that heritage and tradition had often constrained the game's progress and had therefore, in part at least, necessitated the report. The exhortation to reimpose the overriding conservatism of rugby arguably led to an inherent restraint on the workings of the steering committee. On the other hand, living with the traditions of rugby seemed to many to be at the heart of New Zealand rugby and demanded continued recognition.

The Boston Group was initially to review New Zealand rugby as it was currently structured. Once the existing position had been determined, the group sought to analyse the game's prevailing strengths and weaknesses, and to determine the issues and opportunities facing it. The group then recommended appropriate strategies, structures and competitions to best serve the requirements of the game for the future.

The report identified four inherent and historical strengths in New Zealand rugby: international leadership both on and off the field; a domestic competition that is strong both financially and competitively; high levels of customer satisfaction reflected in high public interest and support; employee welfare where the interests of 'employees' (players and officials) were served effectively.

The report identified nine major strategic initiatives the NZRFU 'should consider adopting to take the game into the twenty-first century'. They were:

- A strong and financially viable international calendar
- Revised structure of premier and supporting domestic competitions
- Grow and distribute central revenues
- Introduce mechanisms to ensure an even and financially stable competition
- Scheduling of fixtures to maximise attendance and TV markets
- Focus expenditure on a few stadia
- Continued emphasis on developing marketing and the rules of the game
- Revised governance structures for the game

• Work with the International Rugby Board to enforce similar principles worldwide.

If enthusiasm for change was widespread among players, supporters and the media, it was not reflected among the game's provincial administrators. The report was intended to be implemented in a three-year period. The Auckland, Otago, Hawke's Bay and Canterbury Unions introduced boards of directors but had to negotiate the change process without guidance from the national institution that had initially commissioned the revolutionary report. The NZRFU in December 1995 finally accepted the recommendation regarding the disestablishment of the present council and introduction of a governing board. Provincial unions have progressively, albeit not always swiftly, moved towards more business-like structures.

In that year before the World Cup, debate over the All Black coach appointment intensified. Typical on the one hand was the 26 August 1994 *Evening Post* editorial: 'Hart people's choice for All Black coach'. Conversely, on 19 August there was a Channel 3 sports programme with a call-in for the people to 'vote' for the All Black coach, which recorded a majority for Mains.

Following a huge June 1995 test victory against Canada, the All Blacks travelled to South Africa to compete in the third World Cup. They produced an extremely expansive brand of rugby, and were generally accepted as the most attractive team at the tournament. The New Zealanders swept into the final unbeaten, having defeated Japan and England by record margins. The All Blacks lost the final to the host country 12–15 in extra-time, the first major international match to go beyond 80 minutes. After the final it was revealed that nearly the entire New Zealand squad had had serious food poisoning in the two days leading up to the final. 'I don't know what really happened but you have to admire the way the All Blacks, given their illness, gave the final everything' was campaign manager Brian Lochore's view.

All Black winger Jonah Lomu, in his first full season of international competition, became the most popular figure in the rugby world and the focus of attention. He was sought by league clubs, and became the first prominent New Zealand rugby player to be targeted by American football clubs. Increased business acumen was shown by the national governing body as the NZRFU announced, on 9 July 1995, that it had taken out the name Jonah Lomu as a registered trademark, meaning they would henceforth have commercial authority over its use. Only eight months previously the All Black coach had confided to the au-thor: 'I just don't know if Jonah will make it. He has immense promise and I have faith in him. However, the World Cup preparation requires mental hardness and extreme physical fitness. We'll see.' And the world did see!

Rugby commentators from around the globe praised the style of play attempted by the All Blacks and the standard to which it was raised. Gerald Davies stated that 'All Black rugby is now, by far, the most excit-ing rugby played by any country.' He enforced this message by adding: 'This Rugby World Cup needed the All Blacks. With their presence, the quality of the competition has been raised . . . This was rugby that every other country should attempt.'

On their return to New Zealand, Mains' 'Innovators' were given a parliamentary reception. Prime Minister Jim Bolger thanked the team for the 'entertainment, satisfaction and sense of pride' they had given New Zealanders during the World Cup. Bolger's comments reflected the impact of the All Blacks' campaign upon the public. At least 33 per cent of the potential New Zealand audience watched the World Cup final, although the total is likely to have been larger because of the many people watching at clubs, bars and parties.

Rugby has dominated the cultural and social life of New Zealand for nearly a century. It remains New Zealand's major game in 1998, with a high participation level, viewing audience and generation of income. By every measure rugby is our biggest sport. It has the most players, greatest income, highest profile, largest crowd and widest television exposure. In 1994 there were 148,000 registered rugby players, com-pared with 137,000 in 1988. The $78,000 spent on coaching in 1984 rose to $543,000 in 1994. NZRFU surveys indicate that 22 per cent of the general population note rugby as their first choice of sport to watch or play, followed by league (12 per cent), outdoor cricket (7 per cent) and netball and tennis (5 per cent). The mystique of the All Black con-tinues down the years, as illustrated by typical faxes received by the All Blacks before, and after, a recent test match. A Silver Ferns netball team fax advised: 'Have rearranged the lounge furniture. Had the workman in to check out the telly. Brought in the chips and drink. And already taken the phone off the hook. Make our day — good luck.' A branch of the New Zealand National Party wished the team luck: 'Relax and let it happen as we know it will. Forget the media — as we try to!' 'There are a lot of us over here who think you are all the best. We just don't get the opportunity to say it very often . . . ' declared Elizabeth, a 'totally unbiased supporter'. There has been a flood of 'you're the greatest' faxes, kids' drawings and hideously mis-spelt messages from teachers and pupils alike.

Historian and social critic, Jock Phillips, argues that the sociology of rugby remains largely intact, with a large part of New Zealand male culture still identifying itself with the ideal of a 'rugby playing Anzac'. Phillips acknowledges the male population of today does not share the emotional involvement with rugby that their fathers experienced following the 1956 Springbok tour. Men are moving away from team sports into more 'self-directed' alternatives, such as the individual sports of skiing and surfing. However, Phillips admits the 'heart of the culture will be following the All Blacks to such an extent that winning is vital'. Although undergoing something of a metamorphosis — forced upon it by the changing nature of New Zealand society — rugby retains strong traditional elements which have changed little since the days of informal rules and regulations.

Rugby has historically had a strong appeal to the New Zealand male, especially as the country's representative team has traditionally ranked at the very top of international rugby. Critical reflection on the development of rugby in New Zealand and its present state reveals a sport once entrenched as the country's national game retaining strong appeal, but facing challenges as the nation's premier football code. A New Zealand international test referee comments:

> Rugby union has probably passed its peak in the New Zealand way of life. Other sports are improving their international standards and, with extended television coverage, are gaining an improved image on the world front, and getting more support at home. A much greater variety of well-run sports has arisen over the last twenty years and has cut into rugby's domination. Even yachting has had great national support recently.

The lives and careers of All Blacks have, as a result of a small population and large rugby public, interwoven with club players, national achievers, people in public office and members of the private sector. There are many examples of influence and interaction by past All Blacks at the public level. In the late 1990s, Wilson Whineray is chairperson of the Hillary Commission, Tony Steel is a Member of Parliament (as have been Chris Laidlaw and Graham Thorne), and successful businessman

Joe Karam has become a national figure in his advocacy of a convicted murderer's innocence.

Today, New Zealand rugby management is faced with many challenges. The NZRFU recognises the need to respond to changing demands now confronting their traditionally amateur sport, and must consider the transformation of the professional stages of rugby's development. Given the pace of change in the game during 1995, the provincial and national managers of rugby face pressures to change the long-standing structures and administration of New Zealand rugby.

New Zealand continues to live with the All Black tradition. The vignettes of All Blacks giving their mystique a local habitation and a name are many in the writer's experience . . . At a Dunedin hotel as the test intensity builds, a small boy is brought by his mother to see Grant Fox. Foxy meets this little fan every test week in Dunedin. There is no publicity . . . Mains is signing a letter to a small boy terribly injured in a smash . . . Hart makes himself available for a meeting, despite a crammed timetable . . . A small girl and boy come up to the All Blacks in their dining area and stand, too overcome to speak, until Zinny greets them: 'Where abouts are you two from?' . . . The letters from a kid hardly old enough to write, whose parent writes a note of explanation on the back: 'You are Dale's heroes. There is a picture of each of you on her bedroom wall, and she knows all of your names . . .' Today, there is no forgotten All Black. For better, perhaps, the public read in their newspapers that 'All Black stands for parliamentary selection', or for worse, 'This is the face of a conman! He is . . . the disgraced ex-All Black.' The All Black title is a life investiture. In the 1990s Christian Cullen and Jeff Wilson are more readily recognised than the prime minister and deputy prime minister. Jonah Lomu rules.

David Russell of Otago University was engaged in a study of élite athletes and sport commitment. He was surprised by the essential niceness, intelligence and articulate nature of the All Blacks. These '90s representatives were also seen as men who play hard but fair sport. The All Blacks also have pride — in personal, team and traditional dimensions. Personal pride comes from recognised achievement and self-imposed demands to 'do the business' and to meet the team needs for individual excellence. And, today, there is a professional career providing an undertone. Team pride comes from the integration of 21 men into the All Blacks who are playing a test. Technique, tactical nous, the sub-units in the team, leadership roles in key moves or calling play,

	Saturday, 10 December 1994 – Planned Activities
7:00am	Meet in main foyer.
7:05am	Depart by bus to Swimarama for aqua-aerobics session.
7:20am	Aqua-aerobics session
8:20am	Depart Swimarama for Waipuna.
8:40am	Breakfast
9:30am	Team meeting, Carbine Room
9:45am	Depart Waipuna for Pakuranga Rugby Football Club
10:00am	Group 1 Strength training technique Group 2 Speed training Group 3 Workshop
11:00am	Group 1 Workshop Group 2 Coaching session Group 3 Speed training
12 noon	Drinks break
12:15pm	Group 1 Speed training Group 2 Workshop Group 3 Strength training technique
1:15pm	Lunch
2:00pm	Either at Pakuranga Rugby Football Club or back to Waipuna for afternoon workshops
2:15pm - 2:45pm	Dietician
5:00pm	Saturday session ends
5:15pm	Bus back to Waipuna
6:00pm	Depart by bus from Waipuna to dinner
8:30pm	Leave restaurant
9:00pm	Arrive in park for Coca Cola Carols in the Park. Group of ALL BLACKS® to appear on stage with Sir Howard Morrison
10:00pm	Depart park for Waipuna

interpersonal acceptance and support, cohesion in the task ahead. And there is the ever-present tradition, symbolised by the black jersey, of expectations, of matching the standards of predecessors, of meeting public demands. First and foremost, make no mistake, is the personal pride and commitment. The passion is fuelled by the person and the team — and then the public will is served as a result. 'There is not an amorphous heart-rending "play it for New Zealand" ethos in the All Blacks — if we are playing for ourselves and each other, then we are playing, in the end, for New Zealand,' asserted Ant Strachan, reflecting the views of others.

Demands facing rugby in the 1990s, such as the implications of professional sport, the Boston Review's generation of changes in rugby administration, public expectations of the All Blacks, and ever-present changes to the rule book with the resultant premiums placed upon leadership, are challenging the game's administrators. Despite these, today's game of rugby is still played on a field readily recognised as an adaptation of The Close at Rugby School in England, where the game originated. Much of the modern nomenclature and custom is rooted in the public school practice of its early exponents, such as the touchline, where the first player to touch the ball over the sideline would put it back into the field of play, or the visible sign of the goal posts, shaped as they have been since 1846. The grounding of the ball over the opponent's line, enabling the player to 'try' for a conversion, would not appear alien to nineteenth century public schools. Internationally, the moves to standardisation have included the terminology of player positions and jersey numbering, although New Zealand's naming of field positions is still not identical to that of other countries. Inside it all, the rugby tradition is still alive.

4

Life in the centre: the veteran All Black

I get stopped by people in Ponsonby. I get letters from nuns . . .
Frank Bunce

Frank Ereni Bunce is a professional rugby player. He is an All Black with a social conscience. Born on 4 February 1962, his playing weight is some 94 kg with a height of 1.83 m. Educated at Mangere College and in the environs of South Auckland, Buncey has played for Auckland (1986–91) and North Harbour (since 1991). After playing for Western Samoa in 1991 at the World Cup, he wrote his name large on the turf as a rock-hard defender and aggressive attacker. Bunce was then headhunted by Laurie Mains for the 1992 All Blacks as the first choice All Black centre and, after five years with Mains, found that John Hart also came to a rapid recognition of the qualities his predecessor had valued.

Frank Bunce has experienced the All Black life for longer than any current All Black. He is an example to Pacific Island youth, a busy father, and a pleasant person to spend time with. We talked over lunch late in October 1997.

Has the professional era changed the All Black ethos? Is living with the All Blacks still very similar to the period before the professional era?
Basically the All Blacks are still the same. The pride and commitment have been the same for all the years I've been with them. The routines are still pretty much the same. Some of the younger guys have a new way of doing things — they seem to hang loose a bit more, do things a

Haka — a famous All Black tradition. Here the 1967 team perform at Twickenham in front of the Queen and Prince Philip.

Whatever the decade, All Blacks have always given their all for their country. Dowdy shows the effects of playing a test match against the physical Samoans on 31 July 1993 (*below*) and Fitzy grimaces after the infamous ear-biting incident (*right*).

For the 1949 All Blacks, travelling to South Africa was a leisurely experience on board ship. Here a group of players say farewell; Kevin Skinner is fifth from left. (Kevin Skinner collection)

The pace and mode of travel have both changed in recent decades. After a Bledisloe Cup game, the All Black entourage leaves Sydney with the help of Koala Tours.

Golf is a popular recreational sport for the All Blacks. Fitzy *(top left)* looks a bit uncertain at the prospect of Olo being in charge of the cart, but Loey seems happy enough.

Same game, different clothes! Here Fred Allen *(above)* tees off a green in Cape Town during the 1949 tour. (Fred Allen collection)

The 1949 team *(centre left)* on a rest day during the South African tour. Captain Fred Allen is on the far right. (Fred Allen collection)

'Well guys, this is just like the weather in Dunedin.' The All Blacks *(left)* enjoy time out on the morning of a night test in Sydney.

Even back in 1929 there were links between rugby and commerce, as this poster for a trans-Tasman test match shows.

Commercial concerns of a different nature saw rugby union players depart for the more rewarding fields of rugby league. One such loss to union was Inga Tuigamala, seen here with friend and team mate Iceman, at the winger's farewell party just before he left to play league in England.

bit more informally with the headsets on! In professional rugby the time is now available for your training and a focus on rugby because you've got a good income. But test day tensions and routines haven't really changed.

What are the most memorable off-field moments in your All Black career?
I think our most memorable off-field moments come from our onfield moments. Winning on the field brings special memories off-field. Probably the way we came back from the World Cup and we got that big reception and the following year when we beat South Africa in the series and we had the big parade in Auckland. That's when you realise what it means to the country, when you're an All Black in a crowded area in Queen Street because the public want it. When you meet people like Nelson Mandela and Kiri Te Kanawa, you just stand there in awe of them. To be an All Black does open so many doors. When you are talking to people whom you wouldn't even expect to be rugby supporters, it reinforces how central All Black rugby is to New Zealanders' sporting interests. I get stopped by people in Ponsonby. I get letters from nuns. And, at the other extreme, I know some guys in jail and they tell me how they would gather around a television and watch All Black rugby.

What about your children Frank? How do they find your being an All Black?
My son is 11 and he plays league, actually! I think he thinks that my being an All Black is quite cool. My daughter, who's six, I don't think she understands fully what All Blacks are and how people regard them — like, we're driving along or walking around and she notices people staring at me but isn't sure what the fuss is about! My other daughter is three so she's still free from that. Although Mary-Jane and I are separated the children are the priority for us.

What is a typical week for a professional rugby player when there is no test match?
Probably training and gym work take up the most regular times. It depends how fit I am and what's coming up at the time. When I had my foot injury I couldn't run or anything and wanted to stay reasonably fit, so I was in the gym doing a lot of rowing and things like that. And then there was lots of time at the physiotherapist and rehabilitation. Different regions have different physios and you have a fair amount of choice. I don't think we have to pay — I never have! I don't think anyone does!

If there is a Super 12 match, it's often like being on tour. If it's an NPC match coming up then a lot of the week, such as training, is built around that.

Has the training and fitness environment, that you are in now, changed from the non-professional years?
I think it's always been there but now you're really aware of the support and you have the time to use it. We always have it stressed to us, 'There are lots of good people ready to help and you must ask on any injury, don't muck about.' It's being drummed into you so much, if you've got an injury go and look after it. At the end of the day you want to be playing again.

What are the non-training or non-playing time commitments in your week?
My children. As separated parents, Mary-Jane and I have to work out the week for our three children, and that's compounded by my rugby commitments, and travel, and her work times. It's actually good being a professional player now as I can get up in the morning and get them off to school, then have a period to relax, read the newspaper, go to the gym mid-morning . . . but there always seems to be something! Some media interview or promotion is often part of my day, or I go and have lunch somewhere, perhaps spend a couple of hours, as Michael Jones would say, chilling out, or mucking around, or a friend drops around. Then it's time to pick up the two kids from school. My youngest daughter is at a childcare centre for part of the day.

What is your typical routine for a test match day?
It starts for me with the captain's meeting at six o'clock the night before the test, and then you go and have dinner. I always go to bed quite early. I don't go to sleep but watch television. Then, about 10.00 p.m. or 11.00 p.m., I might take a couple of sleeping pills to make sure I sleep through the night. In the morning I get up and have quite a latish breakfast of cereal, fruit, yoghurt, toast and marmalade. I never eat a cooked breakfast.

Then we have our meetings. The backs meet, and might have a bit of run through a few moves. Depends on what the weather is like, whether we go outside. Look out the window, see what the weather is like for the forwards out there before we decide!

Fitzy's good at letting you go your own way as long as it doesn't disrupt anyone else. The young ones cruise around a bit and do their thing in their sunglasses, but that's their way — to each his own.

At some time in the morning you go and collect your jersey from the manager. It's always been a little ritual. You get handed your All Black jersey, there's a handshake and good wishes. Then back to your room, pack your bag, have a shower, shave if you're a back — the forwards always seem to leave their shaves till after the match. It's a really quiet time then. Some guys don't even talk to each other. Might play a bit of music, watch TV with the sound down, so it's really quiet . . .

I don't have brunch if it's an afternoon test but if it's a night game I will. Then it's assembly time and Harty speaks to us and we move off to the bus, to go to the match ground. At the ground I always take my jersey out of my bag, first thing, and hang it up. Quite a few guys do. Then I go out onto the match ground. I have a look around to get the feel of the place. Look around, soak up the atmosphere, it's part of the warm-up . . . Back into the dressing room. I don't always have the same place in the All Blacks' changing room, although I do in the club and provincial games. I have the same place all the time at the Albany Stadium, when I'm with the North Harbour team, because we're there so often, but with the All Blacks if someone else sits there I don't mind — I'm not superstitious. When I'm back in the changing room I sit down and rub some of that heat stuff into my leg, loosen up, and muck around with a ball for a while. I'll probably go outside the room into a space such as the corridor and run around and chuck the ball around a bit.

Actually, what I do depends on how I feel on the day more than going through the same ritual every time. Depends where you can go and warm up. Some people don't like having other people around, they don't like being talked to, but I don't mind having noise around me. I actually quite enjoy having other people about, basically just doing their own thing.

What is the future after your All Black playing days end?
As you know, I'm still keen on doing social work. I'd like to study to improve my knowledge, not so much to gain a qualification. Helping kids, and young people in South Auckland — giving them some hope, and helping them get a direction in their lives . . . I look back to when I was growing up and I thought South Auckland was the world! You're just grabbed by your own little world when you're young and I was unaware of what else was out there! I still see that now — a lot of people

growing up into that life and doing the same things I was doing. I especially notice this as I talk with my nephews and their friends — what do they want to do with their lives? In the school holidays a fourth form boy, say, finds it pretty tempting to leave school if he's making regular money at his holiday job and thinks he can have that instant money full-time. 'Don't even think like that boy! What about travel? What about getting trained for a good job?' There's a whole world outside South Auckland!

Also, it's sometimes difficult for people outside the area, or outside the various cultures, to understand South Auckland. For example, we have a strong family affiliation in our culture. I find I give away heaps to my family — not because I'm an All Black, but because one of them might have a real need and is getting only a small income. It's just the way we live. I had one older family person ring me up a couple of weeks ago, who had to go to Wellington, and she was tentative about asking me for some help. 'It's a big favour I'm asking,' she said. The money may not have seemed a lot to many people but the $250 to her made all the difference between being able to go and not doing so.

Coaches in New Zealand today have to know Maori and Pacific Islanders and how they are. I gather that was a difficulty John Monie had with the Warriors.

How would you describe John Hart's coaching?
John has done a good job taking the All Blacks into its professional years. He recognises the demands of the professional era upon players and consequently organises time off as there is a lot of pressure on players with the frequency of games, injuries and off-field expectations. He's well-organised. In his role he's more like the English team manager, who is the coach but has a strong coordinating role. All of the coaches get on well. There is no doubt that Harty is the boss. When we actually train, Gordy Hunter runs the backs, Ross Cooper takes the forwards, and Harty is in between. He might bark a few words at you during training but he basically stands there with his arms folded in the classic John Hart pose, or with his head cocked on one side. An especial strength is Harty's thorough preparation, which he does with the team management committee. They have their meetings at 8.00 a.m. He wants to ensure that there is nothing unexpected, no hassle, and they go over the day's outline. He wants to know everything, what's going on with everybody, so that he's not in the dark about anything.

Harty has a basic game plan. He looks at the changes the opposition have made, whether he considers them to be a strength and who they've picked. Will those players add value? He'll go through the team we're playing and discuss, say, Henry Honiball. Obviously, he was picked by South Africa as a strong defender and that might mean his inside back is not as strong, so that player might become our target and we go around Honiball, or move him around. Then that's where we, the players, come in — we've played those guys before, so we can say, 'He does this, or he does that', and John Hart listens and takes notes. So we have the opportunity to give our knowledge but he's in control.

Sean has a clear role in the test match week. He's got an awful lot off the field to do and he goes to all the press conferences and takes a lot of pressures off the guys. He's probably the most professional of all the All Blacks. I don't know if there's anyone else who prepares as he does. During the week he'll make sure the team is tight. At training you can feel if things are loose, or too tight, and he'll do something about it. If he feels we're starting to float along he'll take action. Like getting off the bus at training, he'll have a few words with the guys if he feels that's needed, or with the team at their hotel he'll say, 'At training tomorrow this is what will happen.' He puts the pressure on. You leave the team meeting knowing what is needed, with things tightening up to the right level of tension again.

Fitzy, as a captain, has the prime quality of leading by example. He'll never ask someone to do something he won't do himself. You don't mind following someone like that. You look upon Fitzy like the ultimate warrior, you know. He disregards his own safety, which all compels the greatest respect. On top of that he's matured quite a bit. I think he quite likes that captaincy role now! When Mike Brewer was injured at the time of the 1992 trials and they made Fitzy the All Black captain, I don't know if Sean was that comfortable with it. Now he's in front. Says all the right things — and does all the right things. Pulls on the sponsor's hat for a camera shot, makes sure he has the right T-shirt logo on . . .

Why do you feel the All Blacks still appeal to the public so much?
I don't know. Tradition I guess. Maybe it's the identifying with heroes — the likes of Zinny, Jonah, Christian Cullen and the heap of guys there who capture the imagination of the public. Even the old fellas. Some of them! You know what rugby's like, it's the NZ public that makes it. In a sense it's successful due to John Hart's input. There wasn't support from

all over the country out there before he came in. John Hart has come in and done all the right things, changed everything around and you know the team is successful — you've got the guys that are putting in the performances which have been not only winning but built on our '95 World Cup play. If you think something's going to work with a move on the field, he's all for you trying it because you know you're the only ones out there who can do things and make decisions, and he'll certainly tell you if it's a bad idea. I like his coaching style. He's not on top of you all the time, he breaks things up a hell of a lot — he recognises player's needs . . . In what way? Fatigue — both mental and physical, that sort of thing. He will recognise that and he hasn't got a problem with giving you a couple of days off right in the middle of the year when a lot of coaches wouldn't do that sort of thing. Always well prepared, you know. You can't really pick anything out in particular.

Who would be the best centre you've played against?
Jeremy Guscott of England is quite hard because he's fast and has good balance. He's difficult, but physically it would be Jaapie Mulder of South Africa. When you play South Africa it's different from playing any other test rugby. They are hard guys — the buggers are in your face all of the time! They never give an inch. I guess part of it's the old rivalry. Australia is different. They play more our sort of game. They could be described as playing rugby rather than the opposing team.

Is there a downside to the professional era? Or anything you would want changed?
I'm making a reasonable living as a professional rugby player. The most difficult thing to come to terms with is the feeling that sometimes you seem to be owned by someone, or something, else. I don't like feeling like a commodity. Or being treated like one. One promotion of the All Blacks seemed to have quite different demands — and benefits — for different players, so I think the promotion and marketing of the All Blacks needs care.

And finally Frank, if you were to take only five CDs on tour, or to your desert island, what would you choose?
Elvis Presley for starters! Guns and Roses, some heavy metal, the Rolling Stones and some rap.

5

The force of fifteen: forging a great team

I look at the way they come onto the field, take up their positions, and the coherence in their play. I look for communication, discipline, technical skills, and some sense of enthusiasm, even at the highest level. Consistency in play and the response to pressure with clear leadership and player support are critical.

Olo Brown

There is something special about great teams in sport and in the workplace. They are recognisable as having a unity and force beyond the norm, which activates commitment, frees flair and individual panache, and reveals an ability to pull back the odds under pressure. Such a team has discernible qualities of decision-making and playing excellence. They have excitement and passion, and they dwell in our memories. There aren't many such teams. In rugby they win tests with a convincing dominance and, in the main, shift the balance of the way rugby is played at the highest level.

The All Blacks have always been a central force in rugby. Many times this force has been expressed through great teams. What are the indicators of such teams? In the final decade of the twentieth century the world of management and business is drawing substantially on that of sport to develop workplace coaching and teams. The plethora of publications in this field underline the importance of workplace teams. Virtually none of the management world's manuals, however, are based on actual knowledge of what really happens in the sporting team life and what the coach actually does. So what can the All Blacks tell them? A clear body of agreement comes from the ranks of past and present All Black players and coaches.

A great team has most of the following: excellence in leadership, with a sustaining philosophy and vision for the team and its operation or play; clear goals agreed upon by the team, which the players share and to which they are committed; long-term goals are framed into achievable short-term goals, such as phases of the season, test match weeks and stages of team development; game plans reflect the vision and sustain the players; the development of players as people *and* onfield team members is seen as important; match play stamps a distinctive playing style on the occasion and reveals the game's potential; there is ongoing evaluation of players' perceptions and skills, and continual reassessing of the vision's realisation or possible needs for adjustment; players are selected skilfully and blended in with the prevailing and positive team culture to fit the team's special ethos and goals.

A team may be seen as a group of individuals sharing a goal that has mutual acceptability and to which they are personally committed. Group members have integrative roles which draw upon individual skills, attitudes and positional (or organisational) requirements. A team, traditionally, has a coach and captain — its leaders. The coach, or primary team leader, must have a clear 'philosophy' or set of principles for the sport, which then shape the team. In the All Blacks the philosophy may be simple — as are the best philosophies of this sort — 'Rugby should be a fast, open, and integrated game that fully involves each player at a high level of skill and commitment, and provides pleasure for the team and the spectators.' Great All Black teams include the 1905–6 Originals and 1924 Invincibles. Let's not forget the 1943 Kiwis, Fred Allen's All Blacks, the team of Jack Gleeson and Graham Mourie, the 1987 Exemplars, the 1996–97 Hart All Blacks . . . the list is not necessarily exclusive.

Team philosophy

The philosophy or sustaining belief about the team expresses what the coach or team leader believes with regard to its optimal state and potential actualisation of players — individually and as a unit. More simply the philosophy reflects, 'What are we on about here?' or 'What can we make of ourselves?' All decisions made in a rugby team are based on personal beliefs about what rugby is, perception of self, playing position, the team, core values and ethics, and so on. Those beliefs, the basis for what is decided or done by a team, are hardly ever discussed.

Obviously each coach has a philosophy. Some coaches can recognise and discuss this. Others, usually less successful, reveal it through their actions. The parallel in the workplace is clear. 'Our business provides the opportunity for all staff to experience success through the application of their relevant skills, which will result in sales targets being met.'

But philosophies are not worth a busted dime without tries, goals, contracts or profits. The coach's philosophy, or set of principles or beliefs about the sport, shape what he or she desires for the team. How do they 'see' the game being played? This seeing or vision sets out in the coach's mind, or on paper, the way the team will play. The visions of seemingly disparate coaches like Lochore, Wyllie, Mains and Hart are surprisingly similar — to have a team play fast, open and multi-skilled attacking rugby which is based on the control of set phases and is attractive to play and watch. Then the goals can be set, such as selection, the season's plan, the team's development (as a unit and individually), and the team's environmental needs such as support staff. Too much theory? Maybe, but it's all there in the realities of All Black teams. It's the way good coaches work, folks. Let's look at an example.

A good team at work: 1992–95 All Blacks

In 1992, just like any successful business enterprise, the All Black selectors drew up their vision, or goals, for the All Blacks, then set out their strategy and tactics (the 'nitty-gritty' aims along the way, if you like), for their vision.

The vision
To establish a playing pattern for teams selected by the All Black selectors, compatible with the following criteria:
  (a) Success
  (b) The playing philosophy of the All Black panel
  (c) Best utilisation of the strengths and resources of New Zealand rugby
  (d) Being innovative and evolving, with a view to re-establishing New Zealand as the leader in World Rugby
  (e) Fostering spectator interest, player enjoyment and marketability.

The selectors then set out their selection policy based on this, including 'Re-assessing the experienced, well-performed provincial players that have not been selected in recent seasons.' (This policy led to the selection of players such as Frank Bunce and John Mitchell.) The goals which resulted from the selectors' vision included 'To strive for unity in New Zealand rugby', which led to eight further goals, being identified. They selected a captain, Fitzpatrick, who was a key figure in disestablishing the previously existing Auckland cliques in the team.

The All Black team was to portray rugby through its 'playing style, as an attractive exciting game for players, spectators and administrators', and 'to begin rebuilding by introducing selected new players and retaining sufficient experience to assist development of new players'. Jeff Wilson, Lomu, Ieremia, Hewitt and Justin Marshall were all subsequently brought in. The selectors were also concerned to 'develop the team to be a role model for rugby and to produce individual personalities in the game,' and to 'set standards of behaviour and discipline in the All Black team.'

Despite selection errors and injuries at key stages, the goals were realised. The All Blacks in that 1992–95 period did include role models, produce individual personalities, exhibit the expected behaviour, blend old and new players and play an innovative and evolving style of rugby that, in 1995, re-established New Zealand as 'the leader in World Rugby'.

A key element of strong teams is that once the aims are set out, as generated by the vision, the team leaders must select players who can achieve them. The writer had five weeks with a major provincial team in New Zealand and surveyed the players on their goals. Half the team played primarily for enjoyment and half were mainly motivated to win. The coach's prime goal was to win. Team talks, in game plans and coach–player interaction, were oriented to winning, which did not fully motivate — or was not as highly relevant for — those players who had enjoyment of the game as their main driving force.

Job descriptions

The All Black selectors, at the end of 1991 and early 1992, drew up the positional requirements for their vision and goals to be realised. The obvious parallel in business is the job description for each team member fitting the organisation's strategic plan.

We Recognise The Need To Have A Fall-back Position
FULLBACK
1) Defensively complete: *Tackles*
All angles
Takes high kick
Positional sense

2) Attacking skills: *Creates overlaps*
                           Punches centre
                           Runs outside wings
                           Astute use of blind

3) Astute reader and user of end-phase ball.
4) Counterattacks with good judgement.
5) Should be big and strong. *(Create a fullback with the pace of wings.)*

WINGS

1) High fullback skills level.
2) High work rate.
3) Full range of 'beating man' skills.
4) Understanding of defence patterns and covering.
5) Encouraging ability to play left and right.
6) Pace, big and strong.

MIDFIELD BACKS

(Two types — could play as a combination or, possibly, two of the same type — second option not preferred)

A

1) Good distribution skills.
2) 100% tackle — all angles.
3) Defensive intelligence and discipline.
4) Range of attacking kicks — ideally left and right.
5) Big and fast.

B

1) Quick reactions.
2) Line breaker — good footwork, etc.
3) Good distributor.
4) Quick and dangerous from broken play.
5) Defensive intelligence, discipline and flexibility.
6) Range of attacking kicks — ideally left and right.

FIRST FIVE-EIGHT

1) High distribution skills.
2) Ability to make decisions.
3) Must have three options: *Pass*
                                          Kick
                                          Run

HALFBACK
1) Clears ball quickly, accurately and with variation of length and speed — Full range of passing skills.
2) Must tackle — especially around ruck and forwards.
3) Full range of tactical kicks.
4) Runs.
5) Runs loose forwards.
6) Directs his forwards.
7) High work rate.
8) Speed to tackle and the breakdown.
9) No fear.

No. 8 AND BLINDSIDE FLANKER (They are interchangeable.)
They are complementary to the loose forward trio and team pattern.

A

The Buck Shelford type, whose strengths are:
1) Taking ball up from scrum.
2) Ball winner at six in line-out.
3) Very good block in line-outs for jumpers.
4) Support player for flankers.
5) Very good distribution skills around scrums.
6) Very good liaison with halfback.
7) Strong, aggressive tackler.
8) Good understanding of moves around scrums (communication) and defence patterns.
9) Strong, compact physique.

B

1) Main ball-winner of back three.
2) Enough speed to support three-quarters.
3) Good running and passing skills.
4) Strong, aggressive runner.
5) Good understanding of moves around scrums and defence patterns.

OPENSIDE FLANKER
1) Speed and acceleration — extremely fit.
2) Can play on the ground or in the air.
3) Very good continuity skills.
4) Attacking player.
5) Real pressure player — hungry.

6) A lot of rugby intelligence.

7) Ability to fit into all defensive patterns.

8) Ability to win some ball at the tail of the line-out.

LOCKS — Two types

1) One should be a very good scrummager for right hand or tighthead side.

2) Wins own ball and nullifies opposition.

3) Speed to breakdowns to play an effective driving role at rucks and mauls.

4) Good body position at second phase.

5) One should be an exceptional jumper for guaranteed ball when needed.

6) Prepared to interchange line-out positions.

7) Tackles around legs and is part of a defensive and attacking pattern.

PROPS

1) Must be able to keep the scrum up and push.

2) Good leg position for locks to push on.

3) Effective block and support for line-out jumpers.

4) Good body position and must be in the second phase and driving.

5) Aggressive with ball in hand.

HOOKER

1) Accurate line-out thrower — he is the best line-out forward in the team.

2) At scrum time he pressures opposition.

3) When required he must play the loose forward role.

4) Must be able to tackle like a loose forward and act as cover on the blind from a line-out.

Given that the ultimate goal was to be in the final of the 1995 World Cup some four years on from drawing up the above, the player requirements were met. Adhering to these brought in Mehrtens, Lomu, Osborne and Kronfeld. The same team goals and prevailing style of play brought the selectors' confirmation of Christian Cullen and Justin Marshall in 1995.

Once the team is selected, to fit the broad vision and goals, the captain is a key figure. In established teams, the captain is already known and has an informal role in providing views on possible selections. It is vital that the players know why they have been selected, and that there is an opportunity for the coach and player to talk on a one-to-one basis to reinforce in each player's mind the valued aspects of his or her play. Mark Cooksley replaced an injured team mate in the All Black scrum for a test and was then dropped to the reserves for the next test. 'I really appreciated Laurie ringing me up as I thought I had played well and deserved to stay in the test team. He explained that Kamo and Rob were the test locks at present and that he was pleased at the way I had played. I think what helped me was him pointing out that I was in the top three All Black locks.'

Players in a team have certain positions. In the workplace context this is sometimes overlooked. What is this person's role? What special knowledge is required? Does each person have the technical knowledge to carry out their role? How does the team gel? Is there opportunity for interchanging positions? How do we draw upon team members' special role knowledge?

An All Black team has many dimensions but all are present, to varying degrees, in lower level teams, and each has its parallel in the workplace team. Coaches, administrators and team leaders must consider all of the following.

TEAM

Team culture and traditions
Team goals
Team leaders: appointed, emergent, informal
Team development: long term, match week
Resources: human, equipment
Player goals: as players, as individuals
Perceptions of team mates
Language and communication
Physical environment: team rooms, training
Team meetings: frequency, purpose, participation
Social context: team activity, interaction
Team roles: duties, official roles
Support staff and advisers: medical, liaison, other
Match focus: train as for match

Court sessions and social rituals
Field positions: discuss with each player
Social functions: purpose, attendance
Technical skills: assistance, development
Cohesion: relationships, room allocation
Training: when? where? why?
Induction: 1-to-1, welcoming, mentor
Time usage: plan week
Rituals and bonding: how, purpose
Ethnic identity: recognised in actions
Players' personal lives
Relationships: positive, a little distance
Selection of team captain
Evaluation of leaders: how this is done

Postive team culture

Central to the team's development is the team culture. The team culture is, essentially, the way things are done in the team — not the formal aspects such as the game plan, training or appointed roles, but the informal nuts and bolts of the team machine which are based upon team values and actions. This is often ignored by team leaders, who may not realise that to change some elements of the culture can positively — or negatively — affect the team and its results. How are new players welcomed into the team? At meal times, do the players sit at the first vacant place or seek their little group? Mains and Hart have been insistent, along with Fitzpatrick, that there should be no cliques in the All Black team. Indeed, players were warned before the 1992 tour of Australia and New Zealand that if a clique was formed, the coach would have the ringleader sent home.

The communication pattern is a positive or negative aspect of team culture e.g. 'In my first six weeks on tour I don't think the coach spoke to me once.' and 'I really appreciated Laurie phoning me before the team was announced when I'd been dropped to the reserves.' John Hart is careful to maintain a 'whole team' ethos with the All Blacks and to ensure that, in a large squad of 36 players, there is a prevailing unity and positive team culture.

An example of the All Black team culture is the haka. This Maori dimension of the national team is not necessarily well understood in its history and meaning inside the All Blacks. (The NZRFU, when asked by the writer for the background and meaning of the haka, sent a page photocopied out of a primary school book showing diagrams of the haka actions and its accompanying text.) Graham Mourie, one of the great All Black captains, saw the haka as a forthright traditional challenge with residual memories of 'we live, we die, we're coming to plunder and kill.' Andy Dalton saw it as 'a sheer challenge. We were giving a challenge and the challenge was rugby. It's not so much in the words of the haka but the impact of the challenge.' Buck Shelford brings his Maori perspective to the traditional act: 'If you weren't going to do the haka properly you denigrated Maoridom. If I was involved we had to do it properly. If the All Blacks weren't going to do it properly, I wasn't interested in doing it.'

Test match day reveals diverse scenes inside the All Black team culture. All of the reserves act as 'duty boys' to provide support for the test fifteen. A player not selected for the game always expresses best wishes to his successful rival — with a word, an arm around the shoulders, or actions of support. Bonding is reinforced with customs such as line-outs in the car park (an unnecessary act in strategic terms, as all forwards surely know the calls by test day!). The physiotherapist's room becomes a meeting place. In the changing room, after the silent bus trip to the ground, there are individual rituals that make up team culture: the place each person sits, mental preparation, mutual urging, the captain's dominant role, the strapping of limbs, a cross drawn on a wrist, the hugs, the close physical grouping of the whole fifteen after all management and reserve persons have left the test changing room, the presentation of first-test ties. And, of course, there is the long-established accolade of the All Black bus back seat. The longest serving All Blacks have traditionally taken the test bus back seat, excluding the captain, and possession is zealously guarded. Michael Jones is a good Christian person, but with jawbone in hand he will lustily smite any invader of the back seat! And Zinny or Loey or Bruiser haven't been too concerned about the niceties of human propulsion or explaining theories of force and immovable objects when repelling young All Black invaders of the back seat. They just do it! Which illustrates another element of great teams — they have a core of experienced players who possess proven skills, provide in-team leadership and maintain team culture.

Team culture contributes to the team's development. The 1994 season review by the All Black coach and critical consideration of the looming year of a World Cup show a coach's analysis of some aspects of an All Black team's development.

We've got to look at our line-out. That's the one area that's cost us in every test apart from the first test against Australia in '92. It's been a critical element in our losses. I check the videos of each test and the players' techniques are always 100 per cent so perhaps it's the bad choice of options. We need to look at the player interaction, especially between the key line-out guys and the decision-making. V hasn't selected the line-out options wisely, that's been disappointing. It comes down to the use of player W as he's the only one with the right decision-making capability. Player W has to have back-up though and that's a problem. You need intensive mental preparation between the line-out decision-maker and the coach and then its over to the player's on-the-spot judgement. There has to be intense mental analysis and mental awareness and preparation. We'll look at simplifying the calls so there is no margin of error in relaying calls and possibly using physical signals as we don't want to simplify calls so that they become detectable. We need to look at the need to support players earlier. Referees are not doing anything about the illegal play of other teams doing this. I think we've got enough good line-out players.

I haven't wanted to show too early what we're taking into the World Cup but we have tried out tactics over the two years without persisting with them. We need big men to put pressure on the opposition and they must have mobility and ball skills. We used runners quite effectively in 1992 until they were countered by other teams. We attacked Australia closely and punched through the middle so we dropped that after being effective against Australia and Scotland (Player T was excellent in these). Then we found a failing in the test against England when the tight five were a yard off the pace and found they couldn't get the whole thing started, so we have had to fix that and move on.

Good teams develop traditions and myths which provide basic values and sustain team culture. Earle Kirton illustrated this when talking to the All Blacks after a test loss. 'Old All Blacks came up to me and said that they could never remember an All Black side being physically weak . . . I lost two All Black games but I didn't get the passing parade inquisition last Saturday [test] night. The old All Black fraternity, some of you will be part of that soon, they don't want the legend to die. The greatest part of their lives is revisiting young men recreating what they did.'

This is reinforced by the genealogy of All Black influence. Sean Fitzpatrick is an outstanding All Black captain and a great All Black, who is a strong influence upon the modern generation of players. Son of an All Black (Brian Fitzpatrick, 1953–54), Fitzy had a close relationship of trust with his All Black coach, Laurie Mains (All Black 1971–76), who, in turn, had been mentored by Vic Cavanagh. And they each had All Black heroes. Fitzpatrick recalls the day he saw an All Black, Grant Batty, at a club centenary and the impact of a 'real All Black's presence'. He sees himself now helping to keep the dream alive.

Standards and expectations

Expectation — of the individual and of the team — is high in a great team. This is illustrated by a survey the All Blacks squad completed prior to the World Cup team selection. One question asked what should be done 'in the team's best interests' with a player who was not up to the required fitness levels in the tests at the World Cup camps in early 1995. The sample of player responses illustrate team values and expectations inside the All Blacks. 'Approach that player and lay down the requirements necessary for his and the team's best performance . . . Assign him a training partner . . . If this player is being lazy then he does not have the World Cup or the team in his best interests . . . If he's not putting in the hard yards we shouldn't piss around with someone who doesn't care enough for the jersey . . . '

The demands made by an outstanding team upon itself must be high, attainable and understood by all team members. Each player has a role and his own self-expectations, as well as clearly understood team expectations. An All Black scrum practice illustrates such self-imposed standards.

The coach addresses the new caps: 'What about you Shane? You know the basics, is there anything you want to know? Alama, what about you? Do you want to chat after practice? Do you want to go over what your role specifically is?' At training the coach pulls the team together to emphasise key elements and expectations. On the dot of 4.00 p.m. he is demanding a player's perception of a team error, 'You tell me, Lamby, what happened here.' Five minutes later the forwards group gather to clarify their expectations for the scrum . . . Then it's time to put these into a training session. Onlookers watch and listen.

On the scrum machine the expectations of team mate upon teammate are high. The eight concerted bodies thrust their force into the scrum machine. Again and again . . . The sweating scrum breaks up and the 40-test veteran prop speaks directly to the six-test lock: 'Get down Rigger.' 'Rigger, you gotta get down.' Then the reality is emphasised: 'Rigger we're playing bloody South Africa. You're just too high, your shoulder is right up Fitzy's arse.' The scrum sets and resets. Mark Cooksley is really getting into his work now after his team mates' bluntness. The coach gives a rare individual compliment: 'I can see you working in there Rigger, that's bloody good.' The captain's voice heaves up from the front row: 'Good work Rigger, that's really good work.' The scrum eventually breaks up and Loey pats Rigger on the shoulder with an accompanying grunt of approval. The All Black scrum's self-expectations have been set, and met . . . the listeners nod in approval.

The fulfilment of self- and team-expectations is felt most acutely in the All Blacks' changing room, as Grant Fox noted in retirement. 'The thing I enjoyed most about test rugby was the dressing room after the game — that's what I'll miss most of all. In the ten to fifteen minutes after the test, with only the team in the dressing room, you feel relief first, then satisfaction for getting the job done.'

'Team spirit'

A major element of a great team is cohesion. There is a playing and interpersonal interaction and interdependence which is felt, seen and achieved on the field. The pundits and scientists say it ain't been proven — but the players know it's there. David Kirk, the 1987 World Cup captain, defines team spirit as 'the collective commitment to the cause and to each other.' And nothing helps cohesion as much as winning.

Great teams play well. And while it might please devotees to the coaches-can-turn-any-team-around philosophy to believe otherwise, if you haven't got the players, then you're as likely to win as to carry a gallon of beer in a macramé string bag. Great post-war All Black teams have had great players. The 1967 team had Lochore, Gray, Meads, Kirkpatrick, Tremain; the 1987 All Blacks had Jones, Brooke, Shelford, Whetton, Fitzpatrick, Kirk, Fox, Stanley, Kirwan and Gallagher; and the 1995–98 teams called upon Cullen, Mehrtens, Fitzpatrick, Lomu, the Brookes, Ian Jones and Bunce. Which, in part, takes us back to selection.

Reaching the goals: the plan at work

The great team operates within a structure which is designed by the coach to realise the vision, to attain the goals. As the great All Black team of 1995–98 developed, the basis lay in Mains' planning and work for the previous four seasons, and in the World Cup camps which set out basic goals and principles to achieve team development — just as in a business team. John Hart then stamped his mark skilfully on the team by extending these developments in the professional era with fulsome players.

Camp 1. October 28–31, 1994

1. Medical assessment of all players. Where required decide immediate rehabilitation action e.g. operations, physiotherapy, etc.
2. Muscle balance assessments and corrective action required; also injury prevention measures.
3. Physical strength assessments.
4. Provide specialised individual programmes to strengthen any weaknesses.
5. Setting of aerobic base programmes Nov 9 – Dec 9.
6. Review All Black Rugby 1992–1994.
   - i Strengths and weaknesses of A.B. rugby.
   - ii Assessment of tactics and game plans.
   - iii Individual assessment.
7. Nutrition and diet for rugby players during training and matches. (Wives and partners included in this session)
8. Outline summer camp and training commitments. (Wives and partners included)
9. Role of the All Black Club and players' responsibilities to Club sponsors and sponsors of the NZRFU.

Camp 2. December 9–12, 1994

1. Fitness assessments. Updating of aerobic base and physical strength programmes.
2. Vision assessments:— reaction time/night vision — peripheral vision, etc. There are quite simple methods to improve these, which will be employed.
3. Individual skill development.
   i   Players' acceptance of personal skills requiring improvement.
   ii Technique improvement through specialised coaching.
   iii Sprint technique instruction.
4. Option taking and tactical development.
5. Outline 1995 pre-Rugby World Cup match programme.

Camp 3. February 3–6, 1995

1. Aerobic Base assessment and updating of programme.
2. Assess skill improvement and continued coaching and practice of these.
3. Coach and practise unit development and tactics.
4. Option taking — workshops and practical.
5. Spirit training.

Camp 4. February 24–27, 1995

1. Repeat and recap activities of camp 3.
2. Workshops — Tactics and game plan familiarisation.
3. Practice — units tactics. Team tactics and game plans in teams.
4. Invitation match.

1995 Pre W.C. Match Itinerary

Aim: All R.W.C. squad members will have played eight (minimum) 1st class matches by departure date.

Feb	28: W.C. squad friendly at Greymouth.
March	1: Super 10 (4 matches — notes of squad)
	2: Maori fixtures — 2 matches
April	1: Nth vs. Sth — Taupo
	8: All Black Trial (Dunedin)
	Assemble Tues — All tactics, game plans, etc. revisited
	Recap camps.
	11: South Div. Selection vs. Canada
	15: NZ XV vs. Canada

18: NI Div. Sel. vs. Canada
22: NZ vs. Canada
29: Club and rep rugby NZ VX to Fiji
May   6: NZ vs. NZ XV Whangarei
12–13: R.W.C. squad warm up game

WHAT CAN WE DO FOR YOU?
Please support. Structure. Tactics. NZ.

The team development enhanced by such planning may have effects beyond that of the immediate match, season or year. Brian Lochore noted, 'the 1995 team was very special. With the planning that went into them, Laurie's coaching, and the whole team feeling, it meant their next year [in 1996] would be an easier one for the new All Black coach than the first year of All Black coaching had been for his predecessor in 1992.'

In reflection, then, the ingredients of a great team may be seen as exhibiting:

- leadership, with a clear philosophy translated into a vision, expressed simply, that the whole team shares;
- goals developed from the vision;
- a selection policy which balances experience and ability to meet the goals;
- a core of (potentially) great players;
- the development of team leaders;
- close relationship between coach and captain;
- a strong tradition respected by all in the team;
- set standards — in discipline and values — which are adhered to;
- respect for individuals;
- team member contributions which are integral to the team ethos;
- change which is undertaken and managed;
- cohesion on and off the field is strong, with players knowing their roles;
- a positive team culture with high self-expectations;
- success — players judge themselves against their own expectations and the best opponents, and succeed;
- media relations and communication which are open and positive;

- an awareness of the 'others' in sport — the spectators, followers, sponsors and consumers — reflected in team behaviour;
- clear game plans;
- team member participation in decision-making;
- playing skills and strategic understanding;
- enthusiasm for the task and with each other;
- ongoing review.

6

Living with the legends: the All Black captains

As captain your primary role, how you are judged, is to win a hell of a lot of games with dignity and style.

Wilson Whineray

The All Black team does not exist in an environment of élite rugby walled off from the past. For example, the oldest All Black captain interviewed by the writer, Jock Richardson of the 1920s, shared the views of his present-day successors on a range of rugby matters, despite the 70-year gap in their rugby test experience. In 1992 Richardson expressed similar beliefs about the ethos of rugby as did the 1990s All Blacks, and his opinions that rugby demanded too much financially of its players, and that 'the league fellows' had the right approach with payment to players, echoed the thoughts of the modern All Blacks.

The quintessential quintet

The great post-war All Black captains, who were successors to the Richardsons, Gallahers, Porters and Kilbys, may be considered as Whineray, Lochore, Mourie, Dalton and Shelford. Lindsay Knight has suggested that some captains have achieved results that were at least as good or even better than Whineray's, but Whineray's special place in this élite company is that 'he set the benchmark by which all All Black captains are assessed'. Given that such a selection is subjective, the writer sought judgement from Neville McMillan and three of the most published contemporary New Zealand rugby writers, Bob Howitt, Ron Palenski and Terry McLean. Agreement was virtually unanimous on a select group of captains — Whineray through Dalton — but opinion was divided on the merits of Shelford. He is included in the 'great captain' group by this writer on the basis of his outstanding winning record and the fact that experts as different as Wilson Whineray and Peter Thorburn, All Black selector and Shelford's coach, rated him as comparable to the other four exemplary All Black captains.

Wilson Whineray captained his country for 30 tests, from 1958–65. In his team a player emerged with similar leadership qualities. Brian Lochore became, for eighteen tests, a superb All Black captain over the years 1966–70. The legacy of special rugby chieftainship was next borne by Graham Mourie through nineteen tests in the years 1977–82. A British writer, D. Norrie, saw him 'as an All Black captain to rank with the likes of Whineray and Lochore'. Andy Dalton, in his seventeen tests of leadership from 1981 to 1985, was in the 'élite bracket with the likes of Mourie, Whineray and Lochore,' argued Lindsay Knight in 1991. The final élite rugby team leader included in this small group is Wayne (Buck) Shelford, captain in 14 tests from 1988–90. 'He was a very good captain because he had presence,' declared Whineray. Peter Thorburn believed, 'Unequivocally, he is the most outstanding captain I have seen in the 30 years that I have been playing, coaching and watching senior rugby.'

Whatever the era in which the élite rugby team leader flourishes, the foremost characteristics shaping the ethos and parameters of a team's leadership remain constant. All five great captains expressed comments similar to Andy Dalton's on élite captaincy:

> It's experiencing honesty in a team, the integrity and team work, the team spirit. In leading a team in any era you set a common goal effectively and see how people react to this. Their contribution to the teamwork mirrors what we give to the community generally. A rugby team has differing ethnic and religious groups with a whole range of personalities and jobs — its wonderful! Added to that is the discipline required, to play within the rules. It's probably the only consistent discipline a lot of the young people get, the discipline in rugby, given that it isn't necessarily there in other spheres of their lives. There has to be support. In a professional game the money has to come down through the ranks.

Whineray, Dalton and Shelford also emphasised their belief that two long-prized major values of rugby are its inclusion of people of all physical shapes and sizes, and the centrality of continuous play and running with the ball.

Formative years

The formative years of the great captains provide some common themes. These great captains grew up in home environments with fathers, especially, keen on sport as an outlet for young boys, and parents who supported sport involvement. They were given opportunities to assume responsibilities as leaders in their formative years, at school or early in their careers.

Wilson Whineray's father was active in swimming and, as a boy, the future rugby captain played soccer until secondary school. He felt 'something calling me into rugby, the hurly-burly or something', which drew him out of soccer. He also enjoyed boxing, at which he had success, and secretly cherished the belief 'that I could have gone further'. Whineray's father had his sport restricted by the war, but his mother was an outstanding tennis player. His father played rugby until he broke his collarbone and got married, and his mother's family also played sport.

In Lochore's rural community, 'The game [rugby] was played at school and that's the way things were.'

Andy Dalton, as a 17-year-old schoolboy leader, was described in a 1969 programme as 'a fine leader, dynamic when necessary and diplomatic always'. His father, the past 1949 All Black vice-captain Ray Dalton, noted his son's leadership even earlier.

> He was always a leader. As a father I didn't notice it in the early days but when you reflect back Andrew was always leading his younger brother . . . invariably it was he who was leading. I recall a woman at a play-centre run by Dr Neil Begg for his studies. This woman took great interest in Andrew and said, 'He will make a great leader and will make his mark in some way.'

Wayne Shelford's schooldays also featured sport, especially rugby and rugby league, often with his brothers. His parents had both been active in sport, and a cousin, Frank Shelford, became an All Black who played 23 matches for New Zealand as a flanker.

Captain's confidence

The captain's role at the élite level presents challenges across a range of leadership domains. The five great captains noted the primary role of providing confident leadership, but emphasised the demands of captaincy on tour.

The true elements of a rugby team — training, game and social dimensions — need balance, need a oneness. Players have to be at one with themselves and the team, and the coach and captain are critical in this, along with the manager if you are on tour. (Andy Dalton)

As captain your primary role, how you are judged, is to win a hell of a lot of games with dignity and style. There is pride involved, and people at home feel good. You've got to have a hand in the preparation of the team. It's hard to take a team onto the field that you haven't been involved with. In New Zealand you were seldom asked anything by media in my day. You need to be confident in your team and to have an onfield pattern the team can be committed to. (Wilson Whineray)

Brian Lochore ('BJ') usually exerted a similar presence on the field as had Whineray, and noted the need on occasion to change the game plan. 'If you find in the game that the plan is not working, then, clearly, at the first opportunity you get the team together and say, "Look, this is not working so we're going to change what we're doing." Obviously the senior players may have an input into this.'

Andy Dalton saw his role basically involving liaison and motivation. Graham Mourie added to this:

At the risk of being thought arrogant, I believed I was able to make a team more effective when I was captain . . . making all the right little decisions because they're the hard ones to make. I think my style of captaincy was very much a 'hands-on' style . . . 'Okay, at this scrum we're going to do this, at that line-out we're going to do this' . . . reading the direction of the game on the field, changing the tactics at the right time.

These leaders agree that the captain's onfield requirements haven't basically changed into the late 1990s, although the role's demands, in terms of media exposure and public communication, have increased. Indeed, the 1924 captain has recalled the importance of going into a test with variations of the game plan which could be implemented if necessary.

Lochore and Mourie noted the demands on those close to élite rugby leaders. The obverse side of the accolade of greatness in All Black captaincy may be reflected, at least partially, in Graham Mourie's comment that 'retiring as All Black captain left a hole in my life that will never be filled in the same way . . . everybody likes to be important.' He emphasised the captain's onfield leadership role, making decisions through analysing the game, and the off-field responsibilities of representing the team and working with the coach. 'You miss the centrality of that role in your life when it all ceases.'

Personality and social skills

The 1924 Invincibles test captain, Jock Richardson, believed that 'it's your own personality that comes to the fore in captaincy', rating leadership qualities above playing ability, although a captain had to read and direct the game and play with effort 'fast and well.' One of his great successors, Wayne Shelford, said, 'I wouldn't say I was the best, but I tried my best.' In onfield play and off-field interaction, communication qualities were important for each captain, with Shelford emphasising the need for team leaders to follow their natural styles.

> Andy Dalton was a soft spoken guy, but effective. He'd get his point across without raising his voice too loud, whereas I would grab the team by the scruff of the neck and give them a boot up the backside and that would get them going as well. As a captain you wouldn't expect of the players what you didn't expect of yourself. It was very different captaining a Maori team, letting the guys with excitement use that excitement, enhancing that sort of game, letting the free spirit go, all flair, individual skill and ability, but subtly controlled so they played within a pattern. I was conscious of not remaining static in my thinking. It was important to enjoy what we do and to enjoy the means to be successful. Enjoy yourself. Kia kaha.

Social skills are important, particularly on tour, whether the captain be dealing with 'the little things on tour you learn from' or meeting social demands. Veteran of 28 tests, of which 20 were as captain, Wilson Whineray comments:

> Some people are captains and enjoy it but some aren't prepared to put up with the social side, such as a predecessor of mine, Kevin Skinner. Being a gregarious fun-enjoying person I would look longingly down the hall from the front table and see my mates like Tremain and Meads getting nicely lubricated while I was up there with Colonel How's-your-father!

As regards mateship, the five All Black captains felt that team members can become too close to the captain and that, as skipper, 'You need to have a little distance from your team mates.'

> You have to get on with people and communicate effectively, while at the same time you have to stay a little aloof. At the end of the day you

have to be friends, and have their respect. Different leaders demand respect in different ways. Neil McPhail and Brian Lochore demanded respect for different reasons, for the nature of their person, for their humility. (Graham Thorne)

Concern for players and positive captain-player relationships were integral to captaincy. Mourie recalled being unaware that 'Mark Donaldson had never played at Cardiff Arms Park and playing there had meant so much to him. He didn't get a game there on tour and I was offside with him for a couple of years and I never understood why. It was because I hadn't realised the importance of that ground for him.' One of the great captains was critical of a successor: 'It was absolutely criminal the way [he] publicly criticised this young player after a lost match in France.' In apparent contrast, relating to the young All Blacks had been a deliberate action for Wayne Shelford.

> I made an effort with young players, to go and have a drink with them. A lot of senior players won't do that and I get pissed off with it. I was not just there for myself, I was there for the team. I tried to sit with different people at various meals, especially with young guys coming into the team, as I may not really have known them. I suppose I was lucky as an All Black captain that I wasn't an Aucklander. They usually stand by themselves. Same on the bus, I would try to sit with different players. Before games on a Saturday morning, I would go around the boys and see how they were.

Analytical and planning skills

Wilson Whineray draws attention to other roles. 'On a mental level, there is looking at the opposition and analysing their strengths and weaknesses. That was very important, the planning.' 'The other side,' declares Mourie, 'was putting the team together, in terms of the social part, the training side, and the challenge you set for yourself, such as beating the guy you're tackling.'

A noted All Black believed that, even in the cauldron of an All Black test, a sense of the captain's values could prevail and impact upon the team. He noted that players would often see Mourie or the French captain Jean-Pierre Rives smile when one had beaten the other to a loose ball. As the two leaders had a tremendous capacity to relate to each other, that was seen as great for the game. This illustrates an important dimension. 'There was, in all of that, the physical exhilaration of doing something well, whether it was scoring a try or making a tackle. I think it's important to have standards of excellence that you want to attain as a person,' declared Mourie.

> You are aware of the other captain, you're matching tactics with the guy and may well respect him. Captain X of one opposing test side was suave and urbane but you'd never trust him off the field, whereas Jean-Pierre and I had a mutual respect for the way we each played. We were small guys in a big man's world! Bill Beaumont and Jean-Pierre Rives had the respect of their own players and the opposing team. Mark Loane was an outstanding sort of person also.

Despite having similar qualities, the All Black captains' leadership styles and social closeness to their teams sometimes contrast. 'Graham was obviously a great thinker of the game but I always found him aloof. He and I had a distant sort of relationship; he's not the sort of guy I readily got along with. I still don't know what or who Graham Mourie is. That was his style,' comments Andy Dalton, a hooker in Mourie-led test teams. Another captain from this select group, Brian Lochore, commented:

> Wilson Whineray commanded a lot of respect. To be a good captain you have to have respect. He was articulate, a sound person and a good player, and those qualities should be considered. A captain gains players' respect through playing ability. It's easier if you're quite a good player and able to get the players to work for you when you give instructions, and to feel comfortable about that. Off the field, you need to set high standards for yourself in all aspects of your life.

Inside and outside the All Blacks, players have been seen to respond to the mantle of élite team leadership being placed upon them, and their commitment has earned respect from their peers. 'I think of Frank Oliver. Once appointed as All Black captain, he rose in stature and provided effective no-frills leadership,' recalls Graham Thorne. Thorne points out that one day Oliver was known by his nickname 'Filthy' to his team mates while on the next day he had acquired the mana of his new role.

A similarity of leadership under pressure in high-intensity sport and in war was noted by Wilson Whineray, the oldest of the élite group. 'When you decide on what success is, then the qualities of a captain likely to help you achieve this can be better decided. Whatever qualities I might have being captain helped me find confidence. It's a bit like going to war. For those who came out of the war it must have been a wonderful strengthening experience. Leading the All Blacks on tour has something of that.' This sentiment was echoed by Peter Johnstone, another All Black captain, who saw active service in the Second World War.

The quintessential quintet rated themselves on a 1–5 scale (5 being the highest) on rugby team leadership qualities. These included: commitment to team, communications skills, knowledge of rules, achieving team goals in games, maintaining best traditions of rugby, sensitivity to players' needs and perceptions, relationships with coach, onfield leadership, creativity, sense of vision and personal playing skills. High, self-imposed standards and expectations may be reflected in the moderate ratings they awarded themselves, which appear to be lower than those accorded them by commentators or fellow players. Individual perspectives shape answers. Mourie, for example, rated himself 4 in the first category, commitment to team, as 'I always felt a greater commitment to rugby.' Creativity, sense of vision and sensitivity to players' needs were generally the qualities which the group rated themselves slightly lower than for others. This may indicate areas which coaches could examine in order to facilitate full development of their All Black captains.

Onfield leadership

The importance of onfield leadership is central to All Black success. This is reinforced from the vantage point of the longest-serving past-All Black skipper, Wilson Whineray.

> On the field the captain is really of value when there is trouble. When you're getting beaten, that is trouble! Discipline was never a problem for me as we had standards. We had good relationships with the referees and that helped. The other side is the hard part, when you have to change the game plan. There was an example of this when Buck Shelford changed New Zealand B's tactics at half-time against Australia, which made all the difference to that game. You have to change course when you are in trouble, you must have fall-back positions. You have to have players who have faith in you when you want to change. It's like the military thing under fire, when you really need to rely on others when you say something. From the media point of view you're a good captain if you win! A baboon could have captained most games I played with the All Blacks, but some of my best games as captain came when we were losing but pulled the margin back. You don't really notice the clever captaincy from the sidelines or the press box. Dawie de Villiers, the South African test captain, was a charming man, but the guy I had the highest regard for, and still do as a friend, is John Thornett. He was so good on the field. If both captains are friends, that influences the teams.

Whineray may have presented himself a little modestly, as the rugby writer, A.C. Parker, believed: 'You always knew there was a captain on the field when Whineray played, something that was not always apparent in his absence.' This leadership theme — that captaincy affects the onfield play, atmosphere of the game and team's sporting values — is still subject to debate among rugby followers.

John Stewart ('JJ'), the prominent coach who took the 1976 All Blacks to South Africa, provides an insight into the complex demands upon captains.

The last thing I say to any team is 'The captain's the boss and anything he says has my support', and that's the way it is even if it ends in disaster. The captain is the onfield boss. He's got to be able to do things and make decisions. For example, if you are in a ruck on the 20-metre line and it's your ball, what pattern are you going to play, what tactics, what play or strategy will you call — would you run their forwards off their feet or, perhaps, get the ball wide? What *does* this mean? Do the players have a common understanding of this? One tactic is to pass the ball . . . within *that* is a variety of passes (what are they?), *or* you could kick to move their forwards or to get the ball wide. If you are doing this, then you must know who, how, when, the angle, and what individual players are then going to do. But if it's their ball, there's going to be a different set of tactics, a different set of patterns. What if there's a wind, what if it's a high wind, if the wind is with us, if the wind is against us? What alterations to the game plan, to the tactics and patterns if it's raining, if it's heavy underfoot? How does the score affect it? What if we're two points *down* and there are two minutes to play? How different is our response if we are two points *up* with two minutes to play. Ireland lost a bloody test match because they were unable to work that out. They were up with four minutes to play . . . they should have played another fifteen seconds. They should have lain on the ball, questioned the referee, got injured, got up late just in time to stop the whistle, piddled around, lain on it, lain on each other. They should never have lost the game but they hadn't thought these things through. THINK IT THROUGH!

Stewart continues, and directly outlines the captain's needs.

Leadership, charisma and social skills are necessary but he can't be a pisshead! I don't really know the qualities of a top captain. What I have always tried to do is match the guy to the personalities and contingencies of the team at the moment. The planning has to be done before the test, the 'chess' of the thing. I like to set a game with patterns in it and then help players within that and with their technical problems.

The role of the coach includes the grave responsibility of developing the right team attitude and a sense of sportsmanship.

Fred Allen, the most acclaimed All Black coach, saw a priority for the élite captain's relationships. 'He must be a bush psychologist and understand what makes people tick, get on with players and motivate them and understand the game.'

The captain must lead by example. There are other players who can assist in changing the onfield game but there are not many who can read the game well. The captain has to be able to lead, to have the other players look up to him. The way he can take pressure, a loss, is vital. He leads by example both on and off the field. Playing under an All Black captain you know where you stand with him. The team have to know what it's all about. You couldn't get better off-the-field leadership than Brian Lochore's but perhaps, at times, there were some tactical aspects that needed attention. For example, we should have changed our onfield tactics in the South Africa tests. Buck Shelford led by example, whereas Captain Y found it hard. He played off people and went the way the game went.

The captain's qualities are revealed under pressure. The captain and coach must use the ball . . . There will always be times to play with 'shit ball', the bad ball played well often makes good ball further outside. In coaching you've got to get the set pieces right, the foundations, then the second phase, then build on that. You have the moves, now give them options. A lot of coaches try to make their team into robots but you have to give them the chance to do something. The most difficult task for the coach is dropping somebody.

The highly respected B.J. Lochore expressed his belief that the captain influences the game's direction.

You can lose direction if the captain is in the forwards and is perhaps more worried about his forwards than his backs. It just takes a good captain with overall vision to look at where the strengths and weaknesses of the opposition are, and say, 'Right, let's change our tactics and use the blindside instead of the midfield hits. We've tried for 15–20 minutes to break through in the centre . . . why not change it?' Usually a forward captain relies on his flyhalf or experienced back member for complementary leadership on the field.

On 1 July 1950, the British Isles were defeated by a depleted New Zealand team 6–3. The All Blacks lost Johnny Simpson through injury (no substitutes were allowed) and their captain, Ron Elvidge, was severely injured. 'The British Isles did not capitalise on their opponents

128

being virtually two men short, especially in forward play such as in line-outs,' recalled Johnny Simpson, citing an example of poor onfield captaincy.

In the 1970s New Zealand drew with a country of lesser ability. 'Our All Black captain did not change what was happening and attempt to get ball to the backs. We had the legs on them in the backline but for some reason we seemed to need to keep it in the forwards. The plan had been to move the ball.' (All Black coach).

In our last game of the 1929 All Black tour of Australia, we were about fifteen points down at half-time, partly because we had been to the New South Wales Rugby ball the night before! Cliff Porter, our captain, harassed us at half-time, no doubt about it. I can still see him pounding on the floor! He emphasised the honour we should uphold for New Zealand. Although we were tired from the previous night there was then no question of losing . . . (Alf Waterman, All Black 1929)

In the Lions third test, 1966, the Lions were attacking and had us on the ropes for ten minutes-plus early in the second half, when they narrowly missed scoring. During an injury break we were called together and told to concentrate on our defence pattern and just deny them points, and to nail them when we got into their half. We were reminded that if we didn't score when next in their half we would lose. We kept them out and scored three tries in fifteen minutes the next time we were in their half. (All Black 1966–68)

Debatable sport ethics underlie respect for opponents and self-imposed limits of onfield behaviour — a 'players' code' of acceptable physical aggression and retaliation. 'I don't think kicking is acceptable, but I don't mind getting rucked or the odd clip . . . I don't think players, in general, have the discipline of ten years ago . . . a lot of respect from younger players is missing,' observed Buck Shelford, a formidably physical opponent. In his final years of élite team captaincy it was the inculcation of rugby values and skills that brought this team leader most satisfaction. 'In my last two seasons, it wasn't so much the winning that I found enjoyable as watching the team on the field doing their things successfully.'

The need to respond to potential and actual behavioural onfield situations is a permanent possibility for the captain. Jock Richardson recalled having to adjust the team's onfield organisation after Brownlie was sent off against England in 1924. This was facilitated by going into each test with a number of game plan variations.

For Graham Mourie, the success of All Black leadership is judged on three levels: the public assessment of the way the team performs, the private assessment inside the team as to whether it's a happy one, and the image of the game the team generates at the top level. Lochore suggests that 'You can get an idea of a well-led team by watching a rugby game. The first thing is the team discipline, how they arrived, how they ran out and warmed up, and then the telltale signs of how they moved into their positions.' For Wayne Shelford, the indicators of a well-led team lie 'in the style of play they're trying to accomplish, how success-ful that style is, how correct their techniques are in scrums and line-outs, the way the backs run . . . even in the captaincy you can see if he's calling the right moves.' He further notes that:

You need to be able to teach players, give commands and lead by exam-ple. Don't accept the view that the captain is 'the be-all and end-all' of the match team, but you do need an onfield leader. Basically the cap-tain has to have vision to see a game changing and alter his game tactics accordingly. He's got to lead by example, the way Sean Fitzpatrick does, and call the right shots at the right stage of the game.

Andy Dalton recounts a test series against Australia as illustrating the demands placed on an All Black captain.

We had lost the first test, and in the second test they were twelve points up in ten minutes. I remember looking around the faces of the players; there was absolute devastation. The guys had just given up and I got them together and quickly said we're not going to change anything in terms of our tactics, they're still the right tactics, let's just go out and do them. I told them not to worry about the conversion, just let them take that . . . In fact, we came back and won that game. We had discussed at some length the fact that their loose forwards were faster than ours, so we wanted to roll them around and tie them in and that worked, so [our open-sided flanker] had a good game.

Changing tactics as a captaincy skill is illustrated by Wilson Whineray:

We lost the third game of our British Isles tour and then played a com-bined team, Aberavon and Neath. We were struggling in that game in the forwards and it was a hard slog. They got in front 9–0 or so and then [the centre] hurt his knee and [a flanker] had to come out of the for-wards and play at centre. (I never liked putting a forward on the wing, I would rather cover the missing player in the centre.) Then it started to pour down with rain, which flattens everything out, and I thought 'Christ!' I needed more horsepower from the forwards. We kicked the ball into the corner, ran the blind side and incessantly brought the fullback in with a big blind side and had to take the risks. As captain I had to get us back to where a converted try could win the game. We pulled them back and eventually won 11–9. I was sitting in the communal bath after the game, with Ken Gray, Pinetree and John Graham, and a glass of beer, and I remember one of us saying, 'By Jesus that was a close-run thing!'

A further example of the captain's onfield leadership influencing the course of a game, also in Great Britain, was recounted by Whineray:

We were down about 15–0 at half-time. I thought, 'What the bloody hell is this?' You can't just say, 'Let's get stuck in'. (I don't know what that means.) 'Can we score a try in the next ten minutes? Christ yes!' We scored in five minutes. 'Now we need another three . . . ' The guys responded. We rolled them totally. That's really where you are of value as a captain.

It was in this match that Andy Mulligan, the ex-international player and rugby writer, noted Whinerary's personal play and the impact of his half-time talk, which he described as 'working with such devastating effect'.

Selection and training of captains

Selection of the captain is rarely considered in depth by the rugby coaching manuals or courses. 'I remember when I retired from the All Blacks and the question arose as to who was to follow me,' recalls Wilson Whinerary. 'I had a good rapport with the coach, Fred Allen. Who would become the new captain? Two senior players, Kel Tremain and Colin Meads, were probably ahead of Brian Lochore in the public mind. But Brian seemed to have the potential to become a good captain.' The process of selecting a captain, however, is not always clear-cut, as Andy Dalton and others have found on moving from the leadership of captain to that of élite coach! Shelford holds a strong belief that 'giving the captaincy to young guys is a risk, as is the selection of a very young player and placing him under unnecessary pressure'. Andy Dalton shares this reservation:

As a coach I couldn't see any player who stood out enough to be captain. In my first year I had a captain who had a wonderful ability to communicate. I picked a young fellow who had experience with a younger representative team, but he didn't have the respect of his provincial team mates and struggled for form. It's very hard to mould a captain, you have to have an individual who fits the scene. I had experienced difficulties as a young captain 'learning the ropes'. My most difficult year as captain of Counties was my first year, as I was a younger player and not ready for it. There was an age problem, but one player was a strong person who had an influence on others and gave me his support. I lacked confidence. You really need, as the captain, to have the confidence of the person who put you there.

The great All Black captains saw the onfield leadership role being located around the back of the scrum.

The captain can't get too far away from the forwards. It's very important that you get the feeling you're winning the game . . . the ball gets carried out from the rucks, you're winning more line-outs . . . by God we're starting to get on top of those blokes, you're in control! A half-back could probably feel this but certainly having a captain out beyond first-five hasn't been too successful. In a perfect world a loosie is the best position. He can talk to others and liaise with the halfback. (Wilson Whineray)

A loosie, halfback, first-five or second-five is the ideal area, or perhaps the hooker at a pinch, as they play modern rugby as a loose forward. You could have the captain in other positions but you then need another onfield leader in a central position. To be a good captain you need to have a good overall appreciation of what is happening. (Brian Lochore)

The best positions for a captain are halfback, first-five or second-five or the loose forwards, especially number eight. The number eight can feel how the team is going, if your scrum is good, the driving from the back of the scrum. Without the team leadership role a halfback can be free to be dominant in his play. (Fred Allen)

Shelford endorsed such views, although 'At representative level the honour goes to a very experienced player, but there are probably four or five All Blacks who could captain the team.' He sees the loose forwards as the best positional area for captaincy as 'You're where the ball comes, you can see what's developing in the backs offensively and defensively.' Shelford further noted he had not captained many teams prior to his All Black leadership tenure. 'I think everybody's got the ability but must develop it.' Such development can be enhanced through learning from exemplary predecessors, as Mulligan implies. He says of Whineray ' . . . any future leader would have done well to spend time in his company . . . and listen to what he said about leadership'.

In turn, Whineray, the elder statesman of our élite captains, noted the relevance of his academic study with its focus upon interpersonal skills. He suggested that leadership training would be useful. A starting place could be a role description. Brian Lochore, for example, was given the responsibility of captaining his provincial team at the age of 21 or 22, 'but I was never given any explanation of the captaincy role by any coach or official. I think that such a discussion would certainly help a new captain.' Another great captain reflected, 'I found that I wasn't analytical when I started. The thing that got to me was that I didn't particularly want to be captain!' Whineray, a successful business leader, noted the need for rugby team leadership development, raising pertinent points for administrators to consider in advancing leadership skills of élite captains.

> I think I became a good All Black captain. I had a learning curve from when I was at Harvard doing a Master of Business Administration. We spent a lot of time on interpersonal skills. I think I realised when I was appointed to lead the team to Japan in 1958 that the duty of being a captain was a responsibility. ('Christ, this is real!') I realised that the dignity of New Zealand rugby was, in part, resting in my hands. At times I wanted to belt someone, given the friction of the front row, but the thought of the All Black captain being ordered off was unpalatable to me. All Black captains have no leadership training but there are aspects of leadership that can be taught. Even making a speech is not easy. When you really scratch the surface of a 22-year-old, you're pretty insecure. At that point I started listening to speakers. In 1960 came a big mountain to climb. I would be better equipped three or four years later as a touring captain. In Africa there is, physically, an endless stream of big guys being thrown at you and you're almost worn down by attrition. It's a hard tour and a flinty tour in that the media are looking for angles all the time.

Each of the outstanding captains concurred with Shelford's views on the spheres of business leadership and rugby team leadership being broadly similar. 'Once your goals are set out and approached collectively, whether you are a business or a rugby team, once everyone is geared up, it's using the same skills, although you might be a little more distant from a business or shop than the rugby team you are leading.' Lochore adds, 'Captaincy on the field is very similar to captaincy or leadership in business — you've got to be able to lead, to motivate, to help people, set goals.' This perspective prevailed with latter-day captains, an All Black skipper of the 1990s, Gary Whetton, declaring, 'If you weren't successful at running a business you wouldn't be successful as a top team leader.' Another captain, Graham Mourie, averred that 'Leaders get the ear of people . . . the ability to communicate, the respect they are given, individual characteristics, knowledge of the field they are involved in, ability to handle people, being courteous under pressure . . .'

Coach–captain relationship

The coach–captain relationship is seen by all of the All Black captains as critical. It must be very strong, with the coach having confidence in his captain on the field. According to Whineray:

> Neil McPhail, as All Black coach, trusted me all the way. We both wanted to do the simple things well. Good teams do the simple things well. The forwards get the ball and the backs use it. He was a good man and had a bit of dignity. Fred Allen was more one of the boys, a wonderful motivator even if a bit of it was by fear. An example of this was his saying 'There's nothing that clears a man's mind quicker than watching a game from the sideline.' He was wonderfully loyal to those who performed.

Graham Mourie worked very closely with his coach, Jack Gleeson.

> You'd sit down with coach and say okay this is what we're going to do, and if it doesn't go right you can change it. You also have players on the field with a bit of history and you can say, 'Remember that move against so and so.' It might even be from three or four years ago.

Lochore echoed this view.

> Developing the game plan must involve the captain. You have to know the opposition and the moves that will work for your team. He should have an influence upon the tactics. You look at the opposition, work out your team plan and go over it and over it at practice. You need to have an alternative in you mind, and even practise it. You might think you will blow the other team away in twenty minutes but when you find that doesn't happen you must change your tactics.

All five captains saw the coach–captain relationship as important. The coach must strive for 100 per cent effort, team success, the development of a team ethos, and the recognition of individuals' value. Relationship skills were emphasised as a coach priority by each captain. Respect for the coach was essential, as was the ability to analyse the team and opposition and prepare an appropriate game plan to which all the players were committed.

Support of the players

The support of skilled team players facilitates the captain's leadership role. Whineray openly acknowledges the strong support and leadership provided by the five or six provincial captains in his forward pack, who were men of character. 'We laughed a lot.' Shelford observed that 'Team spirit comes from your captain and your coach and, possibly, your senior members. Winning helps this a lot. Having a loss or losses can make spirits go down individually and collectively, and coaches really come into it then to provide real leadership.' One captain recalled a lasting memory of this: 'In the Cavaliers, the team spirit was brilliant, absolutely brilliant, better than any All Black team I've been in. There were a lot of senior players and junior players. The junior players were made to feel welcome. Success is not just winning, it's also the enjoyment on tour, the camaraderie and the friendships you make.'

The players' views of captaincy

How do players inside the All Blacks see the All Black captaincy? Attaining the position of captain was frequently equated with the achievement or bestowal of mana. Bill Collins, 1935–36 All Black, saw the captain 'Like the driver of a team of horses. He is in control and sees where to go.' In achieving this, captains were seen as having clearly noted qualities. 'One captain we had could bring a dead All Black team back to life, whereas another just could not bring us together in tests in my last year. He blew that. We were complacent and he couldn't lift us.' The players want a captain to lead from the front, read the game and provide off-field leadership. There must be a clear game plan allowing for onfield decisions and opportunism.

On the 1924–25 tour, there were four or five game plans for the captain to draw upon to lift the All Blacks' game if necessary. Jock Richardson said, 'The team also studied press reports on various opponents, so we knew their games and could counterattack. You don't go in with your method and play a certain plan without being able to change it.'

A clear impression emerged of a 1930s All Black captain, Frank Kilby,

as 'The best captain. He was fair and told you once and that was sufficient. He never really told you, he asked.' Another All Black, the inimitable Hugh McLean, recalled Kilby as 'giving direction to his forwards
which, if ignored, meant you were liable to get a boot up the arse from
the skipper, even in a match!' A prominent All Black of the 1930s, Tori
Reid, who was also a Maori All Black captain, emphasised the contribution of others to a team leader's achievements.

E hara taku toa	It is not of my own
Ite toa takitahi	But the greatness
E ngari taku toa	Of those who
He toa takitini	Have supported me

One pre-war captain, Cliff Porter, praised in rugby literature by writers who did not see him play, was criticised by contemporary players.
'He was always in the way and criticising players excessively. He would
berate players who were really trying and say, 'Oh Christ, why did you
do that?', and that would affect your play.' Another captain, Jack Manchester, 'should never have been appointed — a nice bloke but no
bloody brains. Charlie Oliver should have been captain, he had brains,
character and playing ability.' Yet another All Black skipper was pungently described as 'not even a captain's bum' for his lack of playing
skill and onfield leadership. In contrast, pre-war All Blacks considered
Tom Lawton, of New South Wales and Australia, as the epitome of good
captaincy. Lawton was seen as a gentleman, intelligent, knowledgeable,
having strength of character and excellent playing skills, and showing
outstanding onfield leadership.

The post-war era saw All Black captains maintaining work careers
disrupted by demands of test series. A well-regarded All Black captain
of the 1950s, Peter Johnstone, believed he was 'just an average bloke
around the farm with no great prospects but I thought if I could do
well in rugby then I can do something else. In the war there was the
same feeling of comradeship and confidence in being able to do something.' Another 1950s captain, the diminutive Ponty Reid, who died at
a comparatively early age after battling Alzheimer's Disease, was praised
by a number of players as 'a hard little man, a thinker and a thorough
gentleman.' 'He led by example, a great little man. The captain should
be a leader of men.' This was in contrast to a 1950s captain described as
a 'political appointment who could speak well but could not communicate with younger players'. Ian Clarke's reflection that 'I think it was a
period when captaincy was stifled', typified views of that era. Some All

Black captains, much respected by players, are seen as having had a greater influence upon their teams' winning tactics than the coaches. One such captain, and later All Black selector, saw the essentials of captaincy as image, character, discipline and tactical ability.

The importance of the captain's respect for the referee's authority was noted by many respondents. In contrast, one rugby legend 'who was a very good leader for his province', is said by a team mate to have 'run around behind the referee in his first test as captain calling him a little bugger!' The lack of one team leader's ability to respond to changing onfield situations in the 1960s was noted by past All Blacks. An example was his slow response to the challenge of the opposition's innovatory two-man line-out in 1968. 'Those were the days when you battened down the hatches and bashed on. When the edge went off for one side, the initiative went with it. We did not discuss an opposition team or study them as we could have. We could have found out more about South Africa and done something about it,' argues Graham Thorne.

Whineray was seen by one of his team mates as 'lacking tactical skills at the highest level. In the third test in South Africa, for example, when there were a few minutes to go, he said that we should throw the ball around, but that decision should have been made earlier.' In contrast, another player suggested that having sought the extra effort 'Whineray got it because you looked up to him.' Another player thought that particular captain's playing position 'mitigated against him seeing the game's overall direction at times and doing something early enough'. One pre-war All Black, Bill Hadley, outlined a different captain's inspirational play, recalling his onfield leadership.

> This captain was the best skipper I ever had. He was a hard All Black. I learnt a lot from him about what modern players call running the lines. In one game he grunted, 'You went the wrong way son.' 'But,' I said, 'that was where the ball was.' 'Yes, but that's not where it's ending up.' The captain often centre-kicked and urged me on, 'In the guts son, in the guts son,' to get me racing up the middle.

All Black captain Bob Stuart considered Brian Lochore one of the great rugby captains. 'He was the ideal captain in every way, very friendly, a great player, unselfish, the last of our number eights to cover behind the backs.' Another captain described Lochore as 'the best captain I saw. Very firm, very knowledgeable, and he set a good example both on and off the field. A good leader in a decent sporting way. I've never seen him do his bun.' He was also 'always demanding of himself and modest'. Reflecting on his role, Lochore believed an élite captain has 'to be a good player, have the ability to make others work for you and set a high standard for yourself off the field.' He wanted to be an example on and off the field and influence the team's tactics, being ready to change the game plan. Another All Black captain stressed the importance of leading by example, taking pressure, reading the game and being respected. 'You couldn't get a better off-field leader than Brian but he had some tactical shortcomings, such as when he should have changed tactics in South African tests.' This captain noted of his own All Black leadership that 'I found it hard as captain and tended to go the way the game was going.'

An All Black coach indicated the onfield qualities of a great captain: 'In one particular series we had the opposition really and truly gone up front and there were lots of opportunities when we could have moved the ball and didn't. They were big and bulky and if another All Black captain had been there, we would have moved the ball out, but we didn't. If he had been there we would have run the ball all over the field and run them off their feet.'

Graham Mourie was commended by a range of players for his intelligence, onfield example, decision-making and ability to draw out top performances from team mates. His input into the captain–coach relationship and influence on match preparation were noted as team leadership strengths by players of his era. A past coach, Eric Watson, commented upon this captain's ability to 'get alongside young players and give them confidence to play their best'.

Andy Dalton was seen by his coaches as a man of few words 'but every word counted.' His personal sensitivity to players, praised by one of his coaches, was also noted by John Kirwan. Both Dalton and Mourie were well regarded by a prominent team mate.

> You knew what Andy Dalton wanted. He never shouted or put you down. He was a bit more relaxed than Graham Mourie, who was similar in personal qualities but totally absorbed and single-minded. Mourie was brilliant at picking things up and changing a game plan, being willing to use new ideas and seek them out.

Wayne Shelford was cited by many past and present All Blacks as one of the great leaders, being especially commended for his example, onfield play and ability to lift the All Black play and influence the course of a match. Support and evidence for this were volunteered from All Blacks across seven decades of élite international rugby. In agreement with his peers, they said he handled well the complexities of play, relationships and onfield decision-making.

All Black captaincy imposes demands which are not always perceived by those outside the team or who only observe the team leader at practice or in competition. Fred Allen was a captain rated highly by his early post-war peers but was markedly affected by injury and onfield and offield pressures when touring South Africa in 1949.

> I was playing well enough as captain. I felt I couldn't do any more. I was doing my best but we were getting all sorts of critical mail. At the next team selection meeting I said, 'I can't do any more so we'll start with my position — I'm out.' I knew that if we ever could have won, then Ron Elvidge would have won it for us. I pulled out of rugby for some time, that's how deeply the tour had hurt me deep down. It really shattered me . . . I blamed myself for that tour but I really had no reason for that.

Elvidge, who led the test match All Blacks in place of Allen, described captaincy.

> The captain is more than a figurehead, he must lead by example and do the right thing at the right time — and lead a winning team! You need the respect of the team, which you get by your actions and attitudes on and off the field. The captain must be a thinking player who can sense the nuances on the field and sum up the opposition and exploit their weaknesses.

The stresses upon players, captains and coaches were cited by a range of past All Blacks, who thought personal support for a captain helped to lessen leadership pressures. Jock Hobbs recalled, 'I was relatively young and had extremely senior players in the team. One player particularly was upset by my appointment. I probably made a mistake in distancing myself too far from the team initially, but some distance from players is needed.' One post-war All Black coach, however, argued that some captains simply did not have the status to be All Black leaders. An All Black who did experience public recognition and acceptance noted the need for a mature coach to guide players and, sometimes, the captain. 'Coming to grips with public adoration was difficult . . . This affected my personal security and gave rein to character traits and actions which weren't good. But I learned not to give up, I learned that from rugby.'

One legendary 'hard man' who became an All Black captain, Kevin Skinner, was reluctant to accept the honour and did not feel he led the side well. He did not easily relate to the social demands and speech-making dimensions of test captaincy. In contrast, one of his team saw this leader as 'an idol, positive and down to earth, strong and kind hearted'. Another of the team saw him as 'a very good captain. He never moaned or groaned or bawled anyone out.' It appears that those who possess leadership qualities may not fully recognise the fact. The other side of the coin is seen in a prominent test referee's perception that 'the first thing that destroys a captain is his own sense of bloody self-importance, X was like that.'

Captains learn other lessons also. For example, Shelford and Hobbs believed that changing priorities as leader influenced personal satisfaction and team achievement. Shelford: 'Towards the end of my career, my emphasis upon enjoying the game, with plenty of positive reinforcement, made results more noticeable. Winning should not be at all costs, particularly not at the cost of team unity.'

The All Black vice-captain's role was rarely discussed by team leaders with their deputies. One vice-captain saw his role and that of his leader as 'the ability to make a player feel part of a team, that he won't let the team down, to generate respect and have a certain generosity of spirit'. Another, Kevin Briscoe, had discussed his role with his captain, Wilson Whineray. 'In essence, his advice was to be yourself, provide the support and leadership when we run into the inevitable sticky patch, keep open communication between us and the group, and have a key role in the selection committee.' Similarly, the role of informal or emergent leaders was noted by a range of players. Player and later coach Alex Wyllie noted the onfield impact of players 'who always had that extra bit of authority to run the show if the captain was buried'.

Absent in NZRFU coaching courses is any in-depth consideration of a team's cultural dimension. One prominent rugby person took pride 'in treating all players equally. I recall the way Maori players would joke about their colour, and they knew I was joking at practice when one of them had a hangover and I said, 'Get up you black bugger.' He didn't mind.' This contrasted markedly with an All Black captain, David Kirk, who emphasised the need for 'sensitivity to the different dimensions added by players' cultural backgrounds'.

In reflection, All Black rugby captains noted their growth in élite rugby team leadership roles and dimensions of life beyond their élite sport. A typical view from an international is that,

> Rugby taught me to organise my workplace people like a team — certain people to certain jobs. 'Management' staff provide the leadership ... there are four different teams overlapping at work, so they can move people from one position to another . . . More than that, it's how I handle people. I think I can relate to and work with my Polynesian staff because of what I have learned through working with Polynesian players. I think I've learned team skills in getting people to work together . . . you learn to deal with conflicts, when to drive team members and when to walk away.

A New Zealand rugby legend and past All Black captain, Colin Meads, declared, 'Captaining is very hard. I didn't realise how hard it was until I took it on. You can never trade the mana, the history, the honour of being the All Black captain.' Meads emphasised the need for coaching courses, with emphasis on the realities of coach–team interaction and the opportunity for coaches to employ what they learned.

An All Black captain of the late 1980s, David Kirk, respected for his intelligence and articulation, asserted that all players had leadership potential. 'It's very important for a team to have a diffused responsibility for leadership. Leadership is a quality rather than an attitude and is based on character and the willingness to do things for other people. It involves confidence, decisiveness and knowing what you want.' He shared his belief, in 1992, that New Zealand rugby administration then had no vision or cohesion in its planning. 'Where is the game and what are the key three or four things we want for élite rugby, for youngsters?'

Captains and coaches emphasised the limited guidance given to prepare them for team leadership. 'When I became an All Black captain nobody ever talked with me about it and what was involved,' declared Brian Lochore, speaking for captains from across the decades. Gary Whetton, reflecting on his captaincy, said he would now handle young players differently and relate in different ways to his coach and administrators from how he did. Sean Fitzpatrick suggested team leader skills could be enhanced with 'schooling and education, understanding what makes people tick, communication and social development'. Fitzpatrick stands on the verge of All Black greatness as a captain. He has held the scrum and All Black team together onfield through virtually all of the 1990s. Colin Meads, from his vantage point as All Black manager, saw Fitzpatrick as being 'very demanding of himself and the team. He relies on Mike Brewer at times but leads from the front.'

Leadership from the front is a most valued quality in an All Black captain. Dubbed Captain Indomitable, Fitzpatrick has reflected on his role at various stages in the 1990s. Initially he saw his prime aims as 'developing man management skills, being more committed and leading from the front'.

> If you are the leader you are captain of the ship, captain of that group. I enjoy the power of being able to make decisions, having the power to do things, and I'm prepared to use that as I've seen segregation in top teams and young players being left out and not being part of [a provincial] team. For example, early on . . . I remember John Kirwan saying in '86–'87, 'This is what rugby is all about — playing for the All Blacks.' We got away from that, moving from pride to arrogance. I want everyone having an input. I hate All Blacks going into bars and being arrogant . . . Enjoyment is the number one factor. (1992)

> Andy Dalton had man management and playing skills. He was always talking of perfection and the fact there is no reason why it couldn't be attained. David Kirk was a very articulate captain and assessed the game well, also having man management skills. He got caught in the controversy over the Cavaliers and that influenced some attitudes toward him. Buck Shelford was totally committed to the All Black jersey and led by example. He would basically die for the All Black game. I thought Buck could relate to all players, from the senior players to the new boys. Gary Whetton didn't say a lot on the field. He was fortunate having experienced players in the team but was a good motivator.
>
> In my first test match as captain the players were unsure of me, and I was uncertain about them. As the week drew on we became more confident and drew together. I was going into the unknown and so was Laurie with me. We'd sit down and talk through what we'd do at training. He's been very good at training and team talks, very good in assessing the players, and Earle complements him well. For me the coach must be able to put his ideas and strategies onto the training field and into a game. A lot of people have ideas but can't translate them onto the field. They have to relate to people and know when to be involved and when to hold back. Leadership is being able to relate to players and lead by example.
>
> Brian Lochore was a father figure as coach. I went through '86 with him, a lovely guy and a good coach. John Hart was a great motivator and tactician. Grizz was an honest man who told you what he thought, and a good coach. (1993)

Off-field demands and media focus on the captain have increased over recent years. Unlike during the immediate post-war years, the élite rugby coach of the 1990s was seen to have a greater responsibility than the captain for the team's success.

The interviews and surveys by the author of 231 All Blacks, who represented New Zealand in the period 1924–94, provided a strong consensus of opinion on the essential qualities of captaincy.

Underscoring the qualities were requirements for the élite captain to have knowledge of the players, knowledge of the game and the ability to handle pressure. Captains seen by past All Blacks as most emphatically illustrating the primary qualities were Brian Lochore and Graham Mourie.

Reflecting on the élite of the élite brings common perspectives on team leadership. Such captains exhibit onfield leadership, playing to a high standard with the prime capacity to read the game, and make sound decisions. They sometimes call upon valued peer opinions and change the game plan set previously with the coach. Ethical values are emphasised, on and off the field. Off-field leadership has an extra dimension on tour, with the need to be strong on interpersonal relationships and relate to all players. A cadre of experienced players provides an important leadership dimension in the team.

7

Living with expectations: the All Black coach

New Zealand's methods are hard and concentrated, but the sustained efficiency produced through the power of the coach, which is the nearest thing to the coaching autonomy in American professional football, is the one certain way of succeeding at international level.

Welsh rugby writer, J.B.G. Thomas, 1996

'Life as we know it will probably cease to exist if we lose the next test,' declared a national newspaper editorial in 1994. And if the game is lost, the coach will immediately be the focus of criticism. All Black coaches are national figures. As the *Evening Post* of 26 August 1994 noted, 'Few subjects ignite more passionate debate than who should be the All Black coach. Worries over unemployment, crime and MMP are swept aside . . . ' The coach does not only attract attention while in office. Past All Black coaches and captains are called upon by sports writers, talk-back hosts, editors, television producers and publishers. In today's rugby culture we read the views of past All Black leaders, mix with them at after-match functions, watch them in televised discussion and have close contact with them as administrators, coaches, mentors or even as family members. They influence their team when coaching, and the public's rugby views when retired.

Early All Black coaches
New Zealand rugby teams have had coaches in various guises and, literally, wearing various hats, since the cloth cap favoured by the first All Blacks coach, Jimmy Duncan. The 1888–89 Natives team had Jack Lawlor, who cost the promoter two hundred pounds payment as a coach

Ron Elvidge *(right)*, a courageous captain against the Lions in 1950. (Ron Elvidge collection)

Sometimes it's a solitary job. Sean Fitzpatrick *(below)* planning for a team meeting.

Three coaches *(left)* share a rare private moment together during the 1976 tour of South Africa: Fred Allen (New Zealand), Danie Craven (South Africa), Carwyn James (Great Britain). (Fred Allen collection)

Below: Laurie Mains, Robin McConnell and a weary Sean Fitzpatrick after the 1993 test against Western Samoa.

Two smiling All Black coaches *(bottom)* — now that must mean a series win! The team emerges undefeated after the 1994 tests against South Africa.

Right: Ric Salizzo (media liason), Earle Kirton (assistant coach), Frank Bunce and Zinzan Brooke take great delight in pointing out an onfield error during training.

Below: The stands aren't always packed. Zinny makes a point to his team mates during a visit to Eden Park prior to test day.

Massage is a great aid to the modern athlete: Frank Bunce *(bottom)* is a keen participant of this particular aspect of training.

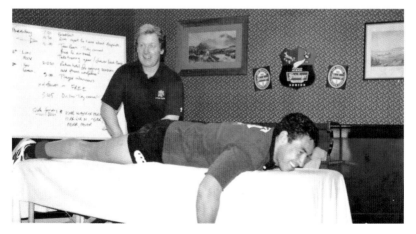

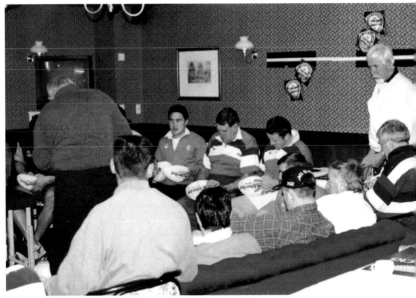

The price of fame — ball signing sessions. Along the back wall are Graeme Bachop, Colin Meads and Sean Fitzpatrick.

Just wait for Zinny's reaction! Brother Rob taped this picture to the wall as a joke, but Kamo and Laurie aren't so sure that Zinny will see the funny side of it.

to teach the team to play Victorian Rules! The NZRFU does not have a complete record of past All Black coaches, but it seems the first All Black assistant manager to perform coach duties was not officially appointed until the 1938 All Black tour of Australia. This was Alex McDonald.

'Alex McDonald could communicate at all levels,' according to Harold Milliken, an All Black on that tour, 'and with different sorts of players on and off the field. He went through all the phases of play with us — the best coach we had. How to pick up the ball was the first thing he made sure we knew, then came the skills and tactics. I think fitness is 95 per cent of it and the rest of it is knowledge, but you've got to have an inherent love for the game. A training session with Alex McDonald would have a warm-up then three lengths of the field at pace until you did his moves correctly. He used to say to us that if we worked out any other moves that we wanted to try, to do it ourselves until we got it right.' Until 1938, according to an NZRFU communication, 'the All Black manager in conjunction with the team captain provided team tactics and strategies.'

In New Zealand home tests Jock Richardson recalls being coached for the test match weeks of the 1921 Springbok series, but the All Blacks first had an assistant manager to act as home test coach in 1956, when Tom Morrison, as convenor of selectors, fitted this role. The first officially designated coach to tour with the All Black team was J.J. Stewart ('Assistant Manager/Coach'), who went to South Africa in 1976. The subsequent team photographs at the NZRFU are not consistent in coaches. (One wonders how there were ever official photographs labelling Jimmy Duncan as coach, or the 1937 All Blacks team photograph with Jim Burrows and Billy Wallace listed as coaches!)

Philosophy and visions

All Black coach Alex Wyllie explains his basic philosophy of coaching.

You have a huge responsibility if you're in charge of New Zealand rugby . . . I get tremendous satisfaction when the team perform well . . . at the end of the day all that matters is the way that the All Black team played. Test match rugby is measured by the win-loss ratio, and you can't argue that. Quality rugby is important, although I would rather play scrappy rugby and win than play good rugby and lose. Overall I want the team playing quality rugby; the winning will come. The rugby must be entertaining for the players, spectators and sponsors, and exciting and challenging for the coaches. The national team has got to be a leader in quality rugby.

I have my coaching style and my philosophy of how the game should be played, in terms of a basic structure and things that are very important to that, but we, the other selectors and myself, discuss often the type of player needed, and the type of play that is best for this particular team, and that tends to strengthen my basic philosophy, and broaden it from the point of view of tactics and, what is very important, to increase my confidence to allow more to happen, in a more expansive pattern — my confidence in myself and in the players and the pattern, both. I've worked very hard to achieve the input of three brains in selection — you couldn't get balance from only one person in a pressure role like this. I know the other two selectors have key roles in keeping this balance.

Laurie Mains, underscores the fact that the starting point for the team's game plan is the coach's team vision.

In my mind I visualise what I would like to achieve with this team. I would describe the game of rugby that I see as my vision for the All Blacks as having a great deal of integrated purpose and activity going on — that creates such pressure on the opposition by retention of the ball, and the speed with which manoeuvres and moves are carried out, that their defences cannot keep regrouping to stop us scoring. Technically, everything being done right. Everyone knows what he has to do in each given situation, and this is brought about not by showing each player a hundred different situations so that he has to remember how to do a hundred things, but by building on a basic philosophy so that he can make his decisions at the time when he needs to.

Playing to this plan needs confidence, self-knowledge and very good vision, and therefore taking the right options, but paramount to it all is communication. This is so important in rugby, as the ball carrier often cannot see the best options and so his support players have got to be his eyes. But time is so short! So little time is really spent on vision, being your team mates' eyes . . .

At the All Black level you'll have team discipline and conforming to the team level, but you don't step in and say, 'Don't have a go yourself.' It's more a matter of pointing out the wrong options. Player Y is a classic example of a player making a break and instead of drawing a man and getting the ball out he tries to beat the next man . . . It may take two or three seasons for the balance to be acquired. If a player is greedy he gets a tune-up, but if he takes the wrong option then he needs talking with. When we look at the options that players take, we have to get to the decision-making process players go through, rather than making hard and fast rules.

Selection skills

Given the coach's clear philosophy and vision, a key role of All Black coaches is that of selection. Wilson Whineray argues for selecting players who fit the coach's intended style of play but also advocates consistency, fairness and recognition of player confidence in the selection process and the coach's decisions.

> The coach must be fair and be seen to be fair from the players' point of view. Put yourself in the place of fullback L, who played for New Zealand B against Australia B. He scored well but the A team was picked and they won their game. Then M, the A team fullback, is injured but N is put into fullback. Player L thinks, 'It's a bit of a blow but I guess I'll be used in an emergency,' but O is put in. So O thinks he's in. Then O and M see P put in and you think, 'What the bloody hell is going on?' Or you take the example of J in the grandstand as reserve halfback, and then they play K, or the example of forward S in the All Black reserves for two tests and then they pick forward R. You must be able to see the logic of the coach.

Selections can bring satisfaction, however! Laurie Mains recalls two examples.

> Grant Fox seemed marginally supportive in his early days with us as a reserve. Then, in the build up to the second Irish test in 1992, he was helping Ant and Walter sort out their game. I said to myself here's a real change. This guy is a real man and a real model to New Zealand kids, helping the competitors for his All Black position make a real success of their jobs, after being the top dog for years. Often we don't learn about the nature or character of players until they face adversity. I would like to think it was because I'd been honest with him. I was delighted with the end result and Grant's reselection as the top first-five.
>
> Zinny Brooke also gave me a great deal of pleasure . . . I thought he played well in 1991 against Australia, but I didn't see him in the top two number eights. In Australia in 1992 I explained reservations I had about him . . . but he handled being captain so well he had to come in for the test. He told me, 'Nobody before has told me specifically what they expected of me.' Ant Strachan was another selected by us, and we were slated. Lyn Colling gave us feedback from the trial, and Earle and I consider ourselves reasonably strong on halfback play. So Ant was selected . . .

A segment of an All Black selectors' meeting in 1994 illustrates the coaches' role in selection considerations.

The three coaches examine the fitness testing reports on All Black trialists. These are compared with their previous test results. Among the relevant factors discussed are attitudes towards training, potential for development, reasons for non-testing and the impact of players' personal lives. The coach is critical of one player on results and declares that he will not make it in a certain position. The other two debate this. They note the increased speed of a veteran back. Time is spent evaluating a raw young player of immense potential. A selector is supportive of the player's efforts in a recent game, appreciating 'the way he had three on one and came off his line and hit the fullback — good stuff!' They discuss the player and his prime learning needs. Another back has 3 kg to lose.

Concern is expressed over a league club here to watch a prime back in a provincial game and All Black trials.

Time is spent discussing another player. The selectors consider his willingness to throw his body around, his sensitivity and how to relate to this, his performance in last year's trial and his excellent approach to training. There is clear concern at the aerobic levels of Auckland players apparently having dropped under that province's training schedule, except for that of the All Black captain, who has his own training programme. A loose forward touted by his local media as a key All Black is lowest in the tests. The All Black coach will ring the provincial coach and discuss the results.

Considerations of the coach's role

Wayne Shelford believed that playing at the élite level provided players with a great deal of experiential knowledge. The coach should draw upon this, and even learn as a playing coach or by 'getting on a close footing' with his captain. The great All Black captains speak with a common voice on considerations of the coach's role, as illustrated by two of their number.

Rugby needs coaches who have thought about the role of the coach. An example of this that's never given much thought is the coach's task of how to maintain the interest of players for a year, or even a season. Some coaches do not value the input of others and see getting others in as a weakness. The more they build themselves up in the eyes of the players the more they fail. (Graham Mourie)

We really don't do our homework on how to coach and too often people do it because it's their turn. Many coaches are too noisy or don't know how to transmit knowledge; for example, in team talk situations you can find no actual knowledge is being transmitted to the player. You'll see a coach shout, 'You Joe, tackle,' but too many coaches assume the player's knowledge about skills and tactics, even at the All Black level. Coaches often blindly label all of the team as being the same, for example, in handling a team talk. They need to understand the quiet guy, those who are steady, the guy who needs a kick up the jacksie and another guy who virtually needs an arm around him. The coach must understand each one. (Brian Lochore)

The support staff assisting team leaders rarely appear in research literature. All Black captains noted the critical value of the rugby team manager. Andy Dalton comments, 'If you've got a weak manager, Jesus it's hard. An outstanding manager is a godsend. A lot of those guys, however, may have never attained management roles in their own particular private or employment roles.' Although their role was primarily organisational it was also critical that managers related to players. Another captain noted an outstanding manager who was 'utterly straight, loyal to everybody and intelligent'.

Wayne Shelford stressed the need for the manager and coach to gain the respect of the players and respect the players as well.

The coach has got to be their friend, their mother, their father, and he's got to be their enemy at times. A lot of coaches are very friendly with their teams but you can get too close. The coach is there for one purpose, to select the best team possible. A good coach must know the game, know the complexities of forward play and back play. Coaches gain respect when they can be friends off the field and have a drink, not take offence at a social jest but be as hard as nails next day. You can't readily compare coaches. For example, one All Black coach was quiet and another was extroverted, while a third was very direct. I can think of other coaches who are the type of persons to pull a player aside and say, 'This is what we'd like you to do . . . ' and to tell the player if they're not playing well, such as, 'You're not making that easy yard.' A big part of the coaching skills is working with the individual, and individuals collectively as team units. You only need one person to fall down and you could be sucking the hind tit all the time!

Less pungently, Whineray noted the need for the coach to adhere to certain standards or principles. Observing that the team has to win games and please the patrons, he is critical of a game plan that embodies, for example, 'continual booting upfield and kicking for penalties by the first-five. That's winning, but you need a better-balanced style to win with style.' He continued:

There is also a moral dimension to rugby and you cannot compromise on illegal or dirty behaviour on the field. The higher the level you're playing at, the less negotiation there should be on bad behaviour. The sinbin and ordering-off should be used more. Everyone in an élite team must stand up for good behaviour and personal standards. An additional demand on today's coach, more than in my day, is that the team leaders and the touring team management group must be able to talk effectively with the media.

Whineray led touring teams in which Brian Lochore was a player who revealed potential leadership abilities. Becoming the next great All Black captain, and one of New Zealand's most acclaimed coaches after his team won the inaugural 1987 Rugby World Cup, Lochore emphasised the need for the coach to get on with people.

He's got to be a people's man. He must be a psychologist and understand what makes people tick. The coach needs to get on with, and motivate, people. He has to have all of the qualities of a captain and realise that all players are different and so you've got to be conscious of their wellbeing. The coach must understand the game. As a coach I learned a lot about players. You had to be a motivator, a leader, a manager and a social butterfly!

This élite leader's skills were further reflected in his role as the 1995 World Cup All Blacks' campaign manager. His interpersonal emphasis was observed inside the concluding team-only session of the All Blacks' Auckland World Cup training camp in 1995, when he emphasised the importance of every squad member.

The extra twenty are very important to the squad. How well you play in March and April will dictate how well the final squad will play in the World Cup . . . the more responsibility the individual can handle, the better the result . . . remember you are representing all New Zealand.

Andy Dalton, who became a provincial coach, perceived the coach needing similar qualities to the captain.

There is, however, frustration in not being able to get out there and only being able to say, 'Come on, this is the way we are going to do it.' It's a humbling experience. The demands upon the coach are heavy, especially upon his time. There are the media and public pressure, millions of watchers, and the sponsors having a go . . . I tried as coach in my first year to establish the team's position in the competition and in the next two seasons to improve on that. Set a goal, say, of beating five or six teams and coming in a certain place in the championship. But it's also a case of seeing what's available, and the best method of using what is available. For example, you need a strong front row for the modern game. And the players must be motivated. It's difficult to change other players' intrinsic motivation. Some players expect support and things to be done for them. Guys would ring me up if I dropped them for a game and say they wouldn't come and train with the team! Coaches vary in their strengths. Hiwi Tauroa had a wonderful ability to communicate with people. He was a guy who could bring a team back from the King Country 'as full as boots', stop them outside the mountain at Taupiri, the burial ground for Waikato Maori, and explain how important it was for the Maori people. This was at twelve o'clock at night. You could hear a pin drop on the bus, but that's the sort of respect that guy had. A great experience to be with him. My coach at university was a wonderful guy at creating a team atmosphere and getting everyone working together. He taught me how to enjoy the game. Barry Bracewell coached me for the first time ever on positional requirements and where to go from set pieces . . . All Black Brian Lochore, as All Black coach, was effective with a quiet manner, whereas Jack Gleeson, who was limited as a technical coach, had a wonderful ability to collaborate and assimilate the thinking and abilities of people in the team. The planning behind our second test against France was a tribute to the man. It was a radical change of style. Had he not had the guts and style to do this we would have been done like a dinner! When I became a provincial coach it was a pretty sobering experience for me as my expectations were higher than those of the players . . . The management and I would be shattered after a lost game but the boys would be saying, 'Well, where are we going tonight!'

Buck Shelford stressed the critical aspect in coaching of match analysis and preparation, which are reflected in the coach saying, 'This is the way we're going to play the game.' The captain then says, 'This is what we're going to do on the field to the coach's pattern.' Shelford emphasised the two team leaders working together. He suggested different emphases may be required of the coach at junior levels of play, although the basic requirements of coach qualities are evident.

Generally, I think coaching is great in this country at the higher levels, but at a lot of lower levels, in club rugby and with second tier teams, it is quite poor, and when the players get through to rep rugby on skill and sheer ability they lack a lot, such as in playing skills, basic tactics, body positions . . . I spent about four weeks with a county side in England trying to teach this one guy to drive straight. By being on the field I could see all the faults they made. A lot of senior players could have passed their knowledge on but didn't, and I got really brassed off with them for that.

An All Black captain predecessor of Shelford's, Ian Clarke, commended him for the onfield leadership that he took into the player–coach role. 'He could take a side from being down and put them in front. It's leadership from the front, "Follow me fellas." It's also tactical and mental.'

David Kirk notes the important duality of personnel management and team spirit for the coach. He reminds top coaches of the different dimension brought to the coaching role by the cultural backgrounds of players. 'The coach must have a context of administration and leadership. Leadership is a quality rather than an attitude, based on character and the willingness to do things for other people . . . John Hart is outstanding in terms of what you need in a coach for managing people. Brian Lochore was excellent. He had an air of conviction and was well respected . . . '

Grant Fox noted that John Hart has been closest to meeting the need for a coach, PR man and expert in management. However, as the ability to coach is of prime importance, Fox also rated Mains very highly.

Laurie Mains was All Black coach for 1992–95. He reformed the unsuccessful 1991 All Black team's legacy, taking his 1995 team to the World Cup final and stamping a new brand of test rugby on the world. The 1995 Innovators, who reshaped the game, were captained by Sean Fitzpatrick, who describes Mains:

> In terms of being a hands on coach Laurie was the best. He was the best forward coach and very impressive with how he thinks about guys and brings out the best in them. He's got the sort of personality that his mood influenced the team — if he was tense then the team could tense up, if he was relaxed, the guys would relax a bit more.

Fitzpatrick saw Mains' deliberate efforts to be positive each morning prior to the third Lions test in 1993 as an example of the impact the coach could have upon the team, with Mains loosening up the atmosphere that was being exerted upon the team from outside and internally from their own self-imposed pressures. On the less positive side, there were times when Mains lost that balance, in his own self-expectations (being harder on himself than on anyone else), in his demands upon players or through overreaction to what he saw as negative criticism, sometimes seeing the media in this light.

Coping with the media places greater demands upon the All Black team leaders today than ever before. Media reports are frequently inaccurate. A couple of examples illustrate this tendency: the reporter who declared in 1993 that Mains had a World Cup plan but two years later said he'd never had any such thing, and the commentators who asserted certain players had not been considered by the selectors when they had, in fact, been the subject of detailed selector discussions. Examples of the latter were Duane Monkley and Mark Carter.

This kind of misrepresentation continued into 1997, when the media described John Hart's team vision and strategic plan as innovations when the previous selectors had also formulated these things, and when Hart was said to have put an end to the beer-drinking environment of the All Blacks — which had not been in existence under the previous leaders anyway! Similarly, there is an unreal expectation of Hart when commentators imply he has a responsibility for the onfield behaviour of leading All Black players when they are playing for their provinces. The obverse is that an All Black coach such as Mains could — and should —have built a more effective relationship with the media. Some misunderstandings may not then have arisen. In the domain of media utilisation, Hart provides an outstanding model.

The great coaches — players' picks
Responses of past All Blacks to a questionnaire clearly confirmed their agreement on five great All Black captains but were not conclusive on coaches, apart from Fred Allen as first choice and Vic Cavanagh, who never coached New Zealand, second.

Fred Allen saw the key to leadership as discipline in the team and oneself. Important also were such teaching techniques as 'walking through the moves, and the knowledge of how to get through to individuals, as long as you are fair and just and have a clear goal. You have to adapt the way you treated individuals. Players X and Y, for example, would get pretty tense so you wouldn't wind them up, whereas Z needed a kick up the arse! You can't kid to All Blacks or go behind their backs, although, for psychological reasons, you might have to tell a little white lie now and then.' Allen emphasised getting the basics right and developing player techniques, even at provincial and test levels. At the interpersonal level he believed the reason for a player's poor form nearly always lay in something outside of rugby.

> It may be also, even at the highest levels, you do have to develop techniques. For example, some players needed to bind properly and know where to hold their hands, to use the arm and body as a spring and . . . push the other fellow down . . . or team techniques . . . Not every good All Black makes a good coach, it's just the way you imbue the players and impart the knowledge. One thing I found was that if a player's form slipped or if he lost his way on tour it was nearly always because of something to do with his personal life, not his rugby.

The views of past All Blacks are reflected in one player's statement that Allen 'had a terrific ability to get the best out of players. He gave some terrific team talks before a game and had a deep knowledge of rugby.' Lochore has noted the relevance of Allen's coaching style to the 1990s. He underscores his discipline, tactical ability and rugby knowledge. Allen was also willing to listen to others. The famed 'Black Panther', All Black flanker Waka Nathan, believes 'Fred and Johnny Simpson worked in well together and Fred became a good forward coach because he listened.' One of Allen's contemporaries describes him as 'a good coach, very volatile, very quick, very knowledgeable, and a hard worker who was quite a disciplinarian'.

Many past All Blacks recalled the impact of Vic Cavanagh, 40 years on, regarding him as the greatest of coaches, as did Lester Harvey, for his communication, simplicity, 'his psychology of the team, his ability to get the respect of everybody, and his aim of lifting players, not slating them'. Cavanagh was skilled at 'reading the opposition, analysing them thoroughly and getting the fundamentals right,' recalls the Otago All Black Ron Elvidge. Cavanagh, described as 'the most clear thinking of coaches' by one overseas writer, influenced a line of All Black coaches and consequent New Zealand rugby successes. A player recalled a 1950 Lion saying of Cavanagh's team that he couldn't believe all players would think as one. Jack McNab recalled Cavanagh's advocacy of reading widely because 'if you can't wait to learn through your own experiences you can learn through someone else's'.

In the pre-war period and into the 1950s, the All Blacks' coaching input usually came from the variable skills of the captain, past players and/or selectors. The assumption that experience and expertise would lead to coaching success was not borne out by such great players as Mark Nicholls or Billy Wallace, who were seen by All Blacks as lacking empathy and teaching skills in their coaching. The influence of All Black team managers as coaches was not necessarily successful and sometimes led to criticism by players. The All Blacks of 1935–36, 1949 and 1960 each provide examples of well-respected men — Meredith, McDonald and Sullivan — who simply lacked the skills, empathy and management qualities necessary to coach at the demanding All Black level.

In contrast, an outstanding All Black coach of the late 1950s, Dick Everest, was extolled as one who 'sat by you as you changed and talked to you quietly. He was a brilliant coach, but in 1960 in South Africa we had Jack Sullivan, who gave the same team talk before each game and lacked the skills of Fred Allen or Dick Everest. It was a very good side that could have been successful with a better coach.' The All Black manager of that team, Tom Pearce, had been a coach who 'was a table thumper with a loud rasping voice, choice language hammering away at you, treating players as though they had no brains. By contrast, I regarded Fred Allen highly as a team coach. He commanded respect and was a very good analyst of the game and knew how to handle men.'

Graham Mourie noted the role of Jack Gleeson as All Black coach:

> He epitomised to me the ability to look at our team, assess its strength and then play a game according to that team's strength . . . I always felt that Eric Watson was a bit maligned by the rugby-playing public and people in top rugby. He took the view that 'I've got a pattern of play which is based on that of Otago province and you guys fit that pattern, and I'll put the best players there that I can to play that pattern.'

Lyn Colling also notes Gleeson as being innovative and fresh in his outlook. Colling saw Gleeson as 'involving players more in decision-making and allowing you to work out options for yourself'.

One All Black coach, Neil McPhail, whose ability was not recognised consistently by the rugby pundits, was recalled with commendation by players for his practical knowledge and concern for players. McPhail, an All Black trialist and Kiwis player who had been a prisoner-of-war, coached the All Blacks on an unbeaten five test tour. He saw his role as 'convincing players you had a game plan and knew the opposition and what you were going to do about that'. He preferred halfback or No. 8 for the captain's position. Players increasingly warmed to him as their association with him increased, although Waka Nathan has noted that sometimes he found it a little difficult to understand McPhail's ideas. He was described as his mentor by one All Black captain. An All Black team manager noted McPhail's 'strong belief in the team concept, encouraging the group to use their talents. Players used their individual talents within the team context . . . Neil never abused a player or shouted.'

Recognition of Fred Allen, by past and present All Blacks, as a great coach is clear, but there is great variation in their views on other coaches. An outstanding Auckland and All Black back, Paul Little, declared, 'I had high regard for Fred Allen's ability as a team coach. He commanded respect and was a very good analyst of the game and knew how to handle men.' This has a similar ring to Colin Meads' description of Laurie Mains: 'He is very sincere, very deep, and demands loyalty . . . I rate him as a coach and he sums up games well . . . Earle Kirton is also a deep thinker.'

> The most difficult aspect of coaching is developing the ability to accurately read the deficiencies of the team and individuals on the paddock. When you're not out there it's different . . . so you have to discipline yourself as an observer to watch for specific players or groups of players . . . obviously video is a great help . . . When it comes to forward play, anybody who sits in the grandstand and thinks he knows exactly what's going on is fooling himself, but he's not fooling any of his players . . . I've always developed a players' committee of experienced and trusted players, and one of the things a coach must have is absolute honesty, so that I can discuss things with them and at length. (Laurie Mains)

According to Alex 'Grizz' Wyllie, 'The coach must be willing to listen to anyone, as there's always the opportunity to pick up something from someone. Listen to your players. You must have discipline but can't run the team like a military camp.' Evidence of Wyllie's coaching skills came from Jock Hobbs, an All Black captain and Canterbury player: 'When he took over as coach we were a shambles in terms of discipline and organisation. Within twelve months we had won the Ranfurly Shield.' That the impact of Grizz's success inhibited some players from speaking up was noted, but he was respected by Lochore, who had full confidence in him. Wyllie argued for élite coaches to move around the country and hold coaching seminars to spread their knowledge of the game. Integral to this, though, is an honest give-and-take of ideas, which may inhibit some coaches. All Black Paul Henderson comments, 'I was a little disappointed in some All Black sides as the players were too scared to say that they thought we were choosing the wrong pattern in case they were dropped.'

A couple of late 1980s All Blacks clearly saw that Wyllie, portrayed to the public as domineering and autocratic, was a shy person who hid behind his gruff exterior. 'He wasn't afraid of change — think of his use of Jim Blair as a fitness trainer with Canterbury — but he was surprisingly indecisive,' said one. He was also fortunate in coaching a very good side.' The other thought 'he went on for a year or eighteen months too long, and it became Gary and Foxy who ran things'.

Key attributes

All Black coaches interviewed by the author placed common emphases on the following as key roles: selection, teaching skills, choice of captain, utilisation of player experience, discipline, coach–player relationships, motivation, tactics, basic skills and training.

Good coaches seek to utilise player talents. One All Black coach, Ivan Vodanovich, commented, 'I made a bloody mistake as selector, picking player X, in the same way as my predecessors had in picking Y for the previous tour, as Y was an absolute bloody flop.' He detailed his All Black selection of an 'architect' of a successful provincial New Zealand team because 'I wanted him to help me with the backs, but on tour he was out injured, overweight and a lazy trainer!' Vodanovich, despite being well respected for his personal qualities by the All Black team, was 'never confident that I was doing the right thing as far as fitness was concerned' and advocated the appointment of dual coaches, as his own backs coaching was not particularly skilled. Another coach noted, 'Looking back on [a particular tour] I should have taken Z as captain instead of the captain we did select . . . I should have known how great he was from the team talks he had always contributed to with real insight.'

J.J. Stewart, assistant manager and coach of the All Blacks in 1974–76, saw the ability to lose as an important quality in a coach. He wanted his players to demonstrate open and clean rugby for the players of tomorrow. In turn, they noted his enthusiasm, his sense of the adventurous, his emphasis on the development of team spirit, the way he involved players in decision-making and allowed them to express themselves on the field. Stewart himself said:

> I think the qualities of leadership apply right across the field, right across your life. Leaders are born not made. It's like a sidestepper — you can make certain skills possible and improve what the player's basically got, but he can't reach the pinnacle unless he's born with it.

Stewart was seen by Terry McLean as the inspiration behind New Zealand players 'being actively encouraged individually to obtain maximum meaning and value from the game'. One of his All Blacks noted his tactical skills, understanding of players and clear thinking. 'JJ could move with the times and had clear communication skills', asserted another. Stewart pungently described the challenge of producing a game plan as 'organising bugger-all people in a hell of a lot of space'. Tactics for this were clarified at a Friday night meeting, at which opposition players were discussed, strengths considered and details reinforced. Stewart considers Fred Allen's book on coaching as still the best there is. Although supportive of onfield communication by his captain, Stewart typically asserts, 'You can be the best talker in the world but if you tackle the wrong joker you're no bloody use,' implying onfield practical requirements as a priority.

Brian Lochore, the All Black coach whose team won the inaugural World Cup in 1987, had been a noted captain. His insights are valued inside All Black rugby.

> The whole guts of coaching is to get 100 per cent effort out of the players. If they get beaten they can handle it, that's the ultimate in rugby. Even if a team is winning at 80 per cent effort I find that annoying. A good example of complete All Black rugby is New Zealand vs. Italy in the 1987 World Cup, when the guys went at it for 80 minutes.

A coach of the 1980s, Bryce Rope, selected players for his pattern of play, 'picking the loose forwards as the first hinge and then the half-back and first-five as the bottom hinge'. He noted the importance of senior players. 'You couldn't change some of the old hands. You could talk to them, but they'd played the best in the world and beaten them.'

Coaches have a clear role in determining the ethical level of play. All Black halfback Chris Laidlaw, who played in twenty tests in 1963–70, asserted, 'Observation and intimidation have both played a vital part in rugby at international level for many years.' The limits are set by the 'unwritten code' which allows, for example, punching, but not kicking. This is justified by test players on various grounds: 'If you don't take action when the referee ignores obstruction or illegal play, then the opposition have an advantage or feel they have overpowered you'. Interference through illegal play gets in the way of playing 'good rugby', and 'Rugby is a game of physical and mental aggression so you can't be seen to give way.' All Black coach Laurie Mains expanded on this view:

There are certain accepted acts in rugby such as legitimate acts of ruck-ing, for example, to get legs out of the way so the ball can come out. It doesn't look pretty but it's a disincentive to the opposition, and as long as it's done in a sensible manner, it's good play . . . Test level rugby is extremely competitive, and if you're a top level line-out forward being held down, and the whole test could hinge on who wins that ball, it's a time when maybe the player has to take the law into his own hands to stop that happening. You always give the referee the first option to stop it, though . . .

I would accept disciplinary action against one of my players for dirty play, but you have to find out the reasons why and look at the severity of the act. There are times when you are driving into a ruck or maul when you actually stand on people. Standing on people is not going to do any harm, but I do not encourage standing on people when the ball's not there — clearly that's another matter. You ruck for a purpose and that's to clear the ball, that's within the laws of the game. If the ball is near a player's head then quite clearly a great deal of caution is required be-cause you do *not* have an excuse, whether the ball is there or not, to stand on anybody's head . . . There can be no mitigation for stomping a player's head.

All Black captain and later provincial coach Andy Leslie expressed a similar belief:

Rugby is a physical, aggressive game and if you're not physical and ag-gressive you're second . . . reactionary backhanders and punches do sometimes occur. I think we have to accept that where it is to deal with a cheating player . . . but there's absolutely no place in rugby for pre-meditated punching, in other words, to soften up a player or that sort of thing. That's where I draw the line. Prevention's always better than cure and I always attempt to spell out the guidelines very clearly to my players so those sorts of situations do not arise.

There are accounts of action being taken on the field by All Blacks on behalf of their captain, who could not be seen taking physical retri-bution. 'Wilson Whineray was bent over many times and I could hear him say, "Come on Pinetree, don't let him do that to me," and Tree would take action,' recalls a contemporary team mate. The onus is on the coach and captain to agree on the spirit, ethics and standards re-quired of players — and then to maintain them.

Grant Fox has an acute rugby brain and has experienced Lochore, Hart, Wyllie and Mains as coaches. He gave his views:

At the élite level the coach should seek input from players . . . part of their motivation and desire is fostered by their being involved in policy matters and team tactics, so it helps to keep them interested. Often the coach is an expert on all positions and master of none. To my mind the major quality a coach needs is man management, being able to coordinate the team and get them to achieve goals. He has to cope with his own make up, and external elements such as the media and players' input, so communication skills are vital. These are almost more of a prerequisite than rugby knowledge; the players have the knowledge and the coach has to coordinate them. The guys know what it takes to succeed at the top — that's how they got there. They don't need a rant and rave coach — nobody's going to change you two hours before kick-off . . .

John Kirwan reflected widely held views on the coach. 'He needs selection skills, to consider the team's relationships, get player confidence and plan a pattern which takes account of his team's abilities.' Gary Whetton described the coaching of John Hart as being able to transmit his knowledge so well 'that he could teach an old dog new tricks!'

There are other typical views among All Blacks as to what makes an outstanding coach: 'Coaches must have the ability to impart their thoughts and knowledge to others.' 'At the top level the coach's main job is to blend the players into a team. He also sets the team pattern to the strengths of the individual players. His training should be intense enough to keep fitness and skills sharp yet the players' minds fresh.' 'To be able to recognise the tenacity and talent in players that sets them apart from others. To know the requirements needed in players for test match rugby and to be able to get their selected players to contribute to the evolution of the game.'

The most important dimensions of élite coaching were suggested by All Blacks surveyed from various generations. They provided a broadly consistent picture regardless of background, era of play or duration of élite career. From 231 replies, these were the most frequently expressed requirements for a good All Black coach.

- Complete knowledge of game and tactics — 176
- Plan and implement game plan (including training) — 164
- Communication — 140
- Develop team around its strengths — 121
- Respect and discipline — 117
- Leadership — 84

- Selection   80
- Man management   67
- Organisation   62

Additional qualities included vision, empathy, setting firm but fair goals, analysing the opposition, maximising player skills, loyalty and honesty, and developing positive relationships with players. Coaches identified as having embodied such a cross section of qualities across seven decades are Fred Allen, Jack Gleeson, Brian Lochore and Vic Cavanagh.

Those rare All Black coaches who have been short of such skills include the one whose team 'sent him away on the Friday so they could plan the final strategy!'

A prominent post-war All Black drew together various perspectives of élite team leaders across decades of New Zealand rugby.

> Great captains and coaches are not different. I believe teams are still trying to play the game in a similar manner to what Saxton, Allen, V. Cavanagh Senior and V. Cavanagh Junior were trying to achieve. They encouraged flexibility, playing the game at speed in forwards and backs, and believed all players should be mobile and fit . . . They all preached the same theme: run hard or drive forward until the ball is held up, then spin it. Forwards must be quick to the breakdown. Last to the ruck is first away. A ruck is a drive not a kicking match . . . Fifteen man rugby, as we saw with the All Blacks in the 1995 World Cup, is the realisation of all of these.

Past All Blacks also provided their perspective on the essential qualities of an All Black coach. Of the 107 responses to a survey asking the players to select essential qualities from a supplied list, the following rated most highly:

- Communicates effectively   96
- Respected by players   96
- Good coach–captain relationship   96
- Accepts decisions and results in a sporting manner   96
- Has a high knowledge of rugby skills and techniques   94
- Develops a clear plan or strategy   94
- Takes pride in player achievement   92
- Has enthusiasm   92

A survey of international players yielded an identical list in the same order minus the fourth quality noted above, indicating that test coach qualities are basically seen the same across the rugby world.

Let us move outside the All Blacks for a moment to consider overseas perspectives. Firstly, a cautionary note from a Welsh captain: 'The defining of the word "coach" is important. There are many coaches who are trainers, others who are teachers of skills, others who are analysts of the skills and weaknesses of players . . . and some who are able to put together tactics . . . International coaches tend to concentrate on strategy and tactics.'

The coach's onfield influence fuses preparation, players' skills, commitment and tactical understanding, the coach–captain relationship, players' self-perceptions, and training.

> All his efforts have gone into the game before the game itself. It's up to the players to do the job. He must trust his efforts and players. Apart from the odd message sent out and the important influence of his half-time talk, he can only sweat, bite his nails, smoke or have a heart attack. (South African test player)

> He must ensure that every eventuality that could occur on the rugby field has been covered in practice and subjected to all situations under pressure. (Andrew Slack, Australian test captain)

Off-field, the coach must focus on match preparation and player development, as described by an Australian captain, Peter Johnson. He must:

> manage the team's preparation, including the analysis of strengths and weaknesses of team and opposition. In this way his strategy will evolve. Where deficiencies are found, he should be able, and concerned, to correct them. This applies to individual skills as much as to tactical shortcomings, although at the highest levels the correction of individual skills should be limited. He must set high standards of personal discipline and, with the captain, police these. He is not, and never should be, considered one of the team. Hopefully, he will have an objective view of the players, be able to convince them they can win, and articulate what they, and they alone, can and must do to achieve it. He should identify with the team in defeat and yet avoid receiving equal praise in victory.

In achieving this, other international players suggest the coach should analyse the opposition, structure challenging practice sessions related to the game plan, and pursue long-term development.

> The coach must have a thorough knowledge of the game, rules and techniques in all positions. After analysing the opposition he must be able to plan his match tactics and put over his plans and ideas in a way the players understand and accept. It is very important that he works with his captain and has the players' respect'. (Scotland captain)

The legendary South African captain, coach and administrator Danie Craven noted, 'the coach must be a practical psychologist and educator or leader'.

Overseas opponents of New Zealand agree team leaders should emphasise 'sportsmanship' on and off the field.

> Fred Allen understood and knew the game, a man of great rugby knowledge. Brian Lochore and Andy Dalton both had the capacity to separate a no-holds-barred, take-no-prisoners approach to winning, from real life, where their pleasant demeanours masked an astonishingly competitive edge. Both are gentlemen you'd rather be with than against. (Andrew Slack, Australian test captain)

> I thought Wilson Whineray and Brian Lochore, the only All Black captains I faced, were both outstanding, not only as players and captains but as men. I had and still have the utmost respect for them. I was fortunate to be captained by the All Black coach, Brian Lochore, in 1971 in the President's XV at the Centenary of the Rugby Union. The team comprised players from New Zealand, South Africa, Fiji, France and Australia. He showed in a couple of weeks all the attributes of a captain I have noted, a difficult job considering the diverse group. His ability to analyse the trend of the match and convert it to specific instructions for individuals was astonishing. His method of conveying this made the recipient wish to thank him, even if the analysis was critical. (Peter Johnson, Australian test captain)

Danie Craven stated that leadership is illustrated by the precept that 'The way you live is the way you play rugby.' New Zealand élite rugby team leaders most commonly admired by opponents for embodying this were, arguably, Jack Gleeson and Graham Mourie. Lochore, Dalton and Shelford were others singled out: 'I admired Brian Lochore for his technical knowledge and man management skills.' 'Andy Dalton was always a good player and great captain.' Buck Shelford 'was a gentleman off the park but an outstanding player and motivator on it.'

There is one word that epitomises almost all All Black coaches and captains and that is character: they are friendly but tough and uncompromising. And when (and if) they lose, they give credit where it is due without complaining. They look for the fault in themselves, and then go and correct it. (Clive Ulyate, South African test player)

How is an All Black coach judged? The All Blacks and their overseas opponents agree on what they look for. Onfield the indicators are: how the team develops; the method and style with which a team plays; sportsmanship; reading the play; the effectiveness of the game plan; and the results. Off the field, the indicators are seen as: the team leader's interest in the players' wellbeing; coach–player relationships; motivational skills; team unity; respect; and the coach's ability to be analytical and impart knowledge.

The final words on top coaches belong to today's All Blacks, who live daily with both the coach's expectations and their own. Asked to indicate their expectations of their coach, their responses were broadly similar. The following are typical:

- 'Someone who can devise a plan to win the game and communicate his/her ideas across to the team effectively so the players are able to reach their maximum potential each time they play. Honest, organised and inspirational.'
- 'Is knowledgeable, positive and fair.'
- 'Offers authority, consistency and clarity.'
- 'Can study his opposition, formulate plans and tactics accordingly, and motivate.'
- 'A person who offers guidance, motivation, support, decisiveness and authority.'
- 'Must express his views on how he wants each player to perform and what he wants from the team as a whole. Never leaves the player wondering.'
- 'Consistency, honesty, loyalty.'
- 'A very decisive and open-thinking man who can command the respect, not fear, of the entire squad.'
- 'Should be fair, honest, and have respect for himself and his players.'
- 'Integrity, honesty, ability to transmit what he wants, and a knowledge of rugby — All Blacks don't tolerate fools.'
- 'Inform you exactly of what is required of you in your position,

help improve areas of weakness, provide positive criticism of performances.'

- 'Honesty, consistency and being able to communicate with the team or an individual player.'
- 'Develop individuals and a team to play a style of pattern which suits that team. It's personal, it's aesthetically pleasing and one which will manipulate the opposition and lead to winning.'
- 'To have mana, good personal discipline, organisational skills, honesty.'
- 'Creating a good environment for the players to be motivated to play at their best level. Integrity, honesty, clear and consistent communication of the game plan, good knowledge of techniques and of opposition strengths and weaknesses.'
- 'To be honest as a person, understand the players as people, and plan effectively.'

8

Living with history:
the Springbok rivalry

*There is still something special about playing the Springboks. They are at
you all of the time and the whole history of New Zealand–South Africa
rugby gives a special edge to these tests.*

Sean Fitzpatrick

The seeds of New Zealand's rugby rivalry with South Africa were sown
in the South African (Boer) War, took root in the 1919 New Zealand
Army team and blossomed in the Springbok tour of 1921. Each country had developed rugby as its primary international sport — for the
settler and indigenous people of one land and the dominant white culture of the other. Each country toured Britain in the early twentieth
century to establish a predominance in international rugby which has
rarely been conceded, even one to the other.

New Zealand soldiers, in South Africa as part of the Empire forces,
engaged in rugby, particularly in the Natal area. Two rugby clubs with a
New Zealand focus were formed, in Durban and Johannesburg respec-
tively, and were followed by the 1919 New Zealand Army team to South
Africa as an inevitable link with South African rugby. This team, having
won the King's Cup international inter-series tournament, had defeated
the South Africans at Twickenham 14–5 in the first national team contact. Then, under Staff Sergeant Charles Brown, with a range of players
who achieved All Black and provincial status, the Army team won eleven
of its fourteen matches in South Africa on the way home to New Zealand. A significant exclusion from the New Zealand Army team was
Nathaniel Arthur 'Ranji' Wilson, a 1908 All Black and King's Cup player,

who was omitted because of his skin colour, a legacy of partial West Indian ancestry. Conveniently enough Wilson was included in the Army team in an important match back in New Zealand. The Army team was considered by P.W. Day, the 1937 Springbok manager, to be superior to the 1928 All Blacks.

1921: Springboks' first tour

The invitation from New Zealand for the Springboks to tour in 1921 was readily accepted. The subsequent drawn series, which was hailed by newspapers as a test for supremacy in the world of rugby, saw the raw intensity and fierce physical commitment that were to mark all subsequent contests. There was one win apiece and a scoreless draw. The match against the New Zealand Maoris revealed the two countries' social and political differences. A South African journalist's cabled report home vehemently criticised the support of European, or white, New Zealanders for the Maori team. The lines of division were not inscribed only on the keenly contested turf.

1928: All Blacks in South Africa

Maurice Brownlie's 1928 All Black team, without the peerless Maori duo of George Nepia at fullback and Jimmy Mill at halfback, again drew the series, two tests apiece. Some 90,000 spectators in South Africa saw the All Blacks' 2-3-2 scrum confronted with the then revolutionary 3-4-1 scrum. During the tour the All Blacks adopted the 3-4-1 scrum and this, according to Jacob van der Westhuizen, improved their play 'immeasurably'.

For the All Blacks, Mark Nicholls was not selected until the fourth test, to the pleasure of the Springboks, as in-team politics and personality conflicts affected selections and strategies. South Africa were captained by Phil Mostert, seen by van der Westhuizen, as a popular and experienced player who provided encouragement and an understanding of mistakes. One of the surviving veterans of the series, van der Westhuizen recalls growing up with his brother in a small village near Cape Town where rugby training was non-existent and consequently organising childhood rugby games with coloured boys in the village. Both brothers were to tour Britain as 1931 Springboks. Van der Westhuizen illustrates the priorities of the times when he explains:

As I was a student in 1928 I never had the privilege of meeting the All

Black players personally because I had to return to Stellenbosch after every test. . . In the four tests their rucking and scrums were first class and when they subdued opposing forwards their penetration by the backs was the key to their success. Grand running and quick passing by the backs were the dominant features of their game.

Like van der Westhuizen and Mostert, the Springbok back P.K. Morkel could not understand the non-selection of Nicholls prior to the fourth test. Morkel also did not meet the All Blacks after the fourth test in which 'Nicholls was instrumental in your victory'. As a schoolteacher he had not been able to get leave to attend the trials for the first test. Morkel also noted the All Blacks adapted to the muddy turf of the final test at Newlands more readily than Mostert's team.

1937: Springbok tour

The ritual expenditure of power moved to a different plane in 1937. One of the great touring teams, Phil Nel's Springboks, lost the first test in Wellington 7–13 after the All Black wing, Donald Cobden, left the field injured after fifteen minutes. (Exactly three years later, to the week, Cobden was shot down over the English Channel on his twenty-sixth birthday.) South Africa won the second test at Christchurch after being 6–0 down at half-time, and in the third emphatically scrummed the All Blacks out of Eden Park in front of 55,000 shattered spectators, scoring five tries in a 17–6 demolition.

A 22-year-old tourist in 1937, Louis Babrow saw his captain, Philip Nel, as possessing the key qualities of leading by example, encouraging and praising his players and being a good friend to every member of his team.

In victory and defeat, at all times he was a gentleman . . . Fred Allen of the 1949 touring All Blacks was also such a person . . . The character of New Zealand–South Africa test matches is that of hard, tough, clean rugby. No quarter asked or given but everything within the laws of the game. The 1937 All Blacks were outstanding. They beat us in the first test whilst they played a man short for the whole match . . . Cobden, the New Zealand wing, was injured in the first few minutes.

With the previous South African tour having set the standard for their provincial opponents, the Springboks encountered teams determined to maintain or change their playing record. Canterbury had been the only province to defeat the 1921 team.

Beau Cottrell was our manager, and we were told that we would have to win. Canterbury had not lost to an overseas team since 1888 but the South Africans were an excellent side. We played on 21 August 1937. I remember that because I met a nice girl on that day (she's now married to someone else). We played about four matches before South Africa but about four of our forwards were very light, whereas the Springboks were big and very skilful in the line-outs and, if I may say, bordering on the unfair in their play — a South African hand would hold your jersey or two of them would hold hands to block a New Zealand forward. They didn't need to do it . . . (Canterbury All Black recalling the 1937 South Africans)

The third test in the 1937 series, won by South Africa 8–3, saw N.A. 'Brushy' Mitchell carry an injury into the test. Hugh McLean, the inimitable All Black of the 1930s, recalls the following: 'Brushy Mitchell was a born humorist on and off the field! The day of the final 1937 test, I was working at Smith and Caughey's shop and he came in and saw me. I said, "You're a bloody idiot Mitchell with that poor knee". . .' However, despite the assumption of McLean and rugby writers that it was Mitchell's knee injury that was responsible for the All Blacks' loss, Louis Babrow reveals a new perspective on the decision to play Mitchell. He explains the significance of a different injury, revealing the planning integral to the keenest of Springbok–All Black contests:

Our coach and myself attended the All Black practice two days before the final test. We noticed that the All Black star centre, brought in especially for this match, had a strapped finger which caused him to wince every time he caught the ball or had to tackle someone. We decided to try breaks at centre from the start of the game. Brushy Mitchell just could not cope that day and we burst past him time and again. We scored five tries that afternoon and that has not often happened to an All Black team. It also proved — do not play an injured player, no matter how famous.

The intense rivalry of the two countries is built around an innate pride and physical confrontation. Tori Reid, one of the most respected and durable of All Blacks, played against South Africa in all three 1937 tests, in a first-class career spanning 1929–49. Reid recalls the arch-adversaries in green jerseys:

They were skilled at illegal tactics! They would put the ball in and it came out in front of the flanker. We couldn't make out why Craven was getting the ball so quickly till the referee saw the way the ball was being put in . . . they weren't so much strong men as they were heavy. If we got in a ruck and pushed they would fall over, but we couldn't move their scrum. They weren't a fast or mobile pack . . . I was lock but really wanted to play flanker!

We would have beaten the Springboks in the Hawke's Bay game had Johnston not broken his leg. Colin Wilson had ripped his ankle and at half-time he wanted to take his boot off but we knew if he did, he would never get it back on . . . we had it all planned, under Norman McKenzie. Our Hawke's Bay team talked things over and were going to place the flanker on the blindside so that Craven would have to pass to the first-five and our open-side flanker would go for their first or second-five. We were leading at half-time and then Tom Johnston's leg went — you could hear the 'snap' on the field as it broke. Craven scored in Johnston's absence, as there was a no replacement rule in those days, and that was that.

Desert 'tests'

The Second World War brought its own forms of South Africa–New Zealand combat involving past and future All Blacks. 'One of my greatest moments was in the Western Desert, in 1941, when I captained 101 Division against the New Zealand Division and my old friend of 1937, Jack Sullivan, captained the Kiwis,' writes Pat Lyster, the Springbok winger. And if one still harbours doubts about the centrality of rugby in the relationship between the two nations, look no further than the memorable bleak and showery desert day at Baggush in November 1941 when the 2nd New Zealand Expeditionary Force defeated the South African Division 8–0. One week later All Black Arthur Wesney, who played in the match with Jack Sullivan and Artie Lambourn, was killed in action.

Jack Griffiths, a New Zealand skipper and veteran of 30 All Black games, was General Freyberg's aide-de-camp in the war.

I think rugby in the war did a tremendous lot for morale. You didn't need a compass or spy to follow the New Zealand Division — you followed the sands where rugby fields were marked out . . . There was always a rugby ball around. When the Second Echelon arrived, at the end of 1940, rugby became quite a spectacle. Initially I was a selector with Padre Frank Green and [ex-All Black] Colonel Rusty Page. We were out of the line at the time. Every unit had goal posts supplied by the Patriotic Fund. There was a salt pan area at Baggush with potential as a ground. New Zealand was to play South Africa. We selected our team and General Freyberg [who had been a representative player while a country town dentist in New Zealand] suggested that the team go into camp for a week. Then, to develop strong support, the general said all soldiers were to be route-marched to the ground and back. He ordered the Air Force to give us air cover in case of an attack and the Navy was asked to put out to sea in case of a sneak attack.

Even in wartime when rugby was, ostensibly, a release, the spectre of a loss shadowed that divisional match between New Zealand and South Africa. Brigadier Alan Andrews, later to become the Kiwis' team manager, recalls the setting:

Baggush could have been a tragedy. The Africans had been up in the desert for a couple of months. We'd been there a couple of days and General Freyberg visited his South African counterpart. Bernie agreed to play them in a rugby 'test'. I asked him when the match would take place. 'Next week,' replied the general!

Jack Griffiths came hotfooting it to me saying, 'This is bloody ridiculous!' I spoke to Bernie Freyberg. 'I understand sir that you've arranged a game against the South Africans. When is it scheduled?' 'I told them next week,' replied the general. 'Sir, we can't play next week, and sir, you've got to get in your [armoured] car and make an excuse to postpone it if you want to win the match.' And, of course, General Freyberg really wanted to win!

Jack Griffiths, Jack Sullivan (who was to captain us) and myself selected the team. We dug around and nailed Padre Frank Green to quickly help. He had played for Otago and I think had been an All Black trialist. He trained them up on an area near the beach . . .

The match ground was a big sandy patch with sand hills around. The Afrikaaners had to walk the last two miles to the ground. We had two ack-ack guns, one of ours and one of theirs, protecting us as Italian bombers used to drift around . . .

Artie Lambourn, the 1930s All Black hooker, was in the front row for that memorable wartime 'test', along with other noted forwards such as Jack McLean, Neil McPhail and Tris Hegglun.

Troops had the day off and just before the first scrum went down I said to the guys, 'At the first scrum we'll bloody try the referee out.' So we were just getting into it when the referee, Father Jesse Kingan, blew his whistle and said, 'Free kick, South Africa.' I questioned his call as he couldn't really see what we had done and he replied, 'Artie, I knew you were going to cheat. I remember at Silverstream College when you came and helped the first XV — you told them to always have a go at the opposite front row in the game's first scrum!'

1949: dismal defeats

If ever rugby administration was caught at the scene of the crime it was in 1949. The inveterate chronicler Terry McLean has outlined the change in selection of the 1949 All Black coach, with its undertones of Masonic preference, and all rugby followers of the day have ground their teeth in anguish at the stupidity of sending the 66-year-old assistant manager, Alex McDonald, with the team to South Africa. McDonald had been a 1905 All Black and an outstanding coach in the pre-war era of the 2-3-2 scrum but his skills were now seen as dated. Parker, the manager, was little better in his role, which demanded different skills from those he had revealed as a 27-year-old Invincible and First World War rugby forward. Confined to Otago rugby, meantime, was the outstanding coach Vic Cavanagh, who should have been with the All Blacks. The All Blacks had been picked eight months before the first tour match, they lacked pace and mobility in the forwards, and the selectors had not chosen the best halfback in the country, Vince Bevan, as he was a Maori.

> I think it was a tragedy when Vic Cavanagh didn't go to South Africa in 1949. He would have been absolutely bloody magnificent . . . Alex McDonald was a fine old bloke but he shouldn't have been put in that position. He said to me early in the tour, 'I wish I hadn't come.' We had seventeen kicks awarded to South Africa in the New Zealand 25 and we had none in theirs . . . and then there was the travel and the itinerary of train journeys! (Ray Dalton)

The series was lost 4–0, with Hennie Muller, Aaron 'Okey' Geffin and the referees placed in the dock with the NZRFU. Muller, a loose forward, was stationed out in the backs, and Geffin kicked the goals presented to him by the referee. The All Blacks, sentenced to hard labour, came out of the tour with character, but character doesn't pay the get-out-of-jail points. The greatness of some All Blacks was confirmed by the ordeal, however, such as Kevin Skinner, Johny Simpson and Bob Scott. The leadership of Fred Allen, tour captain and erstwhile coach, and Ron Elvidge is acclaimed to this day by their team mates.

'The All Blacks engaged in hard-driving, moving-forward play in 1949. They found it difficult to change their approach. For me the second test was the perfect game of rugby. The most outstanding New Zealanders were Bob Scott, the front row and Lachie Grant at lock,' recalls a 1949 Springbok. His team mates concur. 'They were determined . . . they played rugby the way we played rugby.'

The prop forward, Aaron Geffin, could be seen as the scoring difference between the sides, taking five penalty goals to win the first test, one in the second, three to win the third, and a winning fourth test margin of a conversion and penalty goal. This Transvaal player was the Springboks' third-choice kicker for the first test! He retrospectively judges the nature of the 1949 All Blacks:

> New Zealand rugby has always been rugged, the forwards hunting as a pack and never dying on the ball. Both sides were very powerful and there was not much to choose between them — Bob Scott was a frustrating fullback and a thorough gentleman off the field. Kevin Skinner and Johnny Simpson were front row forwards — men amongst men.
>
> In 1949 as I perceived it, playing against the All Blacks in the tests, there was the hard and solid play of the forwards. They held to the basics of their game. Get the ball and go forward, run through a Springbok if he is in your way! The foundation of New Zealand rugby is their forward play, which was outstanding in 1949! The front row was short and bulky, their locks were long and lanky and well built, and they were good movers. As a team we were lucky with the penalties and offside in the line-outs. These cost them dearly, especially in the first test. The backline was fast with good runners and the display of the ball was good. The big mistake was to misjudge your Springbok opponents.

It wouldn't have happened under Cavanagh.

The bitterness of '49 bites as deeply, almost half a century later, as it did at the time. A survivor speaks:

> Poor Fred Allen in 1949 not only had to half-manage the side but coach it and captain it . . . he dropped himself as captain, and I blamed that rotten little bastard, Craven. He saw the danger of Fred as our first-five eighth. Against Transvaal Fred was late tackled by Malan all day . . . all Ron Elvidge had to do was to go to Kevin Skinner and say, 'Take that joker Malan out' . . . We left Malan unconscious in the fourth test for twenty minutes.

1956: 'win at all costs'

The defeats of 1937 and 1949 ate away at the body of New Zealand rugby pride like a cancer. They didn't merely rankle, they rose as bile in the throats of every Kiwi rugby supporter. 'Those bloody Boers!' 'Those Afrikaaners who wouldn't even fight in the war!' 'You know they only win at home because of the referees . . . we've got the bloody scrummaging right now . . . '

Unlike the 1959 Lions, say, who could be seen as yesterday's team playing tomorrow's game, the 1956 All Blacks were completely of their time. They won 10–6, lost 3–8, won 17–10, and then achieved an 'It's all yours New Zealand' farewell for the Springboks of 11–5 in Auckland.

Ian 'Chutney' Clarke exemplified the triple values of family, rugby and personal integrity. As the only New Zealand prop to play in all four tests he brought an insightful perspective to the encounters.

> 1956 was something I don't think New Zealand will ever see again. We were going to win that series whatever happened. We had been well cleaned up in 1949. For 1956 there was a series of trials and then a New Zealand XV played the South Island and North Island and then they played The Rest, all in one week. And all very hard games . . . We trained twice a day once we were put into camp. The Springboks really were very hard men! The set play of the South Africans, in my career, was harder than any other country — they were the daddy of them all! Set play is a trial of strength for South Africa, whereas for us it's a winning of the ball . . . They are great opponents though. To me, as a rugby player from New Zealand, if you can't play against South Africa it's like an athlete not going to the Olympics . . . A player who didn't play against South Africa missed out on the pinnacle, the ultimate test.

Ross Brown also recalls the pressure: 'We were drilled solidly that we had to beat the Boks, the whole public demanded it . . . there was unrelenting press talk and general enthusiasm from the public. New Zealand had been staggered by the four test loss in '49 and, as far as I was concerned, the whole atmosphere was pretty tense . . . the public didn't care how we did it.'

The 1956 surgeons in black who excised the disease of rugby defeat do not grow old in the minds of All Black followers. Short back and sides, a smudge of Brylcreem, and a white collar up on the black jersey, they are framed as we knew them — and still live with them in our memories. The fresh-faced Don Clarke, little Ponty Reid, boyish Ross Brown, Peter Jones the shark-eating man, the gutsy Bill Gray, craggy Tiny White, the balding flier Ron Jarden, an ebullient Maurice Dixon, the inherent decency and prideful power of Ian Clarke . . . Every schoolboy — and most girls — of the class of '56 can recite such All Black names. And then there was Kevin Skinner.

Frank Parkinson refereed the first two tests — and also monitored the ride of the Mooloo Valkyries, who swept roughshod over the Springboks in their first tour game, 14–10, thanks to the coaching of Dick

Everest and the game plan commitment of Waikato.

That was hard work, refereeing that game at Hamilton . . . The thing that surprised me was at half-time when I discovered that the score was 14–0 to Waikato, because a touch judge said, 'The score is unbelievable' . . . You know, George Nola got fairly battered in that game. When you're the referee you know that something is going on in the front row or on the other side of the scrum, but it's not easy to pin it down fairly . . .

In the second test New Zealand had the advantage of the Wellington wind in the first half. It was the worst time I ever had on a football field! A dismal day, dismal game, dismal tactics. The All Blacks worked the first-half wind. The Springboks were delighted at the selection of Pat Vincent, the All Black scrum half and captain for this test, as they could read the way he was going to pass. The players got niggly in this match and one New Zealander let me know what he thought of me as a referee. Indeed, when I awarded a penalty, this player was still so despondent that when Pat Vincent asked him to take the kick for touch the incensed All Black told him to find somebody else! But there was trouble right from the first scrum. Apparently the Springboks wanted the whole world to know the scrum wasn't binding properly. First scrum, up in the air and over the sideline! Their hooker, van der Merwe, made such a song and dance about not binding . . . and Kirkpatrick, their centre, thought he had scored but I ruled no try, held ball in goal. After the game he came up to me, very respectfully, and told me, 'I scored you know!' . . . When that series was all over and I summed it up in my own mind, 'Win at all costs' kept coming back, time and time again, 'Win at all costs.'

After the refereeing difficulties with the second test, Bill Fright was appointed to officiate for the final two tests.

I can see that third test now. I thought I could see the way things were from the word go, when the All Blacks didn't put the man with the ball on the ground. I anticipated there would be difficulties for them but Jarden's try then stood out. Ross Brown cross-kicked and Jarden fell down with it over the line — an off-the-cuff effort! I stood and gave the try and didn't look at the crowd immediately. (In the fourth test when Peter Jones scored I would look at the crowd and see all sorts of stuff going up in the air!) I always felt the 'Boks had a policy based around the ball — that you don't surrender the ball. They seemed tougher mentally than most New Zealanders — not that that's necessarily a virtue!

'The whole thing was,' recalled hooker Ron Hemi, 'that the South Africans had never been beaten in a series.' He notes the New Zealand public's demands for a win. 'They got in behind us, but at the same time put the pressure on us.' Hemi has memories of the brief words in the hotel before the All Black team left for the test ground and 'the main team talk coming after we were stripped. Tom Morrison had a say, then Bob Duff the captain. That was all we needed.'

Unlike, say, Wales, to whom an All Black defeat (or win for that matter) is a Welsh rugby victory, a win by South Africa (or the All Blacks) over their arch-rivals is far more. A loss to Wales earns a mouthing-off boyo, but an All Black defeat by the Springboks has always been seen by white South Africa as a justification, vindication and sanctification of their values, lifestyle and racial being.

New Zealand, often quick to criticise the South African rugby administration, has not been averse to bending international rules itself. Don McIntosh, the All Black flanker, or 'breakaway' in fifties rugby parlance, gives an inside picture of the first test preparation:

> The team was announced on a Saturday, and on the following Monday week the whole team went to Oamaru. The All Blacks trained every day with two two-and-a-half-hour sessions, with Tom Morrison, Arthur Marslin and Jack Sullivan. They brought in Bob Stuart [former All Black captain] as the forward coach. We would train at colleges and have little sessions privately, with a lot of emphasis on line-out and forward play. Things were pretty conventional in play. I remember once I appeared in the backline at practice and Bill Gray, at second-five, said to me, 'What the hell are you doing here?'

Bob Stuart had picked up information from the home unions after the drawn 1955 Lions–South Africa test series. The message he got was that the Africans were stronger than New Zealand in scrummaging and back play but not in driving play. Line-outs were even. Stuart, co-opted by the selectors, fixed the forwards on enhancing driving play and tightening up the pack, which had been too loose in 1955.

> We looked on Kevin Skinner as a sitter when he was fit. Don Clarke was initially overweight and not playing consistently well. Peter Jones was two stone overweight. But we felt that they were the sort of people we wanted in the All Blacks. [Which puts paid to South African ideas of Skinner only coming into consideration as enforcer for the third test.] I think the All Blacks played well in the first test freezing conditions, although their bones were so chilled! Even so, I was convinced, as were the selectors, that changes needed to be made. But how do you throw out a winning captain? So Pat Vincent stayed in for the second test.

[The second test at Athletic Park had a strong southerly wind and it was wind-chill weather.] I was scared someone might die out there. We had instructed the team that no matter where they were on the field they were not to kick the ball out . . . Jesus! You would have thought we'd said the opposite! In the second half they slogged their guts out, unavailingly . . . It must have been heartbreaking for the forwards. In the third and fourth tests we could play the guys we'd been holding back, and there was brilliant rugby. The All Blacks' forward drive was compounded with bad selection by the Springboks.

And so to the third test — and every leather-balled Kiwi of the Winston McCarthy era will recall it — and its build-up. Tom Pearce, who came close to 1937 test forward selection and later became manager of the 1960 All Blacks to South Africa, was an NZRFU councillor in 1956. He forced the calling of an emergency council meeting to examine the second test defeat! The three All Black selectors were called to Wellington, although the convenor, Tom Morrison, was entitled to be present in his own right as a councillor. Pearce had allegedly been kept in the reserves for the 1937 All Blacks as *his* play was too rough — for a test against the Springboks! In Wellington he fully utilised his capacity for direct speech — a tendency inherited by his daughter Sandra Coney — and the air was cleared. A day or two later, out went captain Vincent (to be replaced by Ponty Reid), Robin Archer came back from the first test win to replace Mick Bremner, the gargantuan boots of young Don Clarke replaced the tidy lace-ups of Pat Walsh, Ron Hemi fronted up as the hard and mobile hooker in place of Dennis Young, and two other handy fellows were pulled in. Peter Jones, the big Kaitaia fisherman, who played like a grizzly bear on speed when fully fit, took over as number eight from Tiny Hill, who moved in to MacEwan's place at lock. 'I played with some bloody great men,' exclaimed a team mate 40 years on, 'Christ almighty! But for sheer explosiveness, Peter Jones stands out. He only played about half a dozen great games in his life. He could handle like a back . . . '

Kevin Skinner is one of rugby's great test players. On the field he was fuelled with nationalism and an utter commitment to play to his ultimate. He was the archetypal front-row forward embodiment of the credo, sustained into the 1990s by Sean Fitzpatrick, 'What happens on the field, stays on the field.' Off the field, Skinner and his wife Laurie are one of rugby's unrivalled couples. The seeming paradox of rugby's aggression, even, let it be said, occasional brutality, in New Zealand–South Africa tests, does not deter those same combatants from enduring friendships off the field. If there is some Verdun-like belief 'they shall not pass', or proving ground on rugby's testing turf, then many an opponent has also proved worthy of an enduring friendship.

The South Africans were — and still are — monocular-minded in their perception that Skinner was selected as the ex-heavyweight boxing bloke that he was in order to illegally subdue the Springbok scrum. In fact, Skinner had been the most outstanding 1949 All Black forward in South Africa, appointed All Black captain in 1952, and was still only 29 years old in 1956. He was over six foot tall, and weighed in for the test at 15 stone 4 pounds. The first few line-outs changed the South Africans' play, the balance of power in the forwards and, arguably, the result of the series. Referee Bill Fright recalls, 'Koch tried to crash through the line-out and Skinner belted him. Koch had asked for it, breaching the line-out.' Skinner provides his insights:

The third test All Blacks had input from Tom Morrison on the coaching side, and in those days we had the benefit of films. For example, we studied the first test and the second test and worked out aspects of how South Africa would play, and it came off. We all knew what to do. Our basic plan was to use seven forwards and one loosie, and we used Bill Clark to run wide and put pressure on second-five to come back in. Having Tiny Hill and Peter Jones there was a bonus when I got into that side in Christchurch. I hadn't had any association with the All Blacks in 1955. I knew I was putting my neck on the line by being available for selection, and I spoke with Tiny White and Bob Duff when the team assembled. The message I got was, 'They're intimidating us Kevin' . . . Well, I just looked at Tiny and said, 'Well, you're allowing that to happen, Tiny.' Sooner or later out on the paddock you've got to get on top of your opponent. My being there, with my sort of attitude, might have propped up one or two of the older players . . . Even today, Tiny will say, 'It was just like bloody war!' I think the public of New Zealand expected it of us.

It's your mental ability that gets you over the top — if you approach it with a shade of doubt you're a goner. And that's what I was trying to do. The Springbok forward, Chris Koch, was a good friend of mine. Prior to the first test in Dunedin he even got some test match tickets and took them to my mum . . . But in that third test he came through the line-out. Well, you give a guy one warning . . . ! 'If you're going to come across that line, Chris' . . . and having given him that warning, well, I had to follow through when he did it again. They would have no respect for you otherwise. My theory is, if you're on the paddock and you've got a problem and someone's bending the rules, or things aren't settling down, then something has to be done, preferably by the ref. In that third test they were obviously trying to unsettle our scrum. I used to say to the referee, 'Bill it's your job . . . ' If he didn't act, and we got things sorted out, then I would say, 'Now Bill, you sort it out from here . . . '

One of Skinner's team mates, Bill Clark, also recalls his return: 'Kevin went around everyone and wanted to know what the trouble was with the Springboks, and that was a great lift to the team.' Bob Duff, captain of the two winning All Black test teams in 1956, has clear memories of the games.

In that third test, in Christchurch, we were in the situation where it was the pressure that we put on the South African forwards that finally let Jarden score, and the one that Tiny White got . . . At that stage we could feel the Springboks faltering at forward, we were keeping them on the back foot, not a change of basics though. Ascendancy slowly evolves . . . for example, in the line-out you get the ball more, there are more black jerseys in a ruck . . . we've got 'em, we've got 'em . . .

In the fourth test I felt that they tried to copy us with their play . . . Peter Jones was a damned good line-out player, with tremendous speed for a big man . . . Tiny Hill was a third lock and Bill Clark never received the credit he should have got . . . After the Springbok match against New Zealand Maoris, Craven picked Peewee Howe as his fly-half for the final test. That played right into our hands, we would open up a gap and let him in, and close up on him. They couldn't change their players in their backs . . . I have an idea that Howe came back on *our* bus after that test!

An All Black from that 1956 series remembers the opposition. 'When I think of politics and rugby I think of South Africa. South Africans were always regarded as our enemies on the field. They were bloody hopeless to play against in terms of enjoyable rugby. I always enjoyed my rugby but the only enjoyable thing about playing South Africa was beating them.'

The Springboks' recollections give the opponents' viewpoint on the 320 minutes of hand-to-hand intensity.

New Zealand rugby has been the epitome of discipline, commitment and the will to win. They are not always beautiful to watch, but they are terrors to play against. In 1949 I saw a mediocre Springbok team clean-sweep an All Black team that scored tries while Okey Geffin kicked penalties. I felt something was wrong. In 1956 New Zealand gained its revenge. It was a do-or-die effort and resulted in not a great deal of scintillating stuff. An exception was Ron Jarden's brilliant intercept to win the Dunedin test, 10–6, with a try next to the posts. The most out-standing performance I have seen was by a tiny Taranaki XV who held the 1956 Springboks to a 6–6 draw! I have never seen commitment like that from anybody! (Clive Ulyate)

Perhaps the most gifted player on the tour was the centre Wilf Rosenberg, who rated the 1956 All Black forwards as, 'The greatest pack I ever played against. They were tough, strong, and also were not afraid to use illegal tactics. Unfortunately, your backs in that era were not of the same quality.' He continues:

Throughout history, South Africa and New Zealand have been the great rivals. To beat the New Zealanders was priority number one, and I be-lieve the same about New Zealand's view of South Africa. No other coun-tries have had such rivalry as in the days when I played in the 1950s and 1960s. I remember what happened in the 1970s, and every time a New Zealand side came to South Africa. No side could fill a ground as quickly as the All Blacks in South Africa. We could lose to France, British Lions, etc. and it was taken in our stride, but to lose to New Zealand — the whole country went into mourning.

All Blacks still remembered by the Springboks are exemplified by comments of Tommy Gentles, the 1956 test halfback:

Don Clarke was solid and dependable and a great boot. It was soul-destroying to be driven back with huge touch-finders under the old rules. Peter Jones had size and pace and power. Tiny White was a great all-round second-row forward. He was a fine line-out jumper, a clean catcher, very mobile around the field, and involved in powerful, driving play. Ron Jarden was a complete winger who possessed strength, speed, a swerve, good skills and anticipation.

The rivals' memories linger, four decades later.

1960: another hard slog in South Africa
In 1960, Wilson Whineray's All Blacks saw public agitation at the exclu-sion of Maori from the team to tour South Africa. Despite this, compe-tition for places was keen. Mick Bremner had been injured at the onset of the 1960 trials.

All I wanted was an opportunity to try out . . . I was getting changed when a messenger came down and said, 'Bremner you're not playing.' I went up to the stand and Wilson Whineray sat next to me, and he said,

'Mick I think you're up for vice-captain' . . . In South Africa I played in the bread and butter games . . . I was on the selection panel. South Africa was a tremendous experience, a great country to play in. I think that rugby has helped break down barriers.

Jack 'No Comment' Sullivan, a man of integrity and talent as a 1936–38 All Black three-quarter, was not an inspiring coach. While respecting Sullivan the man, Nevan MacEwan indicates aspects of the tour that could have been better developed by the coach. 'South Africa in 1960 meant no easy game. On a long intense tour you had to run the risk of losing a provincial match by letting the dirt trackers play, but we never did that and so we ran our top brigade into the deck. We never had the scientific approach to the game.'

'South Africa in 1960,' says Kevin Briscoe, 'was far more physical than other rugby. Players were hard and really gave you hell . . . and the length of time away was hellish on a family. My wife was six months pregnant when I left. It could be tough for womenfolk at home.' A team mate expands the former theme: 'South Africa were a lot harder, with a lot more will to win than other countries. Once they got that green and gold jersey on, man oh man, they would run into a brick wall.' Briscoe's captain, Wilson Whineray, remembers seeing 'an endless supply of big guys being thrown at his team. You were almost worn down by attrition.'

Another All Black sounds a theme similar to that of Springboks after a New Zealand tour. 'We had no bloody show of winning the series because they had everything sewn up. They would talk to the referee in Afrikaans. Frank McMullen scored in the fourth test and the referee disallowed it. He came into our changing room after the match and apologised!' Referee Burmeister, not unknown to the 1949 All Blacks, who had lost two tests under his rulings, incorrectly ruled against McMullen for a tackled ball after he got up from an ankle-tap and scored.

From the 1956 and 1960 series Johannes Claasen saw the All Blacks, in a similar way to his predecessors, as 'hard, physical, honest and merciless'. An opponent of Don Clarke's in both series, Roy Dryburgh, who captained South Africa in the first two 1960 tests, described 'Camel' as 'a truly great fullback who became a very good friend of mine off the field'. The Springbok captain for the final two 1960 tests, Avril Malan, saw his opponents as 'a very fit team of players who are tough and have a will to win'. Despite the intensity, his espoused values show some balance. 'The spirit of fellowship is a particular quality of rugby and, although it is a sport, I give of my best, but to lose is not the end of the world. Tomorrow is another day . . . '

1965: wins at home again

The nature of South Africa–New Zealand tests geared down a little in intensity in 1965, when Dawie de Villiers' team lost their two tests against Australia and three of four in New Zealand. Francois du Toit Roux, has his own theory on the seesaw balance between the two countries prior to the 1992 encounter.

> Because of your wet fields you tend to concentrate more on forward play and using either the up-and-under or a heavy first-five eighth, to get second phase ball, to get near the opponents' line, and then to attack again with your heavy forwards . . . I believe New Zealand now have a running fly-half. In part, your rugby is a very prominent part of most New Zealanders because you do well nationally. And your people are well suited for the game, physically and mentally . . . every test between our two countries seems to have had the same pattern. On our hard fields we have had the dominance, and on the soft fields you have done better. On the soft fields, your forwards do better when the game stays close to the scrum, but on the hard fields when we stretch the game they tend to lack the speed to the wings . . . in New Zealand there was Colin Meads who was dedicated to the game and played a hard and tough game . . . Graham Thorne was one of the few backs that had his own initiative but Bryan Williams was the best wing I ever saw because he had great speed.

1970: losses away

Whatever the merits of Roux's theory in the 1990s, the winning at home theory was borne out in 1970 when Lochore's team lost the series in South Africa 3–1. Ivan Vodanovich, another well-respected rugby person, was not an innovative All Black coach. 'But there was still the fanaticism to contend with,' recalls a 1970 All Black. 'At Loftus Versfeld, for the first test in Pretoria, the South African team sat in their changing room with their flag over their knees and prayed — then they came out onto the field and hit us with everything they had . . . then the All Blacks got on the piss and they tried to put Winston McCarthy [a New Zealand radio commentator] on the barbecue, and he broke his arm . . .'

Ivan Vodanovich was not out of touch as McDonald had been in

1949. He did not have the flair of a Hart nor the technical skills of a Mains, but in his innate decency lost nothing in comparison with any All Black coach. His honesty comes through in a frank retrospective of the tour: 'We made selection errors and were too much influenced by Hawke's Bay holding the Shield . . . I was never very confident about my understanding of fitness and I don't like coaching the team on my own.'

Lochore, the 1970 captain, won lasting recognition from his South African opponent, Ian McCallum, who saw him as 'a man of presence. He was most gracious in the final defeat of the series, he played his heart out.' McCallum notes the use of only seventeen players by the Springboks, compared with changes beyond that for the All Blacks. McCallum's regard for the qualities of the All Blacks reflects the values of his predecessors and successors. Colin Meads, for example, is seen as 'a modern legend, he never moaned . . . he knew all the tricks, had years of commitment at the highest level and had an essential modesty'.

1976: hospitality and humiliation

And so the tale of this rivalry moves on . . . In 1976, with captain Andy Leslie and J.J. Stewart as coach, the All Blacks set off with a team with which the coach was not totally happy, and lost the series 3–1. There was the re-appearance of Harry Houdini's major assistant, the South African referee, as key penalties attested. The coach recalls:

> When we got to South Africa the nationalism was very much associated with rugby football — it happened to us in 1956 . . . they are delighted to have you so you can be humiliated on the football field. The hospitality is totally marvellous. Under it all the time you're really there to be cleaned out — underneath we're probably the same . . . They played set-play pieces strongly. Doing this slowly does develop big, hard and fast midfield backs — all they do is wait for set play ball and attack with it . . .

What is sometimes overlooked is that the Springboks, who scored fewer tries than the All Blacks but gained from referee decisions, such as when Bruce Robertson was held back from scoring, did have Morne du Plessis. A number of respondents from the 1976 era have noted this captain's qualities. Divan Serfontein shows why Leslie's opposing captain was so well regarded. 'Morne du Plessis was well respected by all his fellow players, as well as by his opponents. He was a dedicated, skilful and disciplined player with a quiet, likeable way of going that oozed confidence and pride. A gentleman!' A team mate adds that du Plessis could combine all players, with their differing backgrounds, languages and religions, into an effective team by his example on and off the field.

The infamous 1981 Springbok tour

The events of South Africa's 1981 tour of New Zealand have been well documented (not least in relatively unread academic journals). The crass expediency of political and rugby interests, coupled with the flood of public protests over the iniquitous practice of apartheid, have been deeply scored in family histories and family divisions in all corners of New Zealand. The lure of rugby, particularly against South Africa, had the capacity to rip our social order asunder. Within the 1981 South African camp the Springbok skipper was seen as a key figure in holding his team together. Halfback D.J. Serfontein provides an insight:

> Wynand Claasen was more of a players' captain than was Morne du Plessis. He would drink with the boys after a match and have his share in the fun etc., but had a lot of respect from all team mates because of strong views regarding rights of players, and he stood up for them. He was always fit, super-fit, dedicated and disciplined. A friendly guy. He had a *major* part in saving our tour of New Zealand in 1981.

Rob Louw, a much respected opponent of New Zealand rugby test teams, particularly values 'the friendship off the field of play and the camaraderie after the match is finished, despite the intense on-field rivalry.' Louw points to the third test in 1981 as an example of the special qualities of New Zealand–South Africa rugby. 'The third test . . . was one match which I will remember for ever. We were fighting it out tooth and nail during the second half and Gary Knight was downed by a flour bomb. We, all of us in the Springbok team, immediately went to help Gary . . . !' A fellow player agrees on the memorable nature of this test:

> There was the fantastic forward play of New Zealand in the first half; our great comeback with tries in the second half through our backs; the energy sapping battle; the aching muscles; the ten minutes' overtime; the blood, sweat and flour bombs; the crooked referee; the fairy tale do-or-die last-minute penalty . . . and the camaraderie afterwards.

Despite the mutual respect, individual friendships and some rose-coloured glasses of retrospect, the tests retain their particular overtones.

A famous All Black, who played tests against South Africa in the days when apartheid policies were rarely questioned, also coached a side that played the Springboks. He reflected, in the 1990s, upon the arch-rivalry of the two countries:

> Even though I'd played South Africa that many times I never felt after the games that I knew them any better. At the time I went along with the belief of 'No Maoris, no tour' but I was really turned off in 1965. I was associated with one side that played the '65 Springboks and two of our players came off with concussion. The South African attitude afterwards was like that of bloody kids. They had won that touring match and made up for 1956! In 1970 we suffered a lot of disruption because of that tour, and went against a lot of opinion to go there, and the bastards cheated us to get us off the paddock. Since that time I've thought they weren't a race I wanted anything to do with. It really made me wonder how we ever ignored the racial thing.

The closing word from participants on the unique nature of official South Africa–New Zealand tests, in the 70 years before Mandela, lies with a great Springbok of the modern era writing to the author, shortly after his nation's epochal day of change:

> I personally, as a South African, hope that we can get together again on an equal footing. I would love to see New Zealand as a normal tourist. I thought your country was a beautiful one as well as the people being really fantastic. The competitive nature of the New Zealand approach fits ours perfectly, and I think the people of both nations have got an incredible affinity towards each other. I was overjoyed at the referendum in South Africa with de Klerk winning by 70 per cent. I also, as a South African, couldn't imagine what it must feel like to be wanted in a country on tour. It is just so sad that we, as Springboks, suffered because of the short-sighted forefathers we had. I just hope that our future governments think for the children of South Africa's future, and I hope our sportsmen and sportswomen never ever suffer as we have . . .

Into the 90s

In 1992, the All Blacks, without the professional era luxury of taking two XVs plus a further half-dozen players, defeated South Africa in their one-off test. 'It was tough but they weren't quite as hard as I expected. They were at us all the bloody time though. They play *us*, whereas the Australians play *rugby*,' reflected Zinzan Brooke. New Zealand followed this in 1994 with an undefeated series win, and then faltered at the goal posts in the 1995 World Cup final, debilitated by apparent food poisoning attacks. In 1996, the All Blacks again won the series, but lost the final test. Whilst there is the risk of devaluing the unique nature of South Africa–New Zealand tests with an increasing frequency of such encounters, the electricity still surges — not with the same lethal currents as in '49 or '56, nor with the cruel and divisive adrenaline of '81, but with a continued forcefield of pride, founded on tradition and still fed by nationalism and confrontation.

The Honourable John Banks MP

New Zealand Minister of Tourism, Local Government, Sport, Fitness and Leisure

Facsimile Message

TO: **All Blacks**
Attn: Colin Meads, Manager
C/- Shoreline Hotel, DUNEDIN

FROM: Hon John Banks

DATE: 8 July 1994   FAX NO. 03 455 5193

I extend my very best wishes to the All Blacks for the first game in the test series against South Africa. It is a great moment for sport.

I'm looking forward to a fine performance tomorrow at Carisbrook. You can be assured that the country and the City of Dunedin will be well and truly behind you.

It is a great honour to represent your country. I'm sure you will do this with pride and passion.

Yours sincerely

Hon John Banks
MINISTER OF SPORT, FITNESS AND LEISURE

23 July 1994
New Zealand vs. South Africa: Test Day

12.58 p.m.

The All Black Team Room. Players come in wearing Number Ones and read the faxes . . . One is from John Banks, Minister of Sport. 'Attention Colin Meads. Best wishes for a series victory tomorrow. Laurie deserves it and the country needs it . . . ' Another is from Andy Leslie, the past All Black captain. 'To Laurie Mains, Colin Meads, Sean Fitzpatrick and team. Supporting you all 150 per cent. Laurie, do to them what we couldn't do in 1976.'

Alama and Buncey are first in, followed by Rigger, Dowdy and Pinetree, who whistles tunelessly, more of an exhalation than a whistle. Meads has played ten tests against the Boks . . . At 1.07 p.m. Sean Fitzpatrick sits beside JK. He shifts in his chair, jiggles his foot, leans forward, bites his lip, and now looks impassively to his coach. Nobody speaks. Tension. Under control. Fitz now folds his arms, picks at his ear absently and clasps his hands in front. I am here with 21 All Blacks, three selectors and the manager. We are 78 electric minutes from the second test kick-off. Tree, craggy and dominant, stands to speak. He has presence. The players still regard him with a special respect. 'Fellas, it's a pretty tense time, and I just want to wish you well. It's a day like the one we had many years ago, and the team talk then was 'Take no prisoners.' It's that sort of day today. We're not going to give it to them.'

Laurie Mains pauses before speaking. 'There're lots of books written on clashes between New Zealand and South Africa. I just want to read briefly from one of them.' In a lower voice than usual, he reads aloud, 'There are rugby playing countries . . . and then there is South Africa. They stand above all as New Zealand's greatest foe.' He warms to his briefly expressed theme. 'Look at Sean Fitzpatrick here. He's a great All Black. *He's* going to give everything he's got for his country today. Can you do it with him? It's time to stand up and be counted. Remember Buck Shelford . . . Let's go.' The players file out silently to their bus . . .

2.28 p.m.

The prideful challenge of the haka, 'Ka mate, ka mate . . . ,' rooted in the antiquity of Maui's capture of the sun, is thrown into the simmering arena by fifteen men in black. The Springboks turn their backs and draw their wagons into a circle . . .

4.18 p.m.

Dressing room. Loey just sits and stares at nothing. Then slowly grins. He's beaten South Africa. Zinny rings his injured brother at the other end of the country, 'Hey Rob, it's Zin . . . ' Alama slowly cuts tape from his knee. Another player sits and repeats, 'Hell, we did it, we really did it.' His cheek is badly swollen. A team mate calls to the manager, 'Hey Tree, I'll keep this one,' and gestures at his silver fern. JK asks Mike Brewer about jersey swapping. 'No way,' replies Bruiser. 'This jersey's a boyhood dream. I'm keeping this one on. A test series against South Africa in New Zealand. My first test series against South Africa — and we won!'

9

Up against the black jersey: the opposition speaks

I sometimes think that your rugby public demands too much from the All Blacks. They are the greatest team of rugby tradition in the world but you cannot expect them to win every time. But they are the team we measure our standards by whenever we play them.

Vivian Jenkins —Wales and Lions

David Campese sums it up in his biography: 'When you are playing the All Blacks you are playing the best in the world.' For over 90 years it has been so, as the world of rugby beyond New Zealand has used the All Blacks as its international yardstick. In the nineteenth century the rugby smiths began to hammer out the game's appeal up and down the country. The spark of the 1888–89 Natives tour flamed into the Originals tour of 1905–6, when the black steel was first forged.

Living with the prospect of playing Gallaher's team was a challenge for every Home Union team. In Wales, the schemers were out observing the All Blacks in matches before the Welsh test in order to prepare for their encounter at Cardiff. Following the tour, some home teams took to heart the colonials' lessons of fitness, backs and forwards combining, specialities of set positions, and training in set play pieces. Biographies and coaching manuals written by New Zealanders, such as they were in the era between the two world wars, were keenly read by the British Isles coaches — usually of a varsity, county or club team — who drew upon lessons learned from that first All Black team.

Legacy of the early teams

A 1930s letter to an All Black from an overseas test player, whose county team had been guided by an opponent of Gallaher's 1905–6 New Zealanders, illustrates the legacy of the first All Blacks:

> We had no coaches, as such, and the captain always organised us a day before our county game — or even on the day! We did get a lot of advice from X. He had been a test player against your original All Blacks and also played in one other match, I think. He was convinced [by the play of Gallaher's team] of the need to have our forwards more mobile and to lift our level of fitness. I still remember him saying to us that if we wanted to learn how to play the best rugby then we should read the book by Gallaher and Stead.

Opponents of New Zealand teams, as long ago as 1924–25, recall the fluid style of their play. Frank Hewitt, an opponent of the Invincibles, described the character of that team: 'The duty of the New Zealand team was for the forwards to feed the ball to the backs, then, if necessary, join in the handling to score the tries. Team work, everyone taking part, was their target.'

In his later years, 'with an artificial knee replacement resulting from joint batterings on the field,' Frank Hewitt (still Ireland's youngest international as a 17-year-old schoolboy), recalls Jock Richardson's team:

> The Irish team were pleased to escape with a 6–0 loss in the whipping rain of the 1 November test. The match at Lansdowne Road, Dublin, in 1924 was tough. You New Zealanders know how to use well-trained energy. Ireland was defeated 6–0, but we were well pleased to keep the score so low. Regarding our preparation for the All Black test there was no coaching. Our only get-together was on Friday afternoon prior to the Saturday game, and this was only an easy-going airing. Playing the All Blacks was, for us in the Irish team, a real challenge. Probably our defence ability was more tested than that of attack, but we did seek to move forward when possible, passing by hand rather than losing possession by kicking.

An England test player, J.C. Gibbs, who opposed the 1924 Invincibles, also recalls these times. The English test players had lived with the knowledge that Ireland and Wales had been defeated and the Invincibles had not yet lost a match on tour.

In my day we had no coaches and even before international matches we did not even have a run-about together nor, as far as my recollection is concerned, did we ever have endless discussions about tactics. We certainly had no more than perhaps one training session and, if they had been wanted by the selectors, quite a few of us would not have been able to spare the time . . .

I was very fortunate because I played against the All Blacks twice, for London and for England, and was one of the few to score a try against them and against Scotland, Ireland and Wales. The national XV met either on the train or at the hotel and, against France, we arrived by boat or coach on the morning of the match. Most of the international XV here knew each other pretty well before the actual test because we had played both with, and against, one another in club matches, county matches and trials.

As far as the match against the 1924–25 All Blacks is concerned, the ball was actually in my hands when the whistle went for the sending off of Cyril Brownlie. The game had been going on for quite a short time when A.E. Freethy, the Welsh referee, called both packs together and warned them that the next player who ignored his warning would be sent off. The next scrum was when the sending-off occurred . . .

One of my regrets is that I was never able to visit New Zealand — I turned down the chance of tours because of the necessity to work and earn a living.

Cyril Brownlie was the first New Zealander, or rugby international from any country, sent off in a test. His dismissal is implied by one scribe, Terry McLean, as resulting from returning a punch by Tom Voyce, but Ron Palenski records Brownlie as kicking Ray Edwards, who was on the ground.

The perspectives of the past, although subject to frailties of memory and inaccuracy of recollection, do alert today's rugby aficionado to understandings of past All Black teams and players. Perhaps our greatest fullback was the 19-year-old George Nepia of the 1924 Invincibles, who played in all matches of their tour. Nepia has been described as a Rock of Gibraltar, as the last line of defence, in an era when fullbacks did not necessarily run with the ball. An international opponent, F.S. Hewitt, recalls him differently, however: 'The Maori fullback, whose name I forget, was always ready to open up a movement from a defensive position.'

Nepia, along with a fellow great All Black and Maori player, Jimmy Mill, was excluded from the 1928 All Black tour of South Africa. Captained by Maurice Brownlie, the team suffered from one of All Black history's worst tour managers. The captain, although respected by his team as a flanker, lacked the ability to relate to his players, let alone the facility to get to know and accept them as individuals. He was one of the tour selectors, who were seen by opponents as lacking the skills to select the best team for each test.

One Springbok survivor of that series saw the All Blacks change their play because of a more enlightened selection. 'I consider Mark Nicholls as one of your best backs and we were very surprised when he was omitted from all the tests except the final one in Cape Town, in which he was responsible for your winning. Amongst the backs I would place Grenside on the wing as outstanding.' This view of the latter player illustrates the diversity of perceptions, as Grenside, who scuttled with a low centre of gravity like a turbo-charged crab, was seen by one team mate as a less than gifted player, indeed rather pedestrian!

The 1930s teams

Despite ruling the rugby world of the 1920s and much of the 1930s, New Zealand and South Africa were still not fully accepted by the International Rugby Board as equals. An Irish player, Veysey Boyle, recalls an example of New Zealand's status on the Board:

> It was my first 'cap' when I played against the All Blacks in November 1935. In Ireland the 'cap' was given to you just before you went on to the field — I was too excited to bother then about it. When that All Black match was over, they took the cap away from me saying they'd just discovered that New Zealand was only an associate member of the International Board and so I was not entitled to it! They said, however, that I could call myself an 'International' and count the match as a cap! Later on, I played for Ireland again and was presented with a cap, but two players who played against New Zealand that day were never selected again and never got their caps back — poor fellows!

The age of amateurism, condescension and patronising attitudes by English and United Kingdom administrators was alive and well. Nepia and others who moved to rugby league were seen as outcasts for life from the NZRFU ranks. There was, however, even in the hidebound New Zealand union, a lack of the extreme attitudes found in the Scottish administration.

J.M. Kerr, who played for Scotland against the 1935–36 All Blacks, took up rugby again at medical school to get fit. In his third season he was appointed fullback for the international in an era 'when one

Not all of the competition is physical. Mark Cooksley and Olo Brown engaged in grand mastery out on Sydney harbour.

A rare team day out relaxing. Jeff Wilson, Frank Bunce, Graeme Bachop and Michael Jones (obscured) uncharacteristically all at sea.

Night games require night training. The All Blacks prepare for a nocturnal session at the Sydney Football Stadium, August 1994.

If you're an All Black you have to play with intensity even during practice, as this line-out at the Hobsonville air base demonstrates.

Liquid refreshment of all sorts gets taken on very quickly after a test match. And the ice is usually on the body rather than in the drinks, as demonstrated by Mike Brewer. John Kirwan seems to have come through this game relatively un-scathed.

John Kirwan's fifty-sixth international — a record for a New Zealand back. Western Samoa go down to the All Blacks at Eden Park in 1993.

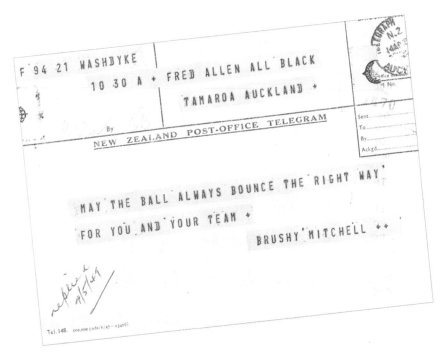

Good wishes and congratulations come in all forms. *Top*: One All Black skipper's message to another on the departure of the 1949 team for South Africa. (Fred Allen collection) *Bottom*: Prime Minister Jim Bolger joins the team in the dressing room after a victory. From left: Olo Brown, Sean Fitzpatrick, Richard Loe, Blair Larsen.

Saturday's match was the practice for the next Saturday's match (including internationals!)'. Kerr recalls an example of the Scottish amateur environment first encountered by the All Blacks of 1905–6:

> The classic example of that era in Scottish football relates to one of my team mates who lived in Glasgow. Submitting his expenses for his test match journey from Glasgow, the gist of the reply from the secretary of the SRFU was roughly:
>
> Dear Lambie,
>
> I have received your claim for 11/4d re travelling expenses from Glasgow. I note that you include the purchase of newspapers which are not a legitimate claim on the SRU. I have therefore deducted 4d.
>
> Yours . . .
>
> You will not be surprised to hear that, not long afterwards, Lambie emigrated to Australia!

This international rugby era evoked by J.M. Kerr is reminiscent of the attitudes extant in the pre-Second World War administration of All Black level New Zealand rugby. Bill Hadley, one of the great All Black hookers, had a similar story of rugby administration. A player with complete physical commitment, Hadley was injured on the 1935–36 tour of the British Isles. Various unconfirmed reports reached his Auckland home area, some of them describing horrific injuries. Bill's new bride, Mary, somewhat distressed at the reports, attempted unsuccessfully to determine her husband's condition. Eventually she plucked up courage, crossed to Auckland on the ferry from their North Shore home, and made her way by tram to the Auckland Rugby Union. At last she reached the secretary, whose reply she recalled vividly over 55 years later: 'He made me feel like an intruder. He looked at me and said, "Mrs Hadley, women have no place in rugby. You will be informed of the state of your husband's injuries through your local rugby club!" It still annoys me.'

Hadley and his team mates were critical of some All Black test teams selected on their 1935–36 tour. The test against England saw the New Zealanders run out to a 13–0 loss at Twickenham, four days into the 1936 new year. From the other side of that test encounter, the England captain of the day provided historical insights some 55 years later on playing the All Blacks. Bernard Gadney, one of England's special test rugby captains, led England in the January match, although the usually inimitable T.P. McLean records in one publication that the skipper was Douglas Kendrew. The revered recorder is accurate, however, in his assertion that three key All Black backs were omitted because of their lateness (or earliness) in returning from a Thursday night New Year's Eve function. The tourists were into their twenty-eighth tour match, whereas England players usually had 'Saturday morning as a working morning, up to the Second World War. It was a job to get time off to play.' Gadney provides the first opponent's inside account of England's approach:

Before New Zealand played England at Twickenham in 1936 the England XV met for the first time at 2.30 p.m. on the afternoon before the match, for a short run about. We had a short talk before the game, when I mentioned three points. They were carried out successfully. This may seem very casual but, in fact, we were all extremely fit. We had a very powerful side. We wanted to win. I had thought, and did think on the day, that England could beat the All Blacks and I said so.

This first of the three points was that we thought we had, by our standards, an extremely heavy and mobile pack of forwards. I asked them to make that point by shoving together as they had never shoved before, as if their lives depended upon it. They did. Secondly, I said we should attack through the backs. We did. Not only were our backs strong good runners but great defenders. I said I would break away from the first scrums, as the situation dictated, and make the breaks diagonally. In those days that drove the defence back and gave one's own backs more room. Say it who shouldn't, this was highly successful.

The key to our situation lay in the second row. Webb and Clarke were enormous and not in their first youth. In those days there was no coach, but a selection committee. John Daniels, the chairman, told me that there was a danger that Webb and Clarke might blow up under the strain, which put the breeze up me! I recall spending the afternoon telling them both the sort of things which I thought would encourage them. But, most probably, I needn't have worried as they appeared to thrive . . .

Alex Obolensky's second move [to score] was spontaneous. As I recall the move, Peter Cranmer appeared to hesitate in his tracks and Olo came *inside*. One or two of us were running with him, Olo was a fine runner . . .

After that England–New Zealand test, in conversation at the dinner after the game, Jack Manchester said to me that never before had he felt such weight from an opposing pack as at the first few scrummages. I made no comment (Jack and his wife stayed here with us, more than 30 years later, and were delightful guests). The All Black test saw not one fist raised, no boot was driven in and the rugby was played in a fine spirit. This left me with a profound respect and warm regard for New Zealanders, and gratitude too.

Despite the less successful win/loss record of Manchester's team, compared with their predecessors, it reinforced a style of play for the British Isles to learn from. A 1935–36 opponent, from the British Isles, noted the strength and impact of the All Blacks upon British play:

> The New Zealand game, to me, always looks as if each player is giving his all. They appear to pressurise opponents in the first half and, to the surprise of their opponents, turn on *extra* heat in the second half. In my day the forwards loved to get in a bunch with the leaders having the ball at their feet — but the All Blacks showed us how much better it was for forwards to get the ball in their hands and pass it. If it went to ground, the next man picked it up and off they go again. After all, it is a handling game although some outhalves or first-fives seem to think it is a *kicking* game!

Post-war teams

Typical of post-war opponents is a more succinct comment: 'The character of All Black rugby is summed up in: determination, enthusiasm, dedication and great play. Marvellous opponents who will hammer your guts with hard play in the game — and fill them with beer after it! 100 per cent.' Even so, the style of various All Blacks teams has often been condemned by overseas commentators as boring 'ten-man rugby', with the backs outside the first-five having their talents condemned to winter in the field of discontent. This criticism, on the record, has been justified in certain eras of New Zealand rugby, particularly that of the 1950s and 1960s.

A famed Welsh player, Haydn Tanner, describes the meaning of All Blacks–Wales encounters:

> Because of history and the national centrality of rugby, Wales versus New Zealand was something special. In most players' lifetimes, it was a one-off game. This involved all the preparation and planning of years, and the history of previous games was only too well known. And yet, in spite of all the history and background, the games themselves were terribly hard but played in excellent spirit. After the game, there were no 'sour grapes' and both teams respected each other.

The 1950s saw the climactic 1956 tour of New Zealand by the Springboks. A member of the latter team provides a reminder of that era, when the whole country lived with the All Blacks under close scrutiny:

> Rugby plays a major role in the life of New Zealand people. It has been said that a New Zealand boy comes out of his mother's womb bearing a pair of rugby boots . . . New Zealand rugby, the great pride, joy, sense of achievement when they wear that black jersey with the silver fern . . . for New Zealand to lose, sets the country into mourning.

A range of overseas opponents saw the back play of All Black rugby becalmed in the doldrums of the 1950s and 1960s, when the forward play virtually provided the whole crew of the cutter. As a 1950 Lion recollected: 'New Zealand has always possessed a fine pack of mobile forwards who, after the war, dominated the team tactics. Possession, position and an efficiency that could be boring at times — but it won the big games!'

1960s and 1970s

In the 1960s a test opponent saw New Zealand rugby as having the positive quality of 'the ability to sustain pressure for an entire match whereas our teams play in fits and starts'. Another noted that, 'Some All Black teams have a reluctance to be creative unless they gain distinct forward superiority.'

This view prevailed with the All Blacks' opponents until the 1970s, when Fred Allen's influence was to impact with more liberal playing styles. An overseas test player, rated by the All Blacks, comments:

> It is their national sport and the All Black teams are well organised. They usually play to a set plan which has been carefully worked out. The selected team is the best to carry out that plan. While the play itself may not always be attractive, it produces results, and one cannot overlook the efficiency. I do think that Fred Allen reshaped your All Blacks from ten men to fifteen. Perhaps it was the Kiwi team influence?

Peter Johnson played 42 tests for Australia between 1959 and 1972. As an Australian captain who confronted a range of All Black and New Zealand provincial teams, Johnson provides compelling accounts of the efforts of the opposition coaches, Alan Roper and Brian Palmer, in developing Wallaby confidence in their ability to take on the All Blacks. Roper's efforts 'to have us halt All Black progress through the forwards made a difference to our resistance in the five tests played against New Zealand in 1962'.

Palmer aided the emergence of Roper, when he convinced a number of us forwards that the All Blacks were ordinary people with an extraordinary desire to win. This, to some extent, took away for us the All Blacks' aura of invincibility despite being more than aware of the win-loss situation over the years. He coached New South Wales to a most unexpected victory in 1962 against the All Blacks.

1980s and 1990s

In the 1980s an international rugby player exhibited a picture of New Zealand rugby that had, in the social reality of that decade, lost its historical accuracy. The viewpoint perpetuated a historical stereotype held, by South Africans particularly, of New Zealand rugby society. 'At the moment every young boy wants to represent New Zealand at rugby football,' asserted this overseas captain, which would seem to be out of touch with the reality of changes then occurring in the wake of the disastrous 1981 Springbok tour and the movement of youth towards individual sports.

Andrew Slack, who captained Australia and played against New Zealand over 1975–86, is succinct: 'The All Blacks are totally uncompromising and committed. Quietly ruthless.' Into the 1990s, opponents of the All Blacks reinforced Slack's views: 'I think there has been a mystique about the All Blacks. However, since the 1987 World Cup the field has levelled more and we have had enough success against them to have some confidence. Having said that, they have been playing great rugby since '94–'95 and their mobile forwards are set up by great tight forwards. But please keep Jonah Lomu on the sideline!' 'I have to say the All Blacks are still bloody hard players — but never dirty. You feel more exhausted after a test with them than with any other team,' adds another contemporary All Black opponent.

Ollie Campbell, the Irish first-five eighth, out-half or fly-half, played against the All Blacks for Ireland and as a 1983 Lion. Describing the All Blacks in the 1987–97 decade of their expansive play, Campbell notes, 'For me, what distinguishes New Zealand rugby from any other is their innate understanding of the *totality* of the game of rugby.'

Whatever the rugby test country, there is an opponent's perspective on the All Blacks. A Springbok of 1994 comments: 'The country is not as fanatical as I expected but the tests are still the hardest of any I have played in. The All Blacks surprised us somewhat with the use of their backs and speeding the game up.' Australian prop Phil Kearns described the 1990s character of New Zealand rugby: 'Its place in New Zealand life shapes, and has shaped, the game itself. The passion and commitment that New Zealand has for rugby is translated on to the field.'

One Australian team leader, with considerable experience of playing New Zealand in test rugby, provides his perspective:

> Winning is, and has been since I've observed the game, the only thing that is important. Winning is vital to all countries but not everything. The style of All Black play is flexible and seems, on average, to actually be that which is thought to bring victory in the circumstances. The style of their play is much more physical, year in, year out, team by team. There is general agreement that if you are going to be belted anyway then you are better being the belter than the beltee! When touring New Zealand, or just playing the All Blacks, we expected it and were not disappointed! All Black play is much more clever than is generally supposed. I think the attacking skills of New Zealand forwards have been totally underrated over the years. Physical intimidation is a cornerstone of the game. As far as 'New Zealand life' is concerned, rugby is the most critical thing in national esteem. Yacht races and cricket etc., seen at the highest level, may touch all the populace, but almost as novelties. Rugby is deadly serious stuff.

Scottish test player Finlay Calder is also struck by the link between living in New Zealand and the play of the All Blacks. His views are a rugby sociologist's meat and drink. 'New Zealand rugby is a direct mirror image of its society. They play an expansive, open game — reflecting outgoing, outdoor people. They play to enjoy themselves whilst striving for perfection.' This perception of rugby as an integral element, or reflection, of New Zealand life is supported by J.P.R. Williams, who believes:

> Rugby is part of New Zealand history. By far the best team in the 1995 World Cup was the All Blacks, playing an expansive game, which has not always been their traditional way. They showed, in their match against Scotland, a game in which they trusted their instinct to pass rather than kick. They had ball retention, Ian Jones in the line-out . . . and Jonah Lomu!

Danie Craven, the Springbok 'maître d' whose administration saw legal and illegal football fare served up on the international rugby menu for some 50 years, described the All Blacks' rugby character in 1992. Craven played against New Zealand in 1937, coached and selected South African teams and was that country's leading administrator for decades after the Second World War. Saint to some, sinner to others, Craven's life centred on rugby. 'The toughness of the players is the major characteristic of the All Blacks, for it is All Black hands which still do the manual work everywhere. It is their nature to lead a hard life, and a tough mind can only be created by physical toughness.' This 1956 attitude was perpetuated for 40 anachronistic years by Craven. Sadly, this picture of New Zealanders indicated a perspective of a past era and a lack of insight into Kiwi life in the 1990s. Craven asserted: 'New Zealand has been known to us as pattern conformists or stickers to patterns. They are also ruckers and blindside experts. To beat them, their pattern of play must be broken or curbed. Do that and you beat the All Blacks . . . there have been no weak New Zealand sides but there have been weak New Zealand thinkers who could not change if they were thwarted.'

Friends off the field

Virtually without exception, the off-field interaction of onfield opponents, the recognition of worthy adversaries and social occasions have been emphasised by players over the test match decades. Paradoxically, given the more open playing style of the 1980s and 1990s, the opportunities for player interaction off the field have decreased in these recent, more professional times.

The voices of test opponents confirm that social fraternisation has not been especially strong in the 1990s as the demands of a greater numbers of tests and shorter tours have increased. The most significant dimensions of rugby's appeal for its international élite, however, are still those of enjoyment of the game and the camaraderie resulting from the end of play. The friendships generated by the game may be a cliché in action for some outside the sport, but are stressed by test player after test player. For some international players, test rugby has led to lifelong friendships with the All Blacks. Understand the onfield battles between Shehadie of Australia and Skinner of New Zealand, two hard-edged forwards, and then you will appreciate the gratitude of the Skinners when Lord Mayor Shehadie took their in-transit daughter under his wing in Sydney. Talk with Vivian Jenkins, that great Welsh fullback and rugby writer, about one of his frequent visits to New Zealand, and the rugby friends' names are unfurled. The doughty 1950s prop H.L. 'Snow' White, clashed vigorously with his Welsh counterpart — and sealed a friendship with him when he was a pallbearer at his funeral in

Cardiff. And this is but a very small group of examples.

Sport may be over-commercialised in some sectors but it still has the capacity to reveal character and attitude in its adherents. Of course players don't have to like their team mates, but in the close interdependence of team sport and its associated social activities, men or women often link closely off the field. Throw in a common goal, mutual trust developed in tense situations and a realistic appreciation of others' skills and qualities, and confine this to a relatively clearly defined age group, and there are likely to be grounds for companionship — mateship even.

Overseas opponents hold a respect for All Blacks who live in the New Zealand tradition of bred-in-the-bone commitment. 'Take Buck Shelford,' stated an opponent of the late 1980s. 'He was an outstanding player and motivator on the field but I found him a gentleman off it.'

It would be a foolish commentator who assumed that test rugby's times are not a-changing. In professional rugby, with the example of league players and their 'day at the office' experience of the code, rugby's modern travel and demanding itineraries, and the increasing number of test matches, the social interaction and much-quoted camaraderie with opposing players will decline. It would still be a fair bet, though, to say that the All Blacks' opponents will continue to prize the test, recall the contact, and value the prospect of pitting themselves against the fifteen in black.

10

Inside the black force (2)

All Blacks v. Lions, 3 July 1993

It is too difficult to envisage how the All Blacks could cobble together a substantial win. Wynne Gray — rugby journalist

The best and most consistent display from an All Black team since the World Cup final in 1987. Lyn Colling

It's a week I don't really want again. New Zealand coach

New Zealand: John Timu, John Kirwan, Frank Bunce, Va'aiga Tuigamala, Lee Stensness, Grant Fox, Jon Preston, Arran Pene, Michael Jones, Robin Brooke, Ian Jones, Jamie Joseph, Olo Brown, Sean Fitzpatrick (captain), Craig Dowd. Reserves: Matthew Cooper, Ant Strachan, Zinzan Brooke, Mark Cooksley, Mark Allen, Graham Dowd

Lions: Gavin Hastings, Rory Underwood, Jeremy Guscott, Scott Gibbs, Ieuan Evans, Rob Andrew, Dewi Morris, Dean Richards, Peter Winterbottom, Martin Johnson, Martin Bayfield, Ben Clarke, Nick Popplewell, Brian Moore, Jason Leonard. Reserves: Anthony Clement, Will Carling, Robert Jones, Mike Teague, Paul Burnell, Ken Milne

Half-time score: New Zealand 14 — Lions 10
Full-time score: New Zealand 27 — Lions 13

Even for veterans like Sean Fitzpatrick and Frank Bunce, the week after the second test loss to the Lions, at Wellington, in 1993, was perhaps the most demanding of their rugby careers. Fitzpatrick had not played or led the team as well as he expected of himself in the test, and Bunce went into the besieged third test week, the series decider, with some trepidation. Fitzy acknowledged, in the *New Truth*, 'I lost it for a while.

I didn't take the right options and I didn't lead from the front. It was a bloody awful experience.'

The media were merciless over the All Black loss, with accusations of the team being 'devoid of character', of 'a directionless second test effort' and of a third test looming where 'a few skills, a bit of flair and some flexibility might also be handy'. Then came the selection of Stensness for his first test, seen by past All Black captain Stu Wilson as 'ludicrous'. Within 24 hours of the test, Stensness was touted as being 'at the start of a great international career'! And, most hurtful of all to present All Blacks, was the justifiable criticism from their predecessors. This became a focus and stimulus for the week — the tradition, history and commitment of men in the black jersey.

Tuesday, 29 June 1993

Spreading with the media wind came the New Zealand public's faxes, some of which were waiting for the team as they assembled, blending pungent expectations and goodwill.

10.14 a.m.

The All Black coach's flight has been delayed and the team will meet at 10.30 a.m. In the Team Room at the Poenamo Hotel I sort out my list of players and team officials so that I can keep a relatively simple but accurate record of the verbal interaction in the team meeting. Here, the Team Room floor has a thick red carpet, with some red and black interpatterns. Three settees, each holding about four guys, are in a semi-circle, with cane chairs placed on one side of the room.

A banner above the side-table of drinks proclaims that the hotel is proud to host the All Blacks for the third test versus the Lions.

John Kirwan comes in, carrying his dress clothes, 'How's your thesis going?' Sean arrives, close-cropped hair and dark jersey and comes over to greet me. He smiles ruefully, 'You've certainly picked an interesting week to be with us.' We chat briefly, and after the week's timetable is known, he will put aside half an hour for discussion with me. (I am keen to check on how he sees his test leadership in the last test and his perspective on this week's leadership.)

Robin Brooke and Frank Bunce sift through the burgeoning pile of faxes, pausing to exchange greetings. (The players seem more preoccupied today, or is it simply that I am observing their arrival more closely than previously?)

10.30 a.m.
What is happening with the team meeting? Some players are uncertain. Some travel plans have been disrupted, affecting arrival times. The team meeting is now scheduled for midday. How does Lee Stensness feel about this on his first All Black day? Would there not be value in having Peter Thorburn, who is here, speak with those present?

10.52 a.m.
Earle Kirton arrives with his suitcase heavy in hand and his trademark scarf. Laurie Mains is with him . . .

John Kirwan wanders in, glances over the All Black posters on the wall, greets a team mate and walks out again. One liaison officer (from the local provincial rugby union) switches on the wall-mounted television, and another rings the Air Force base to check on the All Blacks training there tomorrow, making certain an adequate scrum machine will be available.

Neil, the manager, comes in and greets me. I check on my involvement with the team this week. He is supportive and heads off with my typed record of the previous test week.

I check the letter I have written to Sean and the players and place it with a record of the last test, and an outline of my doctorate, on the team table. It is available there to any player or team official.

11.45 a.m.
Guys have been sitting, coming and going, browsing, idly flicking on television, making a cup of tea, eating fruit and talking. JK, as often, has his own clothes on, wearing a bulky black jacket which is certainly not a sponsor's product. Kamo comes in, 'Gidday mate,' and settles down to chat with JK. Jon Preston makes a cup of tea for his veteran lock room-mate. Graham Dowd arrives in his blue Steinlager jersey, shakes hands, 'Back into it, eh?' Now it's reserve Bull Allen, 'How's it going?' The easy manner of the players is gratifying. Grant Fox arrives in the Team Room, 'Gidday Robin, still at it?' and so it goes as team members fill the sofas and greet each other. The last test was only one week ago. The physiotherapist, Gary Sye, comes in and a couple of players check with him. JT is the only guy in shorts.

Then the test newcomer arrives to a casual 'Gidday Stainless' from one of his Auckland team mates. Reserve Zinzan Brooke arrives, manipulating a toothpick along a row of teeth. He sits down on a settee, and Bull now engages a toothpick as Zinny, whom I had not met before, seems to be checking with JK on my presence. Reserve Mark Cooksley unlimbers his angular frame onto the settee next to Zinny, but then notices the new Steinlager 'Big Game Hunks' poster of the All Blacks. He re-assembles himself into a vertical mass and moves over to check it out. Arran Pene is yawning. (Perhaps the effect of travel?) Buncey, wearing shorts, mooches in.

A television comedy is watched desultorily.

12.15 p.m.

Neil comes in and has a word with a liaison officer about a team call at 12.30 p.m., as a couple of elderly women enter the off-limits room by mistake. 'Excuse me,' smiles one, eyeing the All Blacks a little disbelievingly, and they depart giggling nervously. Michael Jones points them in the direction they need. Graham Dowd shakes Lee's hand and congratulates him on selection. 'How're you doing?' asks reserve Ant Strachan as he passes my chair, and Michael smiles and nods from across the room as he catches my eye.

12.34 p.m.

The All Black captain enters the Team Room, and places a small table and two chairs at the front of the room for Laurie and Earle.

Before the arrival of his co-selectors, Peter Thorburn moves in to address the team. 'I wanted to speak to you guys before Laurie and Earle come in. I've been around the team for some time. You've all been selected but I think many of you feel "Phew, I've been selected again" . . . but are not thinking forward about being selected as an All Black again.' He asks how many players have seen the videotape of the second test loss against the Lions, and tells those who haven't that they should have — and that they should watch it tonight. 'I'm doing this [talk] because I don't get a lot of criticism — I'm the third man . . . They [Mains and Kirton] have copped a lot of criticism in the last few weeks. It spreads into the family of the team and you feel for Zinny and Eroni [replaced in the playing XV] just as you feel pleasure for the guys selected . . . '

Thorburn continues. 'I don't care for the talk about you being playboys or wankers, and those sorts of critics are not worth responding to, but ex-All Blacks who pass criticism do have the right to make us think and examine ourselves.' He is pungently evocative of the self-imposed demands that each individual All Black should have. Thorburn notes

Frano Botica ringing him and emphasising the need to switch on a quarter of an hour before the kick off. There is a similarity between top level play and 'a day at the office. It's the extra 5 to 10 per cent that you give. The most important thing is that test. Why do we sit all that time before a test looking as though we have dropped our watch down the dunny? Are you thinking of the game . . . ?' The selector holds the whole team's attention. He talks about the player's inner self: 'You hear all these words — vision, flair, game plans — that's what you cover at training. On the field you cover your options, getting together during injury times or other breaks. Think about your role on the field. It sometimes requires a bit of mongrel, the work rate you demand of yourself, the "true will to win" are my words. In their team are guys who couldn't tackle an old granny off a pisspot and yet they were driving us backwards with their tackles! Be proactive — for those of you who don't know what it means, it means making things happen!

'In Wellington your ineffective tackling on the tackle bags was bloody awful stuff. How many of you, in your own minds, know you really made a crunching tackle on Saturday?' Thorburn goes on to talk about precision and force in the scrum and the drive. ('What are we trying to achieve at ruck and maul time?') He illustrates commitment by referring to his own, more limited, playing ability. 'At every line-out I thought that ball could come to me . . . although I was not playing at your level . . . Ben Clarke [Lions forward] should never have been allowed to get through an All Black line from a five-man line-out.'

Thorburn now puts the onus on players' responsibilities as a team. 'Call on each other . . . think about what we want to achieve from a move. What do you visualise? Don't leave it for Laurie and Earle and Sean and Foxy. There's a huge amount of knowledge in this group. Have your input, you'll get your chance. Think of our kick-off: why don't you suggest four and four [split of eight forwards]? Why don't we look at our crossovers, kicks along the ground . . .? You guys have to think of these things. Why do we leave one guy to chase it while the others waddle along behind?' Thorburn emphasises support play and 'for the most important five seconds in your life forwards, you are to be on that guy's shoulder . . .

'Look guys, your defensive pattern was very good. They're not a great side, and they play to the letter of the law. We can take hardship where they can't. Look at our rowers who won the world title but who had camped on the side of Karapiro to train their guts out. Use the skills and knowledge *you* have. Don't leave it to two or three people.

'The crucial thing in the rugby world is not to get into a loose mode; it's easy to blame others. A lot of you guys haven't lost a lot of games — and I mean that as a compliment. Don't get caught up in guilt and worry. We spend half of our lives looking back instead of accepting things and learning for the future . . . The success for this All Black family is purely and utterly up here [taps his heart and head] . . . you've got the ability . . . the difference between being successful and being a failure, in business or sport, is purely in here. Give it your application. You owe it to yourselves. You owe it to your "All Black family".' It is a timely and compelling 23 minutes from Thorburn which magnetised the team focus.

1.00 p.m.

Thorburn is followed now by an upfront and visibly annoyed All Black coach. He is getting into the guys from the first sentence: 'I'll tell you what really annoys me is that everything we talked about didn't happen! Is there one person in this room who can say they played to the game plan? . . . If I could have found one hole to crawl into I would have. Discipline is more important than loyalty . . . I have never been so bloody humiliated as to see Poms dominating an All Black team — Poms, not as fit as you . . . all over the top of you . . . do you accept losing a test match? I don't. I don't know why anyone plays at this level, or why I do this job, if we easily accept a loss. Against Australia in the first test we played with guts and we played with discipline and we held our heads up high, even though we lost. We had played our best and you can't ask more than that.'

Mains moves on, sometimes a stereotypical rugby coach, sometimes hitting the jugular of All Black commitment. 'I accept all the shit that's been thrown at me and I'm here to prove the critics wrong . . . I hope you're with me . . . we need guts, we need good Kiwi toughness and heart. Above all, you're All Blacks. What are you going to do about it? I'm going to ask you and I don't want clichés.' It is an unusually pungent and challenging opening. I wonder if it is a little uncomfortably dated for 1990s virtual professionals.

'JT, what are you going to do?' Timu responds that he is going to make tackles, be hard, 'All those things you said . . . ' Mains directly addresses players in turn. They are outwardly grim-faced. Buncey is 'going to do whatever it takes.' Foxy's response is complimented by the coach, 'A bloody good call.' Mains is critical of one player for not taking effective control, but then compliments him, before moving on to Arran Pene, whose game 'will be based on aggression'.

The coach considers action regarding players he sees as cheats in the Lions teams and is emphatic about limits of physical action — there is to be no kicking of players. 'I don't want any bloody kicking at all.' Jamie Joseph (JR) is making a point warning against overaggression and the coach responds supportively. Kamo enters the discussion by noting the need for team and individual discipline. Robin Brooke emphasises that the All Blacks have to compete around the field.

The coach snorts in disgust at 'that guy on TV last night saying he'd rather be a Lion than an All Black — imagine saying that!' He turns to the still inexperienced prop, Craig Dowd. 'How hard are you, Craig? I don't know you pretty well. Can you do the job we're looking for? . . . Sean, what about you? How do you see it?' 'A bit like you Laurie, I wanted to dig a hole and climb into it. We need control, discipline . . . '

'Olo, technically you're one of the best tighthead props I've seen. You can't live on that. I don't see any real fizz. I know it's there and it's got to come out. You're an intelligent guy, look at that videotape tonight and see what you can do . . . look, they climbed into us. Don't anyone tell us that Popplewell and Leonard are better props than ours are. I won't accept that, not for a bloody second . . . Now, if any of you have got any comment, on training or the game plan, or anything I've said, tell me. If I'm not doing something right or I make a miscall, you've got to tell me.' The coach is walking a tightrope here. Time is limited in test match week so there must be some shortcuts and directive statements. However, the coach must also ensure that the players are not pressured to the extent they will not speak up.

The All Black captain speaks. 'I think we've got to put the ball on the ground and ruck more.' The conversation now draws on doing this, as in Australia last year, and giving support for Sean or another runner. Sean asks for clarification: 'Do we go to the advantage line, then the ball goes to the deck, then we go again?' Support from Robin Brooke is discussed. Mains is explicit in his demands of Jon Preston, at halfback, controlling moves and telling forwards what he wants in those moves . . .

The coach now criticises one phase of All Black play which suited Dean Richards of the Lions. 'I don't know who called that and I don't want to know.' There is voiced agreement for a greater part of the week to be spent on team runs and in practice as a team.

Defence is discussed and debated — does the team this week use a drift defence or man-on-man? The latter was utilised more in last year's tests. Implications of the Lions' alignment, and the deployment of forwards, leads Mains to observe that 'what we were also doing Ice, makes it difficult for you to put pressure on their first-five . . . ' He checks on his backs 'reading' the play when Hastings [Lions fullback] is coming into the line and his backs say they can do this. JK agrees with Fox on reading the move and then calling the defence. 'We've got to practise this, get up and knock them down and then switch to drift defence . . . keep them uncertain . . . ' 'Yeah,' adds Fox, 'Aussie are easier to go one out because they are closer.' Mains accepts his back veteran's views, 'If you can read Hastings, I'll wear what you're saying.'

Earle Kirton enters the analysis. He picks up on the theme of old All Blacks being critical of last week's test play. He relates the driving desire of New Zealand divisional players to wear the black jersey. 'Do we pick a mad dog like X who would die for one All Black cap?'

1.45 p.m.

On the bus to training. As we go out of the Team Room Sean asks if Neil has introduced me to the new players. On the bus Neil tells them who I am: 'Robin is with the team this week so feel free to talk with him. He's a big help to Laurie, Sean and me . . . ' (which is an overstatement but one I appreciate). I had not met Zinny, Jamie Joseph or Mark Cooksley before. It's interesting to see the back seat boys in the bus to training are John Kirwan, Sean Fitzpatrick and Zinzan Brooke — some trio! (On the test bus, however, there is no place for the captain at the back. He sits towards the front.)

At Hobsonville air base the training is purposeful. Even Kirwan is not spared the back coach's criticism, especially when he carries the ball one-handed. The game is speeding up, communication is being emphasised and the line-outs are crisp and efficient. Mains stops the forwards, and admonishes them for 'travelling unrealistically fast, that's not how it will be in the test.' The tackle bags are used for a tackling sequence which demands communication. Suddenly Buncey stops, 'Ah shit, I've twisted my ankle,' and is quickly with Gary Sye, the physio.

Olo has more vocal input, and voices his expectations more than at any previous test practice. The emphatic octet drive the scrum machine into the turf, ripping up divots as ominous signals for any observing Lions supporter. The captain pulls his forwards together. 'Let's talk about the scrum, we just about die for it.' He nominates forwards in turn who are asked to say what they feel about the scrum, and to communicate that with each other.

4.07 p.m.
In the showers after training. The front row chat about their limited number of club games this season. Sean has played four or five and jokes about possibly having had to play one instead of playing in this test. 'You know, Olo, this was the first time for a few years I listened closely to the test team announcement!' It is obvious Fitzy feels strongly about his lesser levels of play and leadership in the previous test. Then the All Blacks move on to the mess at the base where there are drinks and a crowded area in which some players are buttonholed by rugby-keen Services people.

6.00 p.m.
Team Room. JK and Rewi (Arran Pene) chat about how cold it was at practice. Players file in, get a cup of tea or sports drink and watch the news. Buncey and JT lie on the floor on their backs. The team will watch the previous test on video before dinner.

The viewing and discussion is more intense and critical than I have observed previously. (For example, a video freeze of the line-out generates precise analysis and a finding that Dowdy had not moved back in the line-out when a move required this.) Then, 'Richards just stopped clear in front of you, Jamie.' Mains freezes another line-out before the throw-in. 'Can you see Winterbottom out beyond the 15 metres? Ice, can you see that? Why not hold the throw until he's drawn in? Fitz, wouldn't it be easier for JP to see that and call it?' A focused discussion results. The coach notes two occasions when Lions, off the front of their line-out, got to JP.

The All Black captain demands a rewind of a video segment. He is a strong figure in this meeting, making notes as he watches. Jamie suggests the Lions know the All Black line-out calls and Fitzy agrees this is probable. The implications are clear.

'Great kick, Foxy,' comes the accolade from some of his team mates after a strategic move. Fitzy raises a point about a hole in the Lions backline — the video is frozen and the gap is apparent. The need to 'suck in the Lions' loosies' is clear, and linked with use of the runners, line-out plays and rucks. 'Once they've been sucked in, then it's red-hot ball JP, and you send play in the direction their loosies have been pulled in from.' There is humour when Ice tries to explain a penalty against him but the video replay shows he was at fault, generating laughter and some wry remonstrations from his mates . . . a little later Michael's team mates and the coaches are recognising a 'Great tackle, Ice.'

The skilled interchanges of the interactive analysis are plentiful. Lineout on the goal line, 'Front lob here, Rob?'; a crooked feed into scrum; the referee incorrectly penalising offside over the line, where it doesn't apply; All Blacks handling the ball but not going down on it; and players in front of Foxy's kick-off. John Timu goes for a high ball and misses it, and is criticised by Earle as there were plenty of catchers nearby, but one of his senior players states, 'It was my fault Earle, I called JT up.'

Sean has a line-out replayed twice until it is clearly seen how a certain opposition forward is coming through. Loey asks his captain for clarification on the move and its counter. It is now half-time on the video and the players have a brief break. The video resumes with similar analysis and the session concludes at 8.00 p.m. The players then chat before their Team Room dinner. They ask Neil if the allotted test tickets include those for partners or not. He is uncertain and will check. Some players revise points together from the video. The atmosphere is purposeful.

Wednesday, 30 June 1993

9.00 a.m.

The coach hasn't slept well, and over breakfast Earle was telling him to switch off for a while . . . The notices from Neil indicate that the ticket for a player's partner is included in that player's allocation. The media liaison officer advises that the two coaches will have a press conference after training today. 'We don't want the media thinking we aren't fronting up because of the pressure of this week.' Foxy, ever to the point, asks, 'Can you find out who they want, as I didn't know last week till after training.' 'Yeah, okay.' The rest of the day is outlined by Neil.

9.37 a.m.

As I walk past Sean's motel unit he calls out to me, 'Robin do you want to grab ten minutes?' After the second test debate how does he see his leadership? 'I did a pretty average job in that test. I didn't do it well. I played badly and when I play badly I don't lead well. I pride myself on playing well and that is part of leading well. This Saturday I must concentrate a bit more, perhaps not so much "more" as to play my normal game. I must play my game well and the leadership will come with this. Like the rest of the guys, I've got to this level, and, as All Blacks, we have to take responsibility upon ourselves . . . we clearly need to switch on and note any signs of guys not concentrating and ensure we have discipline through the training . . . Maybe last week I was trying a bit too hard.'

Sean is now in his second year as the All Black captain. He perceives growth in his team leadership but 'not a lot of change. I'm probably a bit more confident. The guys respect me and that's important. Obviously the public image is higher . . . I don't really know my biggest strength as a captain but part of it certainly relates to being part of a team that's confident and realises their ability. My relationship with Laurie is pretty good and we are quite compatible. We both think along the same lines, our approach to the game is similar. On the field, I basically believe if I play well I lead well. The leadership roles of players like Foxy and Rewi are important. We share a philosophy of "let's make the most of it". We don't want a repeat of the last test — where it's basically having a go and playing catch-up rugby. Laurie's role, related to this, is to instil confidence and firm up our belief in ourselves. We must play controlled rugby to beat these guys. For myself, I've got to relax and get my confidence back. After being pretty shattered last Saturday, I've got to start believing in myself. Positive thoughts are critical. I write down things I pride. I've closely watched the video of that match, the things I did wrong, and different options I could have taken. Given it all, however, there's more to life than rugby . . . '

10.00 a.m.
Team Room. The coach opens the meeting by asking Olo Brown what he is thinking. 'I'm thinking win and that's number one, and the other guy is number two.' Mains turns to Lee Stensness, facing his first test, 'Lee, this game is basically no different from other big games you've played this year . . . You are a good player and Gibbs is an ordinary player and you'll find that out when you knock him over.

'We'll use single runners at training, concentrate on holding onto that ball . . . we're going to use reserves as opposition at training, if it's "hit and run" then keep it realistic . . . let's keep control of the ball, run into the reserves, just over the advantage line, on your feet, on your feet, as soon as you see your mates then feed it back . . . drive across the ball, and then JP's got control. If you're a bit slow getting there, keep out of JP's way.' Mains uses a diagram on the whiteboard to illustrate his points, and then 'Ice is getting the ball from Fitzy here, Winterbottom comes in, drag him in with Richards, but Sean is there and Ice is there, and bang! It's gone! JP, you've got to be there, you've just got to be there.' Kamo checks, 'Shouldn't Sean take Richards out?' Laurie talks directly to Sean to clarify this.

The All Black coach reviews what he perceives as a change in play over recent tests. He notes that in Australia the runners started to disappear. The tempo dropped in the first test at Christchurch in this series and although the captain was effective as a runner, 'The tempo has dropped. Then we said we've got to drive through the middle, and we let our basic pattern drift away . . . That's my analysis. Does anyone disagree with this? For heaven's sake, say so.' In response to a point by JK about players clustering in play, the coach emphasises that 'runners are no good if they are too close.' A related tactic is clarified. Thorburn raises the possibility of a particular move being utilised, and one of the backs replies that it was used yesterday at training as a decoy. 'Why don't we use Buncey as a variation of that move?' asks the coach. 'Peter has pointed this out to me on the video. The gap is there and the 2–4 cut is on . . . The Lions will say "They've brought in Lee Stensness so he can run," so they'll expect that. Well, let's suggest variations to put Buncey through the gap, not Lee . . . ' The coach addresses Arran Pene on the Lions' loose forwards: 'What's the answer?' 'Hitting them at speed, taking them low and staying on our feet.' They are discussing this further . . . Mains demonstrates the desired tackle . . . then, 'The next thing I want to do is clarify the kick into the box.' He is drawing a diagram on the whiteboard and asks about options as 'what they are wanting us to do is to kick it out so they can have a line-out.'

Inga Tuigamala is being complimented on his role in a second test move and then related moves are explored, especially countermoves to the Lions captain and fullback, Gavin Hastings, coming into their backline. (There appears to be more precision here and a greater cohesion from the start of the week in pinpointing tactics than I previously observed. Although the coach and selectors have been very demanding, they have not been demeaning of players.)

The kick into the box illustrates the focus. Thorbs emphasises to JP how important it is to let the scrum know that the bomb has gone up from Foxy. Fitzy checks, 'Are we going to use it from there?' and points to the whiteboard. They agree on the bomb 'outside our 22', and its implications for pushing the opposition into touch. 'If Carling is going to chase the bomb, who is going to move into that hole?' . . . 'We really need a loosie, and if Ice is chasing the kick, it's Rewi who goes back — if it's incidental. Then Lee, if it's planned, it's Frankie to go up . . .' They now concentrate on a blindside move 20 metres from the Lions' line. The diagram is explicit. Richards (Lions No. 8), Clarke (Lions blindside flanker), and Hastings, are located in relation to the scrum, touch, and goal line. The All Blacks 8, 9 and 15 are drawn on the board. There is a short blindside. Who calls the scrum? What is the code call? Who is in it? Rewi must cover Clarke or it won't work. The key players move into even more detail, including confirmation of how and why JT will run inside the wing. There is a suggestion for a missed pass, but Foxy pinpoints a doubt about the calling of this in the heat of play. The coach now checks with the locations of Lee and Foxy. 'What is happening with the scrum?' The code calls and options are settled and Grant confirms one, 'When I call for the ball and try and go through.' It is clear that the move(s) will not be used at a public training today but will be practised tomorrow. One Lion is of particular concern and 'if a guy is going to beat Richards then he's going to need the ball in hand and room to move.'

Further diagrams and moves are confirmed and there is a final agreement on placing the ball.

11.15 a.m.
At practice. Line-outs . . . moving the ball at pace . . . code call moves. There is urgency now. TV3 come up to Sean but the coach calls over, 'Excuse me, would you mind going over to the other side?' There is a good kick by the halfback, which earns a 'Good nudge, JP' from his captain. But now Jon kicks poorly and mutters an expletive. 'You all right?' Sean quietly asks the halfback, as his coach advises, 'I think you should get some height, JP.' Now one of the reserves is assigned to play the role of an opposition Lions flanker . . .

Forward practice pauses. Consideration is being given to Lions in the line-out . . . more practices. Jon Preston is still having difficulty with precision kicking. Peter Thorburn has picked up that Jon is calling 'out' or 'down' while the ball is still in the air . . . Now there is clear communication. On receiving the opposition kick-off, Sean makes a firm point to a fellow forward: 'Kamo's got all the area covered and you're standing in the middle of it — let's do it again.'

The whole team trains together. Some guys are not satisfied with the result of a move. 'Once more?' 'Can we do it again, Laurie?' JK is told he must run in the try, and not ease off assuming that he 'is' scoring. Standing on the sideline, Thorbs makes the point to me that the reserves should be included more fully in this week's practices as 'they could be on the field in the first few minutes.' Other moves are tried and repeated until all are satisfied. The guys are switched on already. They are purposeful and demanding. Fox is prominent in asking for moves to be repeated until everything is in place. Jon Preston is under the supportive eye of his skipper. Sean pulls the team around him, midway between the goal and 22 lines, out of spectators' hearing. 'We've got to take control. It feels good at the moment but we want to beat these guys. Let's get control and lift our desire to win. Do the basics well. You've got to put yourself in the position they were in last week — controlled desperation . . . ' Laurie has the team practise the 'wall', with Arran doing the split 'but it's not the way we'll do it on Saturday.'

Earle has been steadily working with the backs throughout training. Fox puts up kicks into the sun to JT and JK. A rubbish bin truck goes past the ground and Frank Bunce — an ex-rubbish truck worker — grins as they pass and wave. Earle advises him, 'Don't you come off your line in this next move Frankie . . . or you'll be back there with them!' It is a typical Kirton throwaway line.

The three selectors check progress together. They agree that the rucks and mauls are not realistic enough today. Laurie moves with the forwards to the scrum machine, and Earle works with Lee on grubber kicks, making the point that he should be putting them through the gap between opposition backs. Now Lee is doing that.

Practice ends. The guys head into the Takapuna Rugby Club building to get their gear bags and walk back to the motel across the paddock. The building is not noticeably clean, and has one-line slogans painted on the inside passage wall which would provide ready fuel for social critics of the rugby world. It would not be only a gay, Jewish-Asian rugby playing politician who would find the setting distasteful. *A Hebrew is a male tea bag . . . Youth in Asia for rapid pain relief . . . Rock Hudson was a pain in the arse . . . Keep New Zealand clean — eat your beer can . . . Most political jokes are elected . . .*

6.15 p.m.
Team Room. JK, Zinny, Sean and myself talk about the mental side of

rugby. Sean openly discusses his being down in spirit after last Saturday's test. He finds it difficult to relax in some settings. In a taxi he often mentally urges on the driver . . . 'You know, sometimes you wonder if you've still got it, if you're still a top rugby player.' Zinny empathises. JK talks about the use of visualisation and his goal setting each week.

6.30 p.m.
The All Blacks walk over to the Rugby Club building for their official team photograph. Neil is critical of the lack of Waikato players recognised by the All Black selectors. (I wonder about this view being expressed, as those selectors include his All Black coach and assistant coach.) The photographer is late. A game builds up with the playing area including a middle circle of 20 cm diameter chalked on the floor. The guys slide coins along the floor into the centre of the circle. I am asked to have a go. My $1 coin looks promising but turns on its side and rolls away, as does JK's. Then comes the $2 round. Again, I am asked to slide my coin. My slide nudges aside the coach's central coin and I win $26 to derogatory calls from the guys: 'Well, that's an end to your interviews, Robin.' I try to put my winnings into the team funds but players insist I keep them. The guys are openly competitive but seem to accept results with some pragmatism, if not equanimity. After the official photographs another set is taken for the sponsors, Steinlager.

7.30 p.m.
At dinner I am sitting next to Foxy, and I'm just into my mushroom soup when Laurie comes in and asks if I'd like to come through to the bar. I gulp down the soup and join the three selectors, the doctor and physiotherapist. Laurie chats to me about the start of the week. 'This past Sunday and Monday were honestly the worst two days of my life. I was so ashamed. I'm responsible, and I accept that. If they play to the game plan with their utmost effort and lose, I accept that. But last Saturday . . . !'

Thursday, 1 July 1993

9.55 a.m.
Team Room. Fitz is whistling as he sits with arms and legs folded, and now silently watches Wimbledon tennis on television. Inga arrives, and drops onto Ant Strachan's lap where Ant sits on the sofa. The players

are in their familiar black tracksuits. Michael Jones is swivelling the upper part of his body and Zinny is stretching on the floor.

Neil has no team notices so it's straight over to the All Black coach. Kick-off for the deciding test is only some 50 hours away. 'Sleep well, Ice?' 'Not really.' 'Why? Are you ready to go?' 'Yeah . . . '

The coach takes a whole team approach. 'We're getting real close fellows. You were enthusiastic at practice. A bit too loose in the second phase play but I know you're as keen as hell. Today, we'll be as realistic as we can be. We'll do the scrum moves. Realistically, just like Saturday will be. We won't tear 10 or 20 metres over the advantage line . . . ' He checks with Arran Pene on this, then moves to discuss understandings of the reserves, before going on to review possession of the ball on the ground. Then runners . . . Kamo's understanding of the wall . . . options are checked with Dowdy . . . 'red hot ball' is made an imperative upon JP's call . . . runners getting the ball back . . . Now it is Thorbs who asks about JP's ball recovery from a ruck or tactical move and Mains asks Jon to explain how he wants the ball. Foxy and Fitz make key points, and Loey's calling of the scrum is commented upon positively.

The coach is concerned at some 'up and at 'em' comments from players and reminds the guys that 'You can't go rip, shit and bust all day. You know the balance, eh?' A move I am now familiar with is checked through in detail on the left-hand side of the field, on the blindside. A selector makes a point about Michael Jones' role in the move. Ice nods, attentive to the speaker's gesticulations and comments from the other side of the room. Then Arran seeks clarity on whether the move is now a set move or simply an option . . . Foxy points out, 'You're really trying to free Michael and then JP.' 'Yep, he's a key man.' JP asks about his position in this and Zinny murmurs, 'You've just gotta stay there.' This is confirmed. The discussion then moves to use of the high kick, the mortar-like 'bombs', which Sean suggests should be used 'even from our 22, eh?' Laurie advises Foxy. 'Attacking bombs, too, as you see it Grant . . . we'll use double runners. Sean's going to run and unload to Ice and then is with him again . . . I know how hard it is JP, if you're clearing the ball, but you've got to have the players there . . . ' A negative piece of Lions play has a countertactic sorted out.

10.15 a.m.

'Okay fellas, the key to today's training is quarter of an hour on the line-out. Backs, your time is all tactical, for example, you get positions absolutely sorted out on the wipers links. I want some definite discussion on the defensive pattern. Look at man-on-man with some variations. I want all this done in an hour and a half. Then we have fifteen minutes going through our options on the paddock and going back if we need to. Then we'll have ten minutes as match play — and we want it absolutely right . . . Has anyone got anything they want to say or check out?' Grant asks if the team can go through what they will do on getting Lions ball. Mains grins, 'Yep. Now I might get a bit carried away when we get going fellas, so you might have to remind me, or you, Earle!' Jamie feels there will be too many line-out callers at training but his captain tells him 'only Rewi is calling, JR.' Arran then explains the calls to be made, although all are familiar. (There seems to be a focus this week on pinpointing errors and tactical needs, planning from these, and an air of working more precisely. Things are under control.) The line-out points generate a brief discussion and clarity about a drive off Dowdy . . . 'We've just got to think now of the first quarter of an hour. We're going to have the ball and stamp our authority on the game . . . let's get it clear guys, we play in their half.'

On the bus to Sacred Heart College for training, the back seat discussion centres on tattoos, with Michael Jones considering one for his ankle. As the players leave the bus, I stand back in my seat to let the veterans go ahead, but they obviously get off last, as they wait for me to go, telling me that 'It's a little custom we have.'

11.25 a.m.

Andy Haden goes through a technical point of jumping with Robin Brooke, as the other forwards listen attentively. They move into another practice . . . Their coach is concerned at an onlooker filming the line-outs. The manager is sure that there's no problem as the media liaison person 'has seen that spectator.' The line-out is intense . . . the reserve hooker throws in with Fitzy at halfback . . . Rigger (Cooksley) throws Kamo out of the line . . . Haden is reminding players that 'no one's strong at the end of their arm . . . ' Mains thanks Haden for his assistance, saying that it gives the forwards something positive to focus on and get into. The two share the experience of having been in the All Blacks, but the commonality begins, and stops quickly, at that point. One is shorter, one is certainly not; the southerner is a weekend fisherman and conservative, whereas the northerner is urbane and verbally volatile. One of the duo is the All Black coach set on his shared vision for the World Cup in two years' time, the other an open advocate of the appointment of Mains' arch-rival for the task. Uneasy the relationship might be but, for the brief period of meeting All Black needs, it is still an alliance — of sorts. And there appears to be genuine recognition of both figures from the players in this session.

Practice has been going well in patches. Mains pulls the All Black forwards together. 'You guys just walked over here. That doesn't show me you're switched on. Now, we'll do this . . . ' Earle is with the backs. After some vigorous exercises the forward pack is into the line-outs. Arran has the field divided into quarters and relates his calls to Matt. He has named code numbers for a drive from the line-out, feeding the ball, and then a 'Willie Away'. After recording every line-out call, I can now tell the throw, receiver and (usually) the resultant move. Mains has asked Andy Haden to add some new perspectives and reinforcement of basic requirements to the line-outs. Haden believes variations are going to be the key, explains to Craig Dowd a technique for jumping in the front of the line-out, and explores specific All Black-Lion pairings in competition for the ball.

The All Blacks are now training with intensity. Moves are checked and kicks that go too far are reprogrammed but, under it all, the cohesion is really kicking in. The skipper calls the team around him out on the field, beyond the ken of spectators. The veteran backs address their forwards. 'There's nothing more motivational for us than seeing you guys going forward over the top of another team,' points out John Kirwan. His centre, Frank Bunce, reinforces this. 'There's nothing I enjoy more as a back than seeing you guys rucking. At times I'd really like to be a forward when you're giving it everything . . . '

The team moves into a piece of play based on winning the line-out. The ball goes loose but is recovered forcefully ('Well picked up, Craig') and the backline swings into a previously unrevealed missile mode of attack . . .

The backs work on their kicking. Foxy advises JP, as they kick to JK, JT and Inga. The forwards, meanwhile, are at the scrum machine. Sean Fitzpatrick has muddied binding on arm, hand and knee . . . the session is exacting. Then it's the end of the promising Thursday — and of final full-on All Black practice before the test.

12.33 p.m.
Autograph signing. A delighted boy in a rugby league jersey speckled

with league badges is in the forefront of a crowd of signature seekers. As they engage the players, Earle comes over to talk with Peter Thorburn and me about the backs' practice. As always, Foxy has been dominant, even 'grumpy'. The past All Black first-five, Kirton, has overruled the present in deciding on a variant play if Buncey goes through the cut, and the cut-out pass to be used from JP to Lee. The backs agree that man-on-man defence should not be used all of the time.

At the bus, kids crowd the players, voices are saying 'let's go, let's go,' Ice is unsure where his boots are and Grant is talking encouragingly to Lee Stensness about his kicking . . . Winding through the streets of Auckland I partially listen to a debate in the back of the bus on the relative greatness of Tamahou of Te Whanau-a-Apanui and Hone Heke of Ngapuhi. (Here on what seems to be a suburban bus, another paradoxical layer of All Black realities is being peeled back. The mythology of unintelligent rugby players is simply that, at least at this élite level. Then, just as one observes the forward and back players debating the mana of two Maori leaders, and their place in their cultural history, an action or a comment, often by rugby's fringe dwellers, fuels the cynics' fire!) Back at the hotel, the players shower and prepare for the afternoon, which will be spent out on the harbour.

1.20 p.m.
The All Black bus is now at the pier but some players are unsure if the bus is staying, so they can leave bits of gear on board, and do not know what the lunch arrangements are. Television cameras are on the wharf and the journalists seek interviews from the guys but they give a firm, 'No,' and board Peter Thorburn's waiting boat.

For some four and a half hours the team environment is laid back, isolated from media and public expectations, and conducive to relaxation. It is an excellent call by the selectors. The blizzard of criticism from outside the All Black tent is in abeyance. The team emerge to bask in some private sunlight. Some have a quiet drink and chat somewhat idly, and the inevitable and intent card school is immersed in their ultra-competitive task. The food is healthy, enticing, and wonderfully presented. The fresh fruit platters disappear faster than a politician's election promise. The wine is mellow. At 4.00 p.m. the boat is virtually stationary, rocking gently in the shelter of one of the gulf's islands, and hopeful lines are cast by a group of intrepid fishermen. A smattering of players continue reading their books. A few small groups engage in a competition to solve some rugby puzzles. The coach is chatting with a couple of players about his own seagoing boat and the escape it brings from everyday demands. The four o'clock radio news evokes a response from the All Black captain, Sean Fitzpatrick, 'Gee, we didn't even feature — great eh?' Out here, in the haven of a luxury boat, this self-imposed seclusion is appreciated by all of the team.

Mains leans on the bow into the flicker of breeze and unfolds his mental and physical reaction to last Saturday's test play and his team's decisive defeat. Over long, pleasant glasses of Stonyridge he describes his self-imposed tensions. 'I reckon I had two hours' sleep on Saturday and four on Sunday. I thought, "Why am I doing this?" Then I thought through where we had come from and that we needed to hold the belief in ourselves — which I have — and plan simply to win the series.' He reflects also on the NZRFU 'brains trust' of great players which had been disbanded and discusses the positive value of the input of ideas on rugby's future from such persons as Wilson Whineray, Brian Lochore and John Graham.

6.10 p.m.
Back into the lights of cameras and Auckland city. The evening places no demands on player meetings, team talks or formal functions. It is the final phase of gearing-down individual and team tensions. Tomorrow is the day before the series decider. Within the team, the initial self-anger has passed into self-demands, and now a mood of quietly expressed confidence has emerged. Training has been more specific, guys have not become overtensed and the team appears to have a clear understanding of what is needed for Saturday. (It appears to me that this week is emerging as better structured, more specific and with a greater integration of the goal and task, understanding, commitment and tactical confidence dimensions than I observed in the Irish test in 1992.)

Friday, 2 July 1993
9.45 a.m.
After breakfast. In the All Black coach's motel room we are 30 hours out from the third test and its 30,000 demanding voices in the match arena. The discussion with Mains is wide-ranging and, as is his custom in such conversation, frank and unrestrained. We discuss the need for players to have time to reflect before they answer the coach's questions in the compressed period of a team talk — time for them to critically

consider the meaning of the coach's question and its implication for the players' role in a move. (Perhaps players could be nominated before the coach's key explanation of a tactic, so that they are prepared to respond . . . The relative merits of positive affirmations, such as 'We're going to do this' rather than 'We can't do this' and 'When I do my best I don't fail' rather than 'I don't want to fail' are the subject of discussion . . . energising words, and simple breathing and relaxation exercises, are considered.)

Laurie is pleased with the team time on the harbour yesterday. He muses on his experiences and interests. 'I can enjoy the experience of fishing and I love being out on the sea but I just catch enough fish to eat. I used to hunt, but now I don't like shooting or killing . . . Deer are magnificent creatures and I don't want to harm them . . . It's not part of my nature.'

Before meeting with the test players today, the coach will note some points for clarification. These are based, in part, upon: killing the ball in the tackle; Winterbottom and Richards, two of the Lions' loose forwards, entering rucks from the All Blacks' side; and Peter Winterbottom's actions at the back of the line-out. He is discussing these with me as the All Black manager enters. Neil wryly expects that the referee, 'Being a good Frenchman, will do things his own way at the end of the day.' He notes that the Lions' management won't agree to a whole team swap of jerseys but will leave the exchange over to the negotiations of individual players . . . The relationship between the coach and manager is superficially in accord but lacks personal warmth and an ease of interaction.

'Today,' says the coach, 'we'll get the guys out to Eden Park. That's their environment. We'll practise short line-outs, "Lion's ball" at line-outs to be won by us, and clarify a couple of points about our defence . . . ' Earle Kirton is due in Laurie's room now. (At times their differing adherence to set times and punctuality throws uncertainty and even some tension into the relationship and can colour player perceptions. At other times, it may be an irritant, or the difference between an ordered but sometimes tense individual, and an idiosyncratic but aware colleague.) Waiting for the individualistic Kirton, Mains expands on coaching: 'I get a real buzz out of the guys I've coached telling me how they are coaching their teams. I think I'd like to leave such guys with a belief in the need for a coach's honesty and commitment . . . I think I'm becoming more open in my approach. Certainly, I'm more open now than at any time in my coaching career. The Group for the '90s [a rugby brains trust, primarily constituted of prominent ex-All Black leaders] opened up my mind further. My critical reflection, that they set off, has now countered so much of my previously dictatorial style!'

Mains muses on the fusion of the week's training in tomorrow's test. 'I want to keep that team feeling we've got this week. One seemingly small thing is an example of this. At Christchurch, when the backs went out on the field before the test, Buncey dropped the ball and the crowd yelled derisively. This morning Foxy came to me and asked if the backs could stay inside the changing room, and not be required to go out on the field before kick-off to loosen up and adjust to the setting. I said it was fine by me. One councillor even rang me to say that I never had the Otago backs outside before kick-off, and was concerned at the crowd's comments to Buncey. We're having the whole team inside for tomorrow's test before they go out for the start.'

10.25 a.m.
The players assemble in the Team Room. One of them asks who has a bath in their room. Ten players have. Sean looks more tense than anytime earlier this week. More intense. Foxy and Fitz check that the video tape of the All Blacks' win over Australia in the third test last year will be here for viewing later today. On a vacant chair the city newspaper's headlines inform the All Blacks, 'Imperative Victory Demanded'.

A couple of players critically comment upon the scallops 'being a bit dodgy' but then the coach arrives. Numbering now — where a player or 'duty boy' calls out successive numbers and the team members, who each have an allocated number, indicate their presence. It is an efficient and rapid check on attendance. Neil runs through the day's programme. At 4.55 p.m. Sean will want the line-out drills run through in the car park, then the team will meet for the video at 5.30 p.m., which will be followed by the captain's meeting with the players. Tomorrow, after the test, players' partners will have to arrange their own time after the match until the test match dinner time. He explains the procedures for jersey swapping. 'Nothing else? Over to you, Laurie.'

The coach takes the team through the visit to Eden Park and raises other points in discussion. 'So we're clear in our minds about starting the game — we'll give that a bit more emphasis at the Park. It's an important factor for our own self-confidence to produce a good start. We've got to do everything right for this match . . . You Aucklanders, you know

Eden Park. If the crowd really get behind you they hum and fizz.' Among specific points raised, Mains notes that, 'There are two things I have in my mind. I have this bloody vision of Dean Richards stepping around the rucks.' He demonstrates the way Richards does this 'and I'm really pissed off about it. What are you going to do about it, Arran?' The coach quickly adds, 'No hurry, no hurry, some of you others think about it too.' He notes a prop's body language, 'Olo's got the answer but let's wait a moment.' Pene replies and the coach then asks, 'Is that how you see it, Craig? That's what I like to hear, Rewi and Dowdy.'

Mains expresses his annoyance at the Lions' illegal tactics and checks on counters for this. Taking out the opposition with tackling that really drills them is envisaged. 'Sucking in' the loose Lions forwards is another key task . . .

Given the Lions' propensity for standing their loose forwards out of the pack there is a need for the vortex of the All Black pack to 'suck them in' by compelling the opposition loosies to add their weight and endeavours to the set phase. Given that setting, the All Black backs and loose forwards can operate on their well-trained merits with greater opportunity to breach the Lions' backline. 'We're tackling them out fellas, we're tackling them out.' He checks on player queries. Foxy definitely wants practice of his team winning Lions' line-out ball. His captain sits quietly intent, his eyes on Laurie, his head on his hand. Fitz then checks, 'Does everybody know what we are doing on the tap moves?' The players nod or quietly affirm their knowledge. There is a question from the first-five and the skipper discusses it. Laurie addresses his onfield leader, 'Sean, let's clarify one point, what are you gonna call?' 'Let's go.' 'If the ball's there on the mark you just get it and go . . . ' adds Foxy. Voices now call out, 'Hey, on free kicks and penalties?' 'Let's double-check this,' declares the coach. 'Okay, let's say you're first there, what would you do?' The response is a little too general. His coach wants specifics so questions them further, 'Yes, will you look to see if the support players are there?' This generates a number of player voices firm in their messages that the team mates *have* to be there. Peter Thorburn adds an incisive confirmation. Arran Pene states that he will be there. Mains picks up on this, pointing out that players' awareness here will be tested in such match situations — that Rewi is making a commitment to his mates in front of them . . . The body position of one Lions forward is noted by the coach as a strength for the opposition and a couple of succinct points in support of an All Black counter are explained.

Tap kicks are discussed only in terms of Lions retiring. 'JP, you can pleasantly point out, "10 metres ref" to the referee,' states the smiling coach. 'Is there anything else?' (I have the distinct feeling that, when he asks this, it is not the rhetorical question it appeared to be in such a team setting a year ago, but is now a genuine seeking from players of any missing piece of the jigsaw of tactical understanding.) Sure enough, JK raises a point, 'Laurie, let's just have a word on discipline in our own half.' Mains refers to the second test try after half-time when the All Blacks were penalised for putting in the ball crookedly. He is informed by the front row that Preston had *not* put the ball in on a crooked line. Olo ventured that the Lions had been penalised for an incorrect feed and he thought the referee penalised New Zealand to even things up! 'There's an important point here fellas,' inserts the attentive Fox. 'Hastings had fifteen shots at goal in the first two tests. That doesn't happen to All Blacks, fellas . . . we can't do that.'

On the whiteboard, the All Black coach explains a move which has been practised ten times by the Lions in training but was not used in the previous test. As the move relies on Andrews, the first-five, Mains addressed Stensness. 'If Andrews got to there, Lee,' pointing to a field position on the board, 'we'd be disappointed.' The Lions move is checked on with a diagram and 'if their 12 does the cut he's not Lee's man — whose target is he? . . . Yep, you've got it. Let's stick to that. Now, JT you keep note of where their fullback is . . . The key here is you, Ice. If Andrews starts heading across the field you just get in and snuff it.' Mains asks if there is anything else to cover in the rehearsal at Eden Park. Sean asks about line-outs — does everybody understand the line-out variations and their use in the All Blacks' own half?' He adds, 'All we gotta do now is get a bit of controlled hate tomorrow. Let's go . . . ' The team makes its way out to the bus for Eden Park. They are a little too tense for a test week Friday . . . On the bus the coach gets up from his usual seat at the front by the steps, and moves along the aisle towards the back seats. 'Hell, what's happening here fellas, has someone died? We're not going to a funeral you know . . . ' He passes jocular remarks with particular individuals and the mood lightens perceptibly.

11.20 a.m.
Eden Park. Players check out tomorrow's test match changing room. The room has four fluorescent tubes lighting it from above and a russet-maroon industrial carpet underfoot. Gear can be hung on the 41

double hooks or stowed in the 21 lockers. The adjacent room has ten showers, each with two controls for pressure and temperature. There are three basins, two lavatories and a single urinal. Out on the park, a few workers finalise hoardings, mark out the ground, and work on repairs in the virtually deserted stadium. Mains calls the team together and advises them to go down behind the goal post and do some simple exercises before they start any moves. The backs then move off to run through a couple of moves and JP gets in a couple of excellent kicks. 'Top nudge, JP,' and 'Good nudge, JP,' from the coach and JK. Preston's confidence seems to be building this week. This is reinforced by Sean's statement now, outside the 22-metre line, after a JP bomb, 'You do what you see as right, JP. Even if Foxy or I call something and you feel you should do something else, then you do it.' A coded move, 'Frame', is called . . . then a line-out call and a reminder from Foxy, 'Hand signals please, JP.' The practice runs on through, including one planned move with Sean Fitzpatrick out on the wing.

In a huddle with Earle and Laurie, the backs discuss their options. (They contradict the belief that modern-day test players are programmed out of onfield decision making.) JK and Foxy are in favour of some situations demanding a spontaneous response, 'Let's just go.' 'Give it a go at the time, and see what option develops from that.' The forward reserves practise three-man line-outs as the whole team runs through a move in response to the captain's command. 'We'll push their defence to that point there, and then swing it straight back without confronting them.' Such a move, often known as 'Postie', after Craig Innes of the 1990s All Blacks, is a virtual replay of a move used by Midland Counties, at Leicester, to inflict the only defeat of the 1931–32 Springboks in England!

Now, Zinny is ensuring that Mark Cooksley has a realistic practice of the two man line-out. Graham Dowd and Sean have turns throwing in to the test line-out and to the reserves forwards.

12.00 noon

In the changing room after the light practice, Laurie Mains retrieves his wallet from me, before heading off to meet with the match referee. Ian Jones checks with Rigger on where he would like to sit in this room before the test. Neil is on his cell phone.

On the bus JK and Foxy comment positively on the Eden Park reconnaissance.

Back at the motel, players shower and change for lunch and move into a free afternoon. A number of them wander into the Team Room, where the dining tables are set up, and browse through the faxes. There are lots of business house messages and some family faxes. One, with special significance for the team, is from the All Black flanker, Paul Henderson, not selected for this test. The rhymes on many are execrable — as is the language from some government agencies and, especially, radio stations. Among the milder comments of some are the exhortations to 'kick arse' and 'stick it up the Lions'.

1.10 p.m.
Press conference in the hotel. It kicks off easily: 'Laurie, how did things go this morning, and were there any problems?' 'No problems, we wandered around, got a sniff of the air.' 'How do you rate your chances?' 'What is important is the tradition of the All Blacks and that the All Blacks play well.' The press ask if there is a change in tactics, about videos that have been watched preparatory to the test, and if Earle has given thought to the Lions' drift defence. Questions move on to whether some All Blacks are playing for their places, the meeting with referee Rabin, pressures on the All Blacks, crowd support and line-outs. Lee Stensness, selected for his first test, is the only individual discussed. Earle notes that, 'Lee has played well for the divisional side, for Auckland and in [pressure] matches against Transvaal and the Lions. He has also played six or seven times outside Grant Fox. The prospect doesn't worry him much.'

After the press conference there is a video of the launch of the All Blacks Club, featuring Va'aiga Tuigamala and a Maori lad. It has overtones of current rugby league advertising . . . players leave the team room for their own free couple of hours. Some of them are critical of a newspaper article's content on All Black earnings. The coaches watch the Springboks–France test on videotape. Earle jokes with Laurie about being dour at the press conference and the coach responds strongly to this comment.

4.30 p.m.
On the lawn outside the motel, a few forwards are practising line-out throws and takes. Twenty minutes later, all of the pack are in the car park for their line-out practice. They begin with Arran Pene calling the codes. The now familiar cries of 'third quarter, 8329, two' or 'tall

timber' begin. Some balls come to Kamo, and Dowdy is moving around the line to take them, another to JR and all forwards come around behind Jamie. Some are in their Steinlager jerseys, JR has his cap reversed, Dowdy has a local firm's logo on his T-shirt. Now they try a Willie Away variant, with the ball going from Ice to Rewi. Now Ian Jones and Robin Brooke are dominant . . . A boy of about ten or eleven years shivers in the wind and waits to get autographs. Andy Haden arrives to work briefly with the line-outs, as some backs look down at their team mates from the hotel balcony.

In the Team Room Laurie Mains is talking with his backs. He is seeking their views on his intention to have the whole team inside before kick-off. He prefers the team inside, JK is happy to do either. They are agreed on the action . . . The players then browse through the faxes. One, some 100 cm long, is from a Christchurch radio station advocating 'Bring back [Graham] Bachop' as the All Black halfback and 'Preston who?' as a slighting comment on the test rejection of the former and selection of the latter. It will be hard for JP to avoid seeing this fax.

Ric Salizzo, the media liaison officer, is concerned that Andy Haden has mentioned in print that Arran Pene was calling the All Black line-outs this week. One of the non-playing team members reacted strongly, and even calls this a treasonable action and Ric is clearly concerned. 'Laurie is not to know.' (The reaction all seems a case of going overboard, as any close observer of this week's practices or a video film analyst could pick the line-out caller.) As I went out to the earlier line-out practice, where Andy Haden took part, Laurie had stopped me with a grin and commented, 'Do you know . . . here's something interesting,' and proceeded to tell me about the action, as Neil had informed him. Mains had, sensibly, not seemed unduly concerned.

5.30 p.m.

The Team Room is filling up with players. Olo is comparatively vocal about receiving a card from a small boy who predicts a 54–3 victory to New Zealand, with Olo converting his own five tries! Faxes and letters are passed around and read. Michael is at the fax table, reading. On one table are balls and autograph books which players sign as they come into the room. Sean, glass of water in hand, asks for the heater to be turned down. Then, 'Number!' Zinny is a moment late, 'Buncey, there's a phone call for you,' which is obviously a personal joke of theirs. Neil asks if anyone left their boots at Eden Park today, and holds up a Mizuno bag.

Laurie, armed with the remote control, introduces the video session. 'We lost against Sydney and lost the first two tests against Australia. Now have a look at your own form in that third test and how you did things.' The room is quiet with guys placing their feet up on the chairs in front of them. Grant Fox is unsmiling, arms folded, one leg over the other, as he makes a point to Sean Fitzpatrick. Fitz makes a note on his notepad. (I wonder if all players should be provided with pens and pads?) Fitz has one leg crossed over the other so he can rest his pad, speaks to Foxy, and records another point.

The commentator evokes smiles and chuckles when he observes that 'Richard Loe is back in defence here.' Robin Brooke is in bare feet. Inga leans forward attentively with his head in his hands. There is a penalty by Grant and Mains approves, 'Good nudge, Foxy.' The sight of Jamie Joseph driving into a bunch of tangled players on the ground, with a shoulder into an Australian, brings muffled laughter and a few comments. Campese steps inside Fox on a breakout but there is no expression on the first-five's face watching this replay. The All Black backs move up into the Wallaby 22 and Walter Little finds touch. 'Good play, eh?' from JK. Michael Jones, head on his hand, scratches his chin, passes a comment to the group on Ian Jones' sofa, then leans back and folds his arms. 'Good tackling, JK,' comes from one of the team, near the end of the half, and then an Australian is penalised. Earle points out this illegal action as one 'this year's Lions do all the time.' Halftime. Sean reads a fax, JK gets a coffee, others stretch and stand . . .

Early in the second half the combative Sam Scott-Young is rendered dizzy — the action causing this evokes some comment. Ant Strachan's break is commended by Foxy, and the use of the chip kick causes JK to remind his fellow backs of its value as an option this week. Troy Coker gets into an irate punching mode, generating, 'Yahoos' and 'Whoas' as he is penalised. Mains smiles as he sits on the table with his Mizuno sneakered foot on the sofa top, just behind Lee's head. Campese slips away but is caught by Inga. 'Great chasing, Inga,' from JK. About fifteen minutes into this second half JR scores and earns grunts of approval from his watching team mates. First on the field to reach him, with arms around Jamie, pulling him to his feet is Michael Jones. At 23 All Black points to 13 Sean leans back, arms and legs folded, head cocked on one side. As the onscreen commentators compliment him he is expressionless in his viewing.

There is general laughter at an Ocker voice bellowing from the spectators to the zealous French referee, 'We didn't come all this way to see you,.you Frog.' With six minutes to go there is laughter at a penalty against Australia. The smile on Fitz's face generated by this widens as he watches Inga carry several Australian defenders on his back. Frank Bunce appears to score and throws his hands in the air with pleasure — his viewing mates laugh and cheer lightly as they now see the referee disallow the try because Buncey was in touch . . . The test finishes, 26–23 to New Zealand. Mains asks if the team wants to see the new television advertisement for the All Black Supporters' Club. 'Yep.' There are a few chuckles now, in the loosening atmosphere, as some of the All Blacks can't easily find themselves onscreen. As more images are screened, the backing Carole King song is picked up by the All Blacks, who softly sing along, 'Winter, spring, summer or fall, all you've gotta do is call, and I'll be there . . . ' It is a most appropriate sentiment for the interdependent demands of a deciding rugby test . . .

6.45 p.m.
All Black captain's team meeting. Traditionally, on the night before a test, the All Black captain meets with his players and no other person is present. The coaches, manager and other team persons, by custom, are absent. The switch to turn off the somewhat intrusive noise of a fan cannot be found. Now, the third test players lean forward as their captain talks about the critical first fifteen minutes of the test. He notes the practice and simplicity of the blindside attack planned this week. Then the forwards and backs' mutual trust is emphasised. 'If you guys [forwards] give me the ball I promise you that we will not go back,' comes a quiet pledge from Grant Fox. Fitz relates this to what the players had seen on the video tape earlier. Urgency around the field is stressed, as in that observed test. 'Olo, myself, Kamo, we're part of the same team. It's the mental attitude, guys. We play well tomorrow for ourselves, the guys here, for the selectors and, especially, for Laurie. He was ashamed of us, as he said on Monday. He puts in so much, like us, he puts in more than anyone else . . . We have to win.' Sean then pauses for his words to be absorbed, then continues in the absolutely silent room. 'We were intense playing Aussie in that winning test, weren't we JR? We took them in that test. Now we take it to these guys — not for ten minutes tomorrow but a full test of controlled pressure, of control.' The captain, in his white Steinlager jersey, removes his right hand from supporting his chin to gesticulate as he emphasises the need to 'put these

guys away'. The room is unnaturally silent.

His left elbow is on his knee and his pen is in his left hand. 'We've gotta make it happen . . . I was probably the worst offender in Wellington with penalties. I can't afford any tomorrow. Kamo? Rob . . . ? I know there's not a lot more to be said. It's Lee's first test, let's make it a good one for him . . . Buncey, can you play like you did in that test we saw? JT? Olo? Talk as much as you like. We've talked a lot this week, let's talk it on the track tomorrow.' The only noise is the background hum of the fan. (I do my utmost to write silently as I sit behind the players.) 'Enjoy it guys, these games are great because rugby is *our* game. Pick it up and have a go! As Foxy said, he'll put it in front and we'll keep it going. Skills and urgency — those two things . . . I'll make that tackle. At scrum time I'll be there.' 'We must make that tackle,' rejoins JK. Craig Dowd is motionless, reserve Matt Cooper silently turns a ball end on end in his hand without looking at it, and Michael Jones leans forward, scratching his forehead as he gazes at Fitz. Ian Jones stretches back. 'Anything else?' asks the All Black captain. 'Okay, we do it for ourselves — and for Laurie. It's been a hard week. Let's pay him back.'

The players stand and stretch. They will meet in here at 10.00 a.m. (I go over to Grant and Sean and thank them for allowing me to stay in the Team Room with the players. The captain smiles, 'Well, without that, it would have left a big hole in your thesis — that's fine.' Foxy is succinct, 'No problems, mate.')

Rubbers (masseurs) set up their tables in the Team Room. In the front of this room Grant and Zinny sit on a sofa, intense in discussion with Sean and John Kirwan, who sit on chairs opposite. They move over to the dining tables. At the meal, Laurie and Sean sit together, opposite Grant Fox and myself. Mains makes the point to his captain to slow down play at an 'injury' to one of his players if he needs, or wants, to take stock of play. 'Have a quick word with a senior pro Sean, like Rewi or Foxy, and just reassess things, pull the game plan back into place or, if you feel it is needed, change the plan, or have Foxy put up a few bombs. Keep the pattern going overall.'

Observing the masseurs, some players discuss their experiences in Japan. In massages they had their teeth cleaned, were shaved, scalp massaged, and 'felt clean inside and out'. Sean smiles as he now observes his centre and flanker with the masseurs, 'Buncey and JR would live on those tables if they could.' The doctor is sitting at the end of the table. Sean asks him who draws the numbers for the players to be drug tested. 'They are pre-drawn at random.' The use of drugs and drug testing is discussed. Fitz seems to think he's tested quite often. Foxy grins, 'I haven't been tested — it's obvious I'm not on drugs! When you see me make a scintillating break and outstrip the defence, that'll be the time to test me!'

8.45 p.m.
Laurie Mains sits on a Team Room sofa. Nearby a card group operates, with Robin, Lee, Dowdy, JT, Jamie and Olo. On the masseur's table the captain, in his pale orange underwear, is making the most of a twenty-minute session. Tracksuit gear is strewn over a couple of chairs. The coach has a quiet word with his veteran centre, then we chat. 'In a lot of ways I feel good about tomorrow. I've never been a cocky person and there's always a nagging worry . . . Overall I think we've basically done what we planned this week. There's been a lot of pressure to take off the guys.' He discusses the demands on giving due attention to his business . . .

Saturday, 3 July 1993
Third test match: New Zealand v. British Isles

10.05 a.m.
The activity is limited. Some players lie on their beds, there is a guitar on one motel bed, guys read programmes, a group is in the physio's room, forwards run through line-outs and backs chat while loosening up with some close passing to each other. The coach looks surprisingly refreshed, 'Gee, I slept well last night. I didn't wake up until seven o'clock and then I slept again.'

The 1993 All Blacks drift into the dining area. They are preoccupied. Jamie, Michael and Frank sit and eat opposite Earl, JT and JK. Buncey is in his grey track hooded top and track trousers, wearing his Mizuno sneakers. JK wears his cap and tracksuit. In the front lounge area, the generals, Foxy and Fitzy, sit on a sofa together, as do Olo and JT, and Robin Brooke and Lee Stensness. They are all reading the test match programme. Stainless Stensness is one of the team in his Steinlager jersey, track suit trousers and sneakers. Fitz, immersed in this four-hour pre-test mode wears his creamy white sponsor's jersey.

Lee Stensness walks from the All Black Team Room with a bowl of fruit and his first test match programme. JK wanders in with a small bottle of fruit drink. He moves to the whiteboard to read the message written there.

Commit to win.
Mental hardness — work rate
Hunger — urgency
Do your task at hand
Their line-out throw is your ball — stay awake
Remember the 'State of mind tasks'
Scrum — tackle — drive — concentrate
WIN — WIN — WIN — WIN

— The Phantom!

(At breakfast Earle had asked Gary Sye, the physiotherapist, who had written the notice. Gary didn't know — and thought it had been Earle. Laurie is happy with the message. I suspect it was Peter Thorburn but the Phantom remains unmasked.)

A Maori couple come into the doorway tentatively. 'Who are you looking for?' asks Michael Jones. 'Jamie Joseph.' JR greets them and quietly shepherds them out. The Team Room is sacrosanct territory — especially on an All Black test day.

11.00 a.m.

Grant Fox enters the playerless room. He gets a cup of coffee and sits reading a programme. I get a cup of coffee and sit down three chairs along from Foxy so that he is not disturbed by my presence, nor feels bound to acknowledge me. As I read the programme he looks over after a minute or so and says, 'This is interesting Robin, you should read this,' and points to an article in the programme. The liaison officers are setting up the Team Room for the 12.55 team meeting. They question if they should vacuum clean it. One sits down and reads the test match programme while the other sets up the furniture . . .

Laurie Mains is in the Team Room to get a glass of orange juice. He idly works his teeth with a toothpick. He is cornered by one of the liaison officers who is talking at Mains about the wind and varied matters. The detached coach gives him perfunctory attention and responds with brief comments . . . 'I reckon it's going to be a test that's pretty fast and furious today,' says the liaison officer. 'Might be,' opines the coach. The voluble one goes on talking to the polite but distracted coach . . . Then the other liaison officer joins them and introduces discussion on the Lions supporter caught with hashish. Then he asks after Mike Brewer. They discuss Brewer . . . and Otago play . . . and the test referee . . .

Dear Grant Fox,

Hi, how are you? I'm fine. I have never written to an All Black before. What is it like to be out on the field? My name is Kaysie-Lee Talbot. I have got a brother who is called Douglas and my sister Jessica. Who are your friends? My favourite All Blacks are you and Jon Preston. Can you please write back and write an autograph, on a separate piece of paper. All my best wishes for you and your friends on Saturday. Bye.
from Kaysie-Lee Talbot.

P.S
If you're too busy you don't have to write back and give an autograph.

11.55 a.m.

The All Blacks coach is restless. He's very quiet. In the Team Room a player wanders in to read the faxes, smiles distantly at me and floats out. Mains prowls over to the faxes, sighs, and idly picks up a large card of good wishes and then the video tape. 'How do you see them? How do you reckon the guys are?' he asks me. I reply that the line-outs couldn't be better, that Foxy always insists on repeats of moves that he isn't satisfied with, that the week has had a clear structure, and he has kept pressure off the team. 'Yeah.' He is hardly a mass of glee. I ask him if he wants to go for a walk around the block. 'No, Robin. You never know when one of the guys might want a word.' There is now sunlight outside.

The physiotherapist's room is an unofficial gathering place on test match mornings. Gary is barefoot, working on Robin Brooke. The liaison officer comes in to get the bags that Gary wants taken to Eden Park. The physio sprays the big lock's ankle and straps across his arch with a wide band of sticking plaster. His client, in shorts, lies on the table on his back, arms folded behind his head. Ant Strachan, the reserve halfback, sits in a chair waiting and jiggles his legs up and down in his track trousers. The unit is crowded with boxes, bags and pharmaceutical products, which take up part of the bathroom also. The physio checks on the tightness of Robin's binding and the Auckland lock stands and pulls on his slip-ons and checks out how he feels. Meanwhile, Ant is feeling the cold, noting it in his fingers especially.

Next, Lee is in to see Gary, two hours before the test begins. He browses through a *TV Guide* while waiting in the chair as the physio unpeels some tape. The halfback's foot and ankle are being taped. 'Happy with it?' 'Yeah, that'd be good.' Now the right knee is taped: starting from underneath the physio cross-tapes the joint. They joke about Ant remaining second to Rewi in the tally of visits to the physio. 'But Ice still takes the cake, mate,' declares the ebullient Strachany. Gary attempts to keep the conversation light with Stensness. 'What length of studs are you playing in? Eighteens?' 'Yep. That's what most of the guys seem to have on their boots.' Gary asks Lee if he has a ritual of preparation that he follows before each game. 'No, I've tried to but I never seem to remember what I did last week anyway!' The physio, having experienced numerous test rooms, makes a clear effort to provide advice in a pleasant way about All Black changing room habits. He explains how Frank Bunce, for example, can suddenly switch on and that, although the ritual test preparations are not absolutely silent or devoid of quiet interaction, 'It still wouldn't be a good idea to burst into "Great Balls of Fire" in the changing room!' Then the physio checks that the second-five's foot strapping is satisfactory. It is. 'Good luck Lee, enjoy it.' JR is next in, bare chested, and lies on his back with his tracksuit leg unzipped so his left foot can be strapped. Then Kamo is in, drops in the chair from an often unscaled height and jiggles his bare left foot across his right knee. 'You're happy with that one?' asks Gary and Jamie declares, 'Cheers mate, that's exactly how I like it.' Now his other foot is done. Then it's Kamo's turn. He is longer than the double sectioned, black, padded table on which he now lies.

Now Zinny is in the physio's room. He straps his ankle himself. Kamo has his left ankle strapped ('it's a bit uneven that ground eh?'), and leaves, with a 'Cheers, mate.' Zinny unwinds a plaster roll and commences taping up his calf and ankles.

12.40 p.m.
The All Black captain is lying on his motel unit bed. He waves abstractedly as I pass. His All Black jacket and grey trousers hang on his door in the pale light of this cool test day.

A jacketless Peter Thorburn makes a cup of tea in the Team Room. Neil comes in and gets his sixth cup of tea for the morning. Earle arrives, complete with a scarf winding around his upper body like a colourful anaconda. The two selectors move out to sit at a table by the pool. Matt Cooper wanders in and picks through the faxes and cards.

John Kirwan comes in, wearing his tracksuit, jogs lightly and shakes each leg in turn. Dowdy and Bull come in and read some faxes. (I thought that the guys would be in their Number Ones but they are travelling to the ground in their All Black tracksuits and carrying their bags and suit holders.)

JK drinks a glass of water while reading faxes, JT sits and sips at his drink of water. On test day all of the reserve players assume the role of 'duty boys' and Graham Dowd and Matt Cooper are placing a table in the front, with three chairs for Neil and the coaches. Zinny is the last player in. Robin Brooke and Ian Jones, the two locks, are seated together. The front row sit adjacent to each other. Grant Fox finishes his glass and places it on the front table. Next to him his halfback, Jon Preston, sits and stares. He stares straight ahead, unseeing. He just sits and stares. Now he looks down, his eyes closed. He has been a key figure this week in the coach's efforts to more effectively integrate his role and command. A number of players sigh audibly. Kamo sips at his iced water as the captain arrives. Sean sits, leans forward with arms on his thighs and exhales. Inga shifts in his chair, grey hair flecked in the light.

Neil and Laurie arrive one minute late. The manager congratulates Lee Stensness on his first test and wishes the team well. Now it's the All Black coach, who is direct, 'There's not a hell of a lot to say fellas. Every All Black in the country is looking to you today to play with pride, with anger, and with aggression . . . Let's go and do it.' The team files out silently. I sit next to Peter Thorburn on the bus. There is no talking. Earle and Laurie converse briefly, in virtual whispers, in the very front of the bus. From their North Shore motel, over the harbour bridge into Auckland city, the bus winds through thronging streets as it nears Eden Park. Spectators glance at the bus and, recognising the players, stop and wave, 'Hey, it's the All Blacks.' A man lifts his granddaughter onto his shoulders and she waves to the team. The players are immersed in their self-demands and mental preparation. Nobody physically responds to the supportive onlookers. Nobody speaks. Grant Fox draws an audibly deep breath in the silence on the bus. JK bites the fingernails on his left hand. Sean is breathing heavily. He tells the bus driver the best lane to take. Pulling into the parking area of Eden Park the bus crawls to the back of the stand. Spectators are gathered around the outside entrance of the passage to the All Blacks' changing room, and call to some players by name. The crowd applauds and buzzes with remarks and support as the team files off the bus, single-minded and self-contained.

1.30 p.m.

The players place their gear in the changing room and move out onto the ground. The captain stands by himself by the goal line watching the curtain-raiser game. He unzips his tracksuit top and moves inside. The Lions arrive, with Underwood's headphones plugged in. In their opponent's changing room Fitzpatrick is taping on his shinguards. Only the All Blacks are in this room. Michael Jones is checking his taped right ankle. Neil and Laurie talk briefly to the two liaison officers who have come in to provide any needed attention. Most of the players are still out on the field area, checking the ground and drawing in the enveloping atmosphere. Fitz now tapes his right leg sock to ensure that it will stay up in play as the doctor comes in to check that Neil has the

correct telephone number to ring for the weather forecast. It is 40 minutes before kick-off as JK and Jon Preston come in. Now Ian Jones jogs
up and down the changing room. Zinny sits down as Sean tapes his left
sock. The coach has been leaning on the physio's table but now begins
to pace up and down, with measured strides, his hands in his pockets.
Inga, in his shorts, is pulling on his black socks. Ice is leaning his body
forward on Gary's table as the physio pushes up the flanker's track top
and rubs his lower back. JR is bouncing a rugby ball as his coach speaks
to him. JT sits on the wall bench seat as Laurie moves to him. Mains
leans over to address his fullback, hands on his grey trouser knees . . .

The doctor works on Inga's back. Sean is jogging around the room.
Individual players are immersed in their self-preparations as their captain advises them, 'We'll warm up in here together at ten past two and
we're going out at 26 past.' Sean moves to sit by Lee, making points
with his left hand. Lee is intent upon his captain's comments, a glass of
a red sport supplement drink in his right hand. Nearby, Arran Pene is
rubbing his legs. Laurie has his final encouraging words for Lee, with a
warm pat of Lee's shoulder. Earle moves to Lee with a quiet word. 'We
make it happen. Make it happen,' urges the captain to his team. Dowdy
jogs, JK does likewise from corner to corner. The coach reminds Rewi
about chasing kicks. Pene, rubbing his left leg with liniment, nods. The
air is threaded with liniment. Pieces of tape are on the floor. Mains now
sits alongside Dowdy and talks quietly to him. Fitz now twirls a ball on
his fingertips and commences to jog. The coach is urging Dowdy to
apply himself and 'drive'. The captain is reminding his blindside flanker
to, 'Keep your low body position JR, low body position, eh?'

Just over half an hour left before kick-off. The NZRFU chairman,
Eddie Tonks, and president, Ian Clarke, come in and shake hands with
Sean and Lee and wish them well. Inga walks over to wish Lee well in
his first test, as does Kamo. 'Have a good one Arran, all the best,' comes
from a team mate. Peter Thorburn and Laurie Mains chat quietly. There
is a call, 'Boots, boots,' as the referee and linesmen enter. The coach
adds, 'Get your boots out, fellas.' (The linesmen make, what seems to
the observer, a cursory inspection of the type and length of sprigs, or
tags or studs on the bottom of players' boots.) Sean walks across the
room after the departure of the match officials, his bottom lip curled
up over the upper, he is immersed in himself. The All Black selectors
stand quietly together. Fitz goes out to toss the coin, returns, raises his
eyes and quietly informs his coach that, 'We won the toss. It's their kick.

Let's hit them.' He moves into the shower room, 'Foxy, Foxy, we won the toss.' Fitzy returns to the dressing room, urging his team to be 'totally focused on what we want to achieve — it's each one of us — there's no tomorrow for this one. Fizz — fizz — we will have 80 minutes of fizz.'

Down on the floor, Kamo is on his knees, stretching his back. Mains has his hands clasped in front of his body as he talks with Earle, then they both move to Frank Bunce and Laurie speaks to him, still clasping his hands. Earle chats quietly to me, explaining how he tries to smile slightly to players as he talks to them, 'so as to not add to their tension'. He comments on the backs staying inside today. He doesn't agree with this. ('Every other sport has its players go out before the event.') However, he accepts Laurie's decision. As he speaks, JK races on a diagonal line across the room, blowing and dodging an imaginary marker. Players belch, get rubbed down, slap a ball into their hand, blow, cough, occasionally fart, and cough again.

From the shower area comes the irregular rhythmic scrape of sprigs on the concrete floor as players jog, jump and run. Some go in for a pee. The three selectors stand by the dressing room door. They see JK come back from the loo, disengaging his mouthguard with his tongue. Ant and Buncey pass a ball to each other until Buncey begins his star jumps, his open tracksuit top flapping with the exercise. Craig Dowd is going into his stretching routine, including his squats. He is a formidable but now self-immersed figure. Fitz is quietly dominant. He jogs while urging his team mates to have 'control, we must have control — and heaps of enthusiasm.' Ant is stretching. Someone else goes off to pee. Fitz pauses in his jogging and looks around in a measured gaze. One group has two rugby balls, passing them to each other as they call each other's name. At 2.05 p.m. Doc Mayhew gets the players' attention, 'Okay, let's go down and do our hammies, no bouncing . . . ' As they stretch and warm under John Mayhew's direction their captain is urging, 'We've gotta be more desperate, more desperate than they are . . . ' Arran adds, 'Communication guys, Jamie and Lee, plenty of communication, eh?' Laurie has his hands in his pockets, standing quietly. A pair of forwards engage in light wrestling to warm up as Foxy walks around in his self-controlled body space.

2.10 p.m.
The prime minister enters the changing room but the guys are in preoccupation mode, and their only concern is to win a rugby test in twenty

minutes' time. Lee is in a corner stretching. A player urges, 'We get ourselves into the game, fellas.' Serious. Focus. Intent. The only smiles in the room are from Bolger and his aide. The former calls, 'Good luck, guys,' as he leaves. The All Blacks are now vigorous in their warming up, doing press-ups, sweating . . . they move into a mini-grid and the captain calls for 'one last quality grid, no mistakes.' Laurie surveys the closing scene of this first act, his hands again clasped in front. Still in his runners, Sean, with his jersey collar up, urges, 'It's not going to come off one set phase, it may be two, it may be three — we go with that.' Arran is also prominent, 'Plenty of talk — there are no short cuts fellas.' A back jogs on the spot, as his captain stalks around the changing room, 'How much do we want it — how much do we want it?' There are vigorous responses from his players. A forward reappears and takes a drink. Rewi places his foot on the physio's table and stretches. Again his dominant captain compels, 'Everyone will chase and tackle, chase and tackle.' Thorbs checks with the doctor on whether he will do any stitching of injuries, if needed, and where it will be done. 'We must win,' growls Jamie Joseph. 'We've gotta,' agrees his captain. 'We want it fast,' declares Pene. Jon Preston answers a query from Michael Jones on a move and then checks with Rewi, the No. 8. Laurie checks with Doc Mayhew on their telephone lines being clear and the numbers being correct. (In this way the coach can observe the play from his grandstand seat and telephone the doctor's cellular phone on the sideline with directions for tactics and messages for individual players.)

Thorburn shakes Lee's hand with good wishes for his first test. Mains rarely intrudes on players' preparations but does so now. 'Control the kick-offs. Get it down there Foxy.' Sean is putting on his grease, brushes his very short hair with his hand, has a pee, ties up his shorts string and pulls on his boots. Rewi comes into the room, 'Get 'em first, eh? Get those tackles first.' JK is pulling on his boots.

Peter Thorburn has a quiet word with Arran as he stretches. Foxy is off to the loo, followed by Michael Jones. All boots are now on. (I want to go to the loo, but don't as I don't want to get in anyone's way.) Sean urges, 'Their kick, their kick, we want to dominate from that. Kamo? Rob?' JP and Robin Brooke pass a ball to each other. Faces have grease on them to ease the close friction of forward contact. Lee comes in from the loo as the coach calls his name. They step towards each other and there is a handshake and 'Good luck' to the first-five from Laurie.

Sean wishes Lee well and declares to his team, 'It's our game, its *our* game today.' The reserves are out of the room now, as are the team officials except for the coach, who pauses at the changing room door and calls loudly, 'Good luck fellas, give it all you've got.' Now there are only fifteen All Black test players, and myself, in the changing room. There is a hug between JT and Inga, JK exhorts his team mates and then the players move into a huddle in the centre of the changing room. The 1993 All Blacks now move out, into the supportive arena of some 47,000 spectators . . .

2.35 p.m.
JT is leading the All Black haka. By 3.00 p.m. the Lions are leading 10–0 but the home players feel confident despite the deficit. There has been some ill-discipline, but the week's practice of chip kicks and support for Lee Stensness to use his judgement pay off. He chips a grubber kick through the Lions backs and Buncey is up on it to score. Mains is relatively expressionless but bites his hand at times. This contrasts with the Lions coach, Ian McGeechan, and their manager, Geoff Cooke, who are often voluble. After some excellent back and forward play, the All Black captain scores. It is 14–10 and the week's combined team practices have paid off. At half-time the basics are stressed, along with the need to maintain both pressure and continuity. Fox kicks two penalties in the second half. Mains is on the phone again, this time to tell the support staff that Matt Cooper should stay on the sideline. 'If Inga isn't fit he's got to come off.' A smidgen of a smile on the coach as Hastings, the Lions captain and fullback, drops the ball over his line. The smile widens a little as JP scores. The doc checks Inga. Thorbs is exuberant as Foxy converts, 27–13. Mains grins and comments to Peter as an All Black loose forward drills an opponent and snuffs out a move. At 3.54 p.m. Michael is off and Zinny replaces him. The crowd support is loud and tangible, culminating in a countdown to end the match . . .

There are hugs, interviews and jersey swaps on the field as spectators and media spill around the players. Back in the changing room, JT and Inga engage in their ritual hug. Lee Stensness stays in his All Black jersey . . . Michael has the guitar, the guys are worn and weary, relieved but not yet relaxed. They pick up on their song, 'Stand by me'. The prime minister is quickly in and sits by Foxy. (An exhausted and cynical forward mutters, 'This might help you get some votes.') Photographers are allowed into the changing room and the team group together with their coach in the middle. Bronnie Fitzpatrick, the captain's wife, is brought into the room, standing with Sean for a few minutes. Mains notes that 'the crowd was bloody good'.

The players slump with relief. Joy slowly suffuses their committed bodies. Team mates recall incidents as they pack ice on a leg, wipe dried blood off a forehead and ease socks down scarlet shins. Sean is recounting a couple of episodes with the French referee, Patrick Rabin. 'In the second half when I checked with him on the reason for one penalty, he said to me, "Shut up, you're talking far too much." "But", I said "I'm the bloody captain!"' The second had its own humour, despite the tension of the final stages. In the last few moments Fitzy asked the referee how much longer there was to go, 'about one minute?' The referee's response may have been a sample of Gallic humour, 'We stop when I say so. This is my only test of the year!' 'Yeah,' adds a player, 'and what about . . . ' Most of the guys wear Lions jerseys which they obtained out on the field after the final whistle.

Mains takes off his jacket, munches a sandwich and listens to Buncey. He then unwinds with his shorts-clad captain. The fullback, John Timu, is sitting next to JK when Doc Mayhew approaches, 'Okay JT, let's do it,' and goes to stitch up JT's eyebrow. The media want to interview Stensness and he moves out of the room in his first All Black jersey. A radio reporter is with Michael Jones, who moves back into the team sanctuary and peels his jersey off, revealing red tracks emblazoned across his chest. Jon Preston, who has been the centre of so much guidance and direction this week, is now a test try scoring All Black. He has an ice pack on his left leg. On the table are Tooheys and Steinlager drinks. (I wonder at the drinking of beer so soon after a match injury. This seems at odds with sport science dictates.) Mains and Fitzpatrick move out for interviews — a pleasant duty after a clear-cut series win.

I sit with John Kirwan. He reflects on the confidence felt by the team, even when they were behind on the scoreboard. 'It was tense out there Robin, when we scored that JP try we knew we'd nailed them.' He sees a radio commentator trying to get his attention and responds. He comes back, 'We did our talking for 80 minutes, and now our series against the Lions feels so good, mate! The support in the park was felt strongly by the All Blacks.' Another All Black adds, 'The crowd was unreal, I've never heard the "All Blacks" chant like that before. When the Lions supporters started up we could hear the crowd respond to support us.' Lee is complimented on his chip kick which led to the Frank Bunce try. He describes it, 'I numbered them off and I couldn't see Hastings, so I made a conscious effort to just chuck it on my foot and put it through.'

Lee warms to his recall, 'Even at 0–10 we were pretty confident — we knew we were playing well . . . when the penalty was reversed and they went down our end they were confident and I was a bit nervous then! . . . I didn't want to let down those guys who'd gone before us.'

Inga starts up 'Hoki Mai' and other singers join in. Foxy hobbles off to the showers. JK gives me his All Black shorts and socks as mementoes of this test. I appreciate the action. Foxy is back from the shower and his captain comes in from yet another interview. The All Blacks are told they will go out into the car parks and then to the sponsors' tents. A few heads nod as the guys change into their Number Ones. Sean eases his slacks up over indentations pockmarking his thigh, compliments of British rugby boot makers.

Mains, still jacketless, is grinning as he chats with Peter Thorbs and myself, 'I think I'm about three years and four stone lighter!' He grins at Lee moving past, red weals scored on his side and backside. Inga comes up. I compliment him on his excellent take of a high Lions kick. 'I simply had to, mate.'

5.20 p.m.

The two major team leaders, coach and captain, stand in the centre of a now dishevelled dressing room in conversation with the Iceman. Foxy comes up and generates laughter as he tells the story of one player making a financial gain from the test. 'We were at a scrum in the Lions half when Stainless suddenly spotted a $20 note on the paddock. So here's this guy, in his first test, a series decider, and he crabs across a few steps, keeps his eye on the scrum, picks up the $20 bucks and tucks it inside his All Black sock!'

Sean and I look back over the singular week. He smiles at having felt a little threatened for his place in the team after the second test. 'It certainly caused me to look at things more closely.' But now, an air of contentment and achievement fills the room. Songs. Tentative testing of bruised muscles. Drinks. Sandwiches. Foxy is warmly shaking Inga's hand. Neil presents Lee with his first test tie. Lee replies briefly. The coach speaks. He tells the players that partners are welcome in the Team Room after the test dinner, thanks the team . . . and adds, 'Hey you guys, one thing.' He grins, 'let's be humble eh?' The guitar is passed along the seated players. Zinny passes it to me with a request for some music. Then Michael has it. 'Under the Boardwalk.' JT is smoking, his darkened stitches heavily apparent. Mains is sitting with his first-five. Foxy directs his mates, 'One more song, one more song.' Bags are on the floor, cans are opened, 'I feel wonderful tonight . . . ' The coach has a small bottle of beer in his hand. He looks relieved and is winding down.

6.00 p.m.
The All Blacks, having been under siege from public and media demands for a week, move out into the Eden Park car parks. Some have called in at the Supporters' Club. Media people are having drinks from car boot hampers. Tardy test revellers, moving to the gates, stop to observe or, hopefully, engage the guys. Almost all of the car park crowd are Pakeha. Sean and Laurie move forward to a group and chat with them. Autograph seekers approach players. The occasional car departs, crunching over empty beer cans. Neil talks with a fellow who has hazy eyes, the overcareful speech of an imbiber, and a pair of binoculars slung around his neck. JP looks up to his taller target, who has a cap, long coat and boots. The halfback is listening politely to an account of the All Blacks' deficiencies in the match.

Laurie and Sean chat with me, detaching themselves a little from the public interaction . . . Players now tend to congregate with the more gregarious and younger media people, who are liberally stocked, internally and externally, with liquor. Buttonholed by individuals, the All Blacks are polite and pleasant in response to autograph requests. One spindly grey-haired woman quietly takes her programme around the players.

It is now dark in the car park. Lights flicker and retreating car lights temporarily silhouette the groups and locate momentary shapes behind voices. A couple of my students come up and ask for help in getting Michael and Inga's signatures. This Samoan duo are walking to the bus. 'I'm so proud for the people when I play well,' confides Michael as we board the bus. He and Inga sit alone in the back and softly sing Samoan songs as they wait for their team mates to disengage themselves and return. It is a special post-test vignette. Outside, the hospitality tents are emptying. On the bus, Michael keeps naming the songs and Inga keeps growling them out. Now the bus fills up, a player from here, a player from there, now a duo from the dark . . . and still the test encounters are recalled — as are the feelings of effort and commitment. A forward confides to his seat-mate, a back, 'With five minutes to go, boy, I was absolutely stuffed out there.'

The bus revs up and moves out through remnants of the crowd and cars and slows to pick up the remainder of the team. Olo gets on, shakes Lee's hand and seats himself. 'Number!' Whoops — where's Zinny? And his brother? Rob ascends the bus steps slowly. Recognising the All Blacks, a group of Lions supporters hold up a home-made flag and a sign declaring 'New Zealand beer is still crap.' (Think what you like fellas — just look at the scoreboard when you're sober.) A voice floats aloud in the darkened bus, 'I tell you what — the whole place is fizzing.' The bus pulls out with the winners and the weary. Drink cans are passed along the bus to thirsty team mates, from the well-stocked rear seats. Pulling out, the bus is cheered by all of the car park crowd. There are three cheers from one big group, applause from others . . . A sardonic All Black voice breaks the tired dark in the bus, 'Yeah, clap now, we didn't hear too much from you all week.' It may not have been an entirely fair comment, it may have been a lubricated finger flick at the fickleness of public support, but for now it was a way of saying, 'Yeah, *we did it.*' And so they had.

The evening sees a test match dinner of the usual participants, in which the New Zealand propensity for pumpkin soup on menus is noted by a Lions speaker and a telling point made on his team being the British Isles and Ireland — not the British Isles, as officials and media so often designated them. It is a typical and customary male-oriented occasion. After the dinner, team members and their partners gather at the motel Team Room. As with any group of predominantly young people on a New Zealand Saturday night, there is wine, liquor and beer — but nobody is disorderly, obviously drunk, excessively noisy or rude to others. On the contrary, groups chat, introduce partners, and make newcomers welcome. It is a pleasant, intra-team couple of hours . . . Did I say couple of hours? Hmm. The crowded disco boogies on, and the evening hours unravel into early morning. And every time the test is recalled, the All Blacks have still won . . .

In the hindsight of a mellow post-test Sunday the newspapers make good reading. The test will be one of New Zealand's special victories of the 1990s. The Lions are criticised for their negative play but the All Blacks are seen as having played at pace, varying the game and negating the Lions tactics. The *Sunday Times* reports Fitzpatrick's statement, 'I knew that if we played as well as we trained then we would win.'

Such a week would not always be typical of Mains' coaching reign. Nor would the team always consistently 'produce the goods'. On this Sunday, 4 July 1993, it would be a churlish rugby follower who could not agree with Laurie Mains that there was particular pleasure 'going into the dressing room and having so many players express delight that they'd achieved the game plan.'

This dramatic week had brought a range of insights, rarely revealed first-hand to the public. The feelings of pressure from the public, media and (tellingly) the retired All Blacks, ranged from concerned to absurdly parochial. The team had filtered these out and taken into their motivation the criticism from their peers — past and present All Blacks. A clear game plan was developed, the key elements explained and training was match-oriented and focused on the tactics.

The coach had geared his anxiety down a notch, kept a close hand on the team climate and worked closely with his captain. Only one new player had been introduced, and he was encouraged to play his game within the broad plan, with freedom to make decisions as he saw the need. Critically, as the pressure began to rise, the team had time out. In the wings, the support staff and key personage of Peter Thorburn had played their essential roles. Inside the All Blacks for a series decider had been a compelling week.

11

Living with the All Blacks off the field

At the hotel we were disturbed in the early hours when [player Y] leapt into our bedroom through the window at two o'clock in the test day morning, returning to the team hotel via my husband's room.

Wife of 1956 All Black

Life off the rugby field falls into three broad areas — home test weeks, on tour, and non-test times at home. The behind-the-scenes scenario of a test match week, at home or on tour, reveals a progressive build up to the game, social settings, some player free time, and functions to fit marketing and public relations demands. All Black team activities off the field do vary from home test week to home test week but the basic pattern remains. Away from test match rugby, All Blacks have treatment for injuries, cope with domestic and personal difficulties, enjoy home life, attempt to keep up with study or a part-time career, and meet the increasing demands of professional sport. The last includes fitness training and playing for provincial or Super 12 teams. On tour the All Blacks structure their weeks around test matches, meet the demands of official functions and utilise all 'free' time to relax or act the tourist. Off-field life for past All Blacks reflected a more ordered, slower paced and secure society. The women in All Blacks' lives have received increasing recognition from administrators and social observers in recent decades.

The opportunity to visit new places and meet well-known figures is a bonus of All Black selection. In the modern era the time for off-field relaxation and escape to non-team environments is relatively curtailed. Some off-field activities, such as visiting game parks in Africa, provide memories that privileged — and wealthy — tourists may emulate. But money does not necessarily purchase a meeting with Nelson Mandela or the royal family of England. Touring South Africa gave Sean Fitzpatrick the opportunity to meet President de Klerk.

> He was a relaxed person, sipping on a Scotch . . . and he was clearly surrounded by a high level of security. I was really struck with his armour plated Mercedes up on the road. This did 3 km to the litre, weighed three ton and had lead linings . . . at the other end of the time-out scale I remember the guys going out shooting. One early morning Loey arrived in my bedroom with evidence of the buck he had shot.

Europe offered other interests. John Kirwan states: 'I had done some history at school but when I actually spent a few days there [in Italy] I got quite taken in by all the feelings of history — the age of the place was revealed around every corner. I loved it. That's part of the reason why I went back to play there.'

A typical tour break for a recent All Black team was in Sydney, when the players escaped from the demands of the job out on the harbour. Olo Brown and Mark Cooksley engage in chess battles, a poker school operates, guys sip a beer and talk, a few read books, others chat with their Australian hosts. An electronic skeet (clay bird) gun competition is organised. The targets are catapulted into the air and the guns fire an electronic beam at them. A hit is recorded on an electronic scoreboard. Preliminary heats are worked through and then the final of a very competitive series is held, which results in Olo Brown defeating his captain and an accompanying team researcher.

Living with the off-field All Blacks still often means living with active competitors. Zinny Brooke is arguably the most relentless of these, but others are close. Golf is a compulsive encounter on tour as well as during home test weeks. Few contests over the decades would rival a twosome between Zinny and Mike Brewer. Other players bet on holes, needle each other and 'sledge' with delight. But Zinny and Bruiser bet on single shots, holes and the competition and drive a golf buggy with a spectacular immunity from disaster!

Different players require different approaches off and on the field. Earle Kirton, who played 13 tests for the All Blacks during 1963–70, recalls an off-field evening:

> Before my first test I couldn't sleep and walked across London at 3.00

a.m., watching black cabs and wandering all over the place. Jazz Muller was eating a massive steak in the cafe at the Hilton. (We were told his mother used to leave great steaks out for him to eat at night!) Bunny Tremain told Fred Allen [the All Black coach], who replied that when he was playing as well as that, he could go out at night like that also. 'So there's a lot to knowing your players!'

Media and commercial demands

The media shape public expectations, demands and personal criticism, and may misconstrue or misreport team happenings. Terms such as 'battle lines', 'war' and 'must win' reflect, and add, to the tension. The improvement in media liaison under John Hart has been instrumental in changing elements of All Black–public communication with commensurate positive off-field reporting.

The media feast voraciously on off-field activity. Think of Keith Murdoch or Joe Stanley, for example, and their tour publicity over physical incidents, the 1991 World Cup non-public relations or the 1997 television record of All Blacks' comments when subbed off the field. Off-field behaviour affects public perceptions, as was seen during the World Cup in 1991. In what Phil Gifford described as 'the most publicised public relations disaster', the Wallabies went for a walk in Dublin's main city area the day before their semi-final against New Zealand. They pressed the flesh, talked with the Irish citizens and earned uplifting crowd support the following day. The All Blacks remained in purdah and thus drew more muted support.

Then think of how little is recorded of earlier tours, especially pre-Second World War. Imagine the publicity in today's media if an All Black on tour was apprehended by police after smashing a streetlight on a well-lubricated evening. On the 1935–36 tour Bill Hadley administered a *coup de grâce* to a fancy streetlight in Bristol. The police went to the All Blacks' hotel, knowing they were looking for someone named Bill — and took away Bill Collins! The manager, Vinnie Meredith, appeared at the police station. 'I am the Crown Prosecutor,' he announced (as indeed he was in New Zealand), and secured the release of the innocent Collins.

A test against the All Blacks is big business locally. In one test week in the smallest of New Zealand's four usual test cities, Dunedin, there will be $3 million generated in the local economy; 10,000 visitors to the temporary Steinlager Village; and 15,000 extra litres of the local Speight's beer and 20,000 pies consumed! Off-field engagements for the All Blacks in such a week include hospital visits, usually by the reserve players, corporate lunches, with players dispersed among tables around the room of white-shirted businessmen, and sponsors' functions. In the professional era — and in the years leading up to it — the commercialism of rugby has governed certain periods of All Black test and tour weeks.

Memories of early tours

The inclination of touring All Blacks to keep diaries has been variable. Merv Corner played 25 matches for the All Blacks during 1930–36, and kept a diary on his 1935–36 tour of Britain. It relates an experience of English life unlikely to have come the way of this Auckland bank clerk if he hadn't been selected to represent his country.

Tuesday, 29 October 1935. We breakfasted at 9.00 a.m. and shortly afterwards set out on our Pigeon Shoot. Unfortunately we were a week too late for the best of the season but nevertheless saw plenty of birds, but George Hart and I were the only ones to arrive home with one each. It was great fun but the shooting was much more difficult than we had imagined.

After luncheon we had more shooting [rabbit] and with the aid of ferrets we had plenty of good sport. In my school, my partners being Pat Caughey and Rusty Page, only once could I lay any claim to a kill, but one thing I did bring to earth myself was a pheasant, only to find it a hen, so the game keeper smuggled it home out of sight. A chat followed tea, dressing, then dinner. This evening meal will live long in our memories. The beautifully polished table with Lord and Lady Bledisloe at each end and the visitors arranged along each side, viewing one another over shaded candles, was an experience for all of us. Mr & Mrs Lysaght and their son were present. Mr Lysaght is the 'Old Man' of the steel trade of England and a very interesting and powerful personality. The meal concluded, we all enjoyed a smoke listening to an election speech of Sir Philip Snowden. The speaker's reference to the poverty and unemployed of England was hotly contested by Mr Lysaght and, in fact, seemed to decide the publication of a letter he had written on the subject.

Monday, 11 November. Armistice Day in London found the New Zealand team at the Cenotaph in a section reserved for us. I saw the most impressive sight of my life. The huge crowd thronged round the Cenotaph, the street lined with soldiers of many regiments and sailors, Royalty and important Englishmen doing homage to the brave dead, their heads bowed, ambulance men attending to fainting ladies, old soldiers with their medals donned, that two minutes silence when it seemed that the very heartbeat of nature had stopped, and finally the sounding of the Last Post, could not but touch the soul of one and all of us. I am sure that I will never see so impressive a scene again. We saw the march-past and the wreaths gradually piling up at the foot of the Cenotaph, and then joined the dispersing crowd to return to the hotel.

Monday, 23 December. We went by train to London. We arrived at 2.30 p.m. and just in time to attend a tea given in honour of Jack Lovelock by 'New Zealanders in London' for the purpose of handing on to him a writing desk from the Athletic Association in NZ. Jean Batten was to be there, but a real London fog prevented her keeping her appointment. We also received a gift in the form of a silver cigarette box, suitably inscribed, and one by one we wound our way through the guests to receive our presentation from Sir James Parr. At the same function, we were given a silver ash tray, a Christmas gift from Viscount Bledisloe.

In the evening, Dr Macintosh took George Hart, Eric Tindill, George Adkins and myself to the Bertram Mills Circus at Wembley. Getting there, we saw just how bad a London fog can be for, so bad was the visibility, his Rolls Royce had to be abandoned for the underground railway. We had a grand night and saw a circus that I will never forget. In our party was Mr Torrence, a plus-4 golfer and former captain of the English Walker Cup Team. After the performance we saw the performing fleas and other sideshows before returning home to the Doctor's house for supper.

Past tours entailed weeks of sea travel. For some players this provided memories that lasted all their lives. In 1935, on their voyage to England, players' diaries often noted the doings of 'Doodle' or 'Lanky' Wynyard. The youngest member of the team, sometimes also known as 'Bubs', Wynyard was the major victim in the crossing-of-the-equator ceremony, a day before his twenty-first birthday. Merv Corner recalls:

Father Neptune and his followers took charge of the ship when it crossed the line at noon. Charlie Oliver was Neptune and other chaps who had been over the line made his court. There were only three certificates to be had on the ship so we drew lots for the chosen three and Jack Best, Jack Griffiths and Jim Wynyard drew the lucky and unlucky numbers ... the barber, Mike Gilbert, after covering them with paste and shaving them, handed on his prey to the policemen, who duly delivered them into the pool, where the bears administered a sound ducking.

The following day, Saturday 13 August, brought another entry:

Just before dinner, Jim Wynyard, who was 21 today, was given a dress cigarette case, the presentation being made by Mr Meredith ... A twenty-first birthday comes once in a lifetime, so naturally the team made it an excuse for a night out, and what a night. After several rounds just as the bar was closing, our last order of 50 bottles was made and, as they were all consumed before we finished, it is easy to imagine the night was a howling success . . .

Some 57 years later the poignancy of that young player's death had hardly been dimmed for his fellow soldiers. The untimely cessation of one All Black's dreams came on 2 November 1941. A fellow soldier recalls the episode:

Moments later, I was looking at Jim Wynyard's tank when it was struck in the turret by two armour-piercing shots — just as though one had banged a blanket with a fly swat, dust appeared. It took fire almost instantly; Jim Wynyard appeared in the open turret trying to get out; raised himself to about waist height, then slumped back inside. There was never any sign of his gunner or wireless operator but Snowy Ward, the driver, got out of his separate driver's hatch . . . Thus perished Capt. Jim Wynyard, his driver Peter Fullerton-Smith, and gunner A. Loe . . . poor Jim, he never lived to achieve his ambition of driving a carrier down the Unter den Linden.

Eleven years of potential All Black test rugby were lost, in a period of 32 years, to two world wars with all of their attendant tragedies and bonding memories.

Test weeks

In test weeks, free time is spent quietly with friends or family, playing golf, hanging around the hotel, watching rented videos or relaxing in the Team Room. Some players do a little extra preparation. Mark Cooksley's team mates still remember one of his early tests. On a free afternoon most of the guys were out of the hotel, but the coach noted a figure hunched over the video recorder in the Team Room. He went in, to discover Rigger repeatedly playing the tape of opposition line-outs and writing the tactics and code-calls in a notebook.

A key element in off-field preparation for a test is the coach's meeting with the referee. A typical session covers the rules and their interpretation. In one such meeting the referee explained he wanted the ball cleared quickly. 'When a maul is stationary I will be saying to the boys, "Use it, use it." Discussion covered tackle interpretations, rucks, driving over the top and taking the opposition out ('Clearly, if they're on the ball that's okay, but not if they're a metre or so away'), binding ('The specific law must be followed, bind with the arm or get back, bind on or piss off'), sprigs . . . An international northern hemisphere referee emphasised the importance of the captain's communication — and believed that 'even the coach saying something positive to the referee at half-time is important!' One wonders at the self-confidence of such an official needing reassurance from a coach in the intensity of a test!

All Blacks in court

Another dimension off the field is rugby's 'Court Session'. A feature of most first-class teams, the Court Session is a traditional occasion conducted by those of a more social disposition in which members are subjected to demands to down drinks or face various fines and penalties. Although some teams, not necessarily in rugby, prescribe only beer, the All Blacks allow a choice of drinks, and the emphasis on extreme beer consumption has gone. Some Court Sessions result in an overt or covert clash between the judges and those with formal responsibilities, such as the coach or captain. An example of this occurred after the successful second test against South Africa in Wellington in 1994. Brewer and Loe, a formidable duo, were intent upon a more lengthy bout of drinking than the manager desired. Pinetree Meads prevailed, making it clear that no player was going to leave the Court Session having consumed more than a couple of drinks, as they were meeting their friends and families in public. Drinking was, to meet the needs of the occasion, to be carried out by the mouthful, rather than by the jug or can.

'Tis not always thus! In contrast to the All Blacks, an account of a top team's Court Sessions illustrates this off-field tradition:

> Back at the team motel, before the evening meal, in the Team Room, the Court Session preliminaries are under way. An experienced loose forward and second-five duo are the Judges in charge, as in the previous team court. (They are quick masters of repartee and tolerate little questioning of their powers or decisions, regardless of the fairness or logic of the defendant's reply or defence!) The manager quickly covers a couple of organisational points before the session gets fully under way. He notes the need for good behaviour this evening, and details the duty boys for tomorrow. No outsiders are allowed to be present. In the second match of the observation period the Court Session had included two local union liaison men, and was mainly a series of fines and punishments for individuals who misused numbers and confused sequences,

or alphabetical puzzle segments. Hats had to be worn at that court, and each member was assigned a number. Punishments for not following instructions, or for incorrect answers, or disputing the court leaders' decisions, were inevitably in the form of compulsory drinking . . . of beer, fruit juice, or water — the choice of drink was up to the group member. (This is unlike one national level team whose coach informed me that, upon taking up his position, he found all players had been expected to only drink alcohol. He was so concerned about this aspect of court sessions that he cut them out in that form.) Tonight, we each sit next to our number-mate: 1 and 2, 3 and 4, up to 25 (masseur) and 26 (myself). It is a big circle and everyone has to have on a white shirt. Each person has a choice of drink, and spare jugs of orange juice, water and beer are placed around the floor.

Drinking is to be done by the left hand only. 'Pimps' are named to inform the court leaders of any court member who does not follow instructions, or who is a disruptive influence. A compulsory fast round is called. Each player, in turn, jumps to his feet and unloads the contents of a large glass or small jug down his throat as soon as the player on his left has done so. Any laggard is punished with an extra drink. (I hardly swallow as the water gushes down, mainly in my throat and some on my shirt. I want to be inconspicuous and unnamed by the pimps. A Samoan winger downs his orange juice at the pace he outsprinted today's opposition defence.) The restaurant sends a message to come to dinner, but it is put to the side by the Judges. The ritual continues.

Another round, to break the speed record. Like a single-line Mexican wave of spray we stand, gulping down a drink each, to then individually subside. A chant follows each person by name, building up to the players sitting alongside the Judges. 'Okay, the next penalty is for dishonesty. You must name every woman you have slept with in the last month.' Each player jumps to his feet, gives a name, downs a drink and sits. Player X begins to name a list, but is penalised for lies and boasting, and punished with a fast jug to drink. The restaurant sends another message that dinner is ready.

(The coach and his partner are adjudged guilty of a misdemeanour in front of the Judges for not drinking with their left hand. They are compelled to drink a fast jug, and when the coach disputes the ruling they are ordered to repeat this punishment.)

One of the Judges tells a joke which evokes little response. He declares, 'When the Judge tells a joke it's always bloody funny, so I want to hear you laughing — or face your punishment.' The short and dumpy masseur rolls around in laughter at the team reaction. The Judges finally decide to respond to the now irate final message from the restaurant. The manager checks with the duty players, and everyone heads down to evening dinner.

The Court Session had been informative and the team leadership passed to two players, with the official leaders placed in subordinate roles.

This is a role of the captain and coach not observed at training and practice. Comments made at the dinner table indicated that the captain and coach were respected, in part, because of their ability to participate in such a situation with no obvious rank, yet did not 'overstep the mark' by becoming drunk or behaving in a demeaning way. Examples were given of past team leaders who had not been like this . . .

Friends and relations

Off the field, All Black families suffer threefold when a test is on. There is the intensified and personalised identification with the team and its fortunes, the parental worry about injuries and the Kiwi spectator role in barracking for a win. Watching an All Black test on television with the parents of John Kirwan demonstrated these dimensions. His mother admits, 'I do worry about him. I worry what might happen while the game's going, and I'm always glad when the game is over!' Her husband, Pat, eats his homemade tuatua fritters and emphasises the basic values he attempted to instil in his son as a boyhood coach. Mrs Kirwan adds, 'The basic values are so important. I remember one day at Papatoetoe when the boys were about nine or ten years old. One kid tried to kick one of our team so the whole team was pulled off the field as that wasn't what they were there for . . . ' On screen their son aggressively bundles a Wallaby over the touchline, evoking a mother's response, 'Oooh, don't be so rough — I don't like it when he does that!' Father has a different view, 'Ah, maybe so, but he's letting them know that he's there.' JK had rung his folks and told them of the coach's expectations of him and the need to be more involved in making play, so his parents have an extra dimension to look for in the game. In a break in play, they debate their differing preferences for league (father) and rugby union (mother)!

In test week there is always a fax for the All Black captain from his parents and one for the team from them. Other members of Sean Fitzpatrick's family always send messages. Fitzpatrick's balanced perspective of rugby within the totality of his life, in particular the natural integration of rugby and home life, has created a positive picture of an All Black leader within the team setting. One team talk on a test match Friday was a couple of minutes late in starting as the captain was quietly finishing a brief time with his daughter, Grace. In the social situations in which the players and their partners find themselves, Bronnie Fitzpatrick eases newcomers into the setting and is adept in her support and individual way of facilitating life off the field.

Off-field life for All Black wives and partners has varied markedly. Wives were excluded from most formal and informal rugby off-field settings into the 1980s and 1990s. Cooking, caring for the children and waiting in the car park were more frequent activities than attending a test-match dinner or post-match social event. One spouse recalls:

> In 1956 [my husband] was suddenly picked by the All Blacks and wanted me to go and be with him. He had a single hotel room. I flew down and got to the airport and then more or less crept up and deposited myself in his room. We were pretty frightened. He said, 'We'll have to pretend in the hotel that we don't know each other.' The night before the test we didn't get much sleep . . . it was a time of warfare, we simply had to beat the Boks . . . at the hotel we were disturbed in the early hours when [player Y] leapt into our bedroom through the window at two o'clock in the test day morning, returning to the team hotel via my husband's room as he didn't want the selectors to know! . . . It was absolutely archaic in those days, the approach to All Black wives.

All Black wives and partners of the later 1990s note the off-field changes.

> The players are away so much that the women have to be considered much more than in the 1950s. Many wives and partners turn up on tour at the same time as their menfolk, and have a much higher profile than in yesteryear. In a recent fashion supplement of a daily newspaper, the wives of two current All Blacks were interviewed about their choice of clothes for watching matches, attending after-match functions, etc.

The main change is that the women now have professional rugby partners and are often given a high profile because of their more public careers. Thanks to singular efforts over the years by such All Black wives as Trecha Hayden, administrators' attitudes towards players' partners and wives were challenged to change. Before the World Cup, Laurie Mains and Kevin Roberts arranged for wives and partners to be flown to Sydney for time with the team. That was much appreciated. Under John Hart also there are clear efforts to consider wives and partners.

An All Black's time away from home impacts on wife or partner and on children. Grant Fox, on retirement, pointed out how the years of touring and test match weeks had affected his children. There was difficulty, at times, in getting to know his son and daughter again, and some key stages in their young lives had not been shared with their father because of his All Black duties. A contemporary, Frank Bunce, comments: 'The public see the glamour — and nothing else in my life would bring me such recognition or open so many doors — but they don't see your kids look at you as though you're partly a stranger. They don't know how you feel when it's your child's birthday, and you are missing it — again . . . '

Sex and the silver fern have never been alien to each other. The off-field engagements of the 1888–89 Natives team included the romance between Davy Gage and an English gentlewoman. The 1905–6 Originals were officially affected by severe influenza but the players have passed on unofficial accounts of syphilis contracted in ports far from home. Rarely have the All Blacks, however, been seen in similar vein to French or Lions teams and their liaisons. Contrary to the view of certain social critics, few sports or workplace teams could match the 1950s All Blacks for unbroken marriages.

It would be absurd to believe that off-field life for any sports team does not include a degree of sexual dalliance or the odd gratuitous relationship — and not only among single players. Double standards are at work in some cases, but the usual reality of touring is that of training, travelling, sightseeing and competing.

A recent All Black and his girlfriend provided insights into touring and perspectives on women and rugby while at an end-of-season function. She commented on the segregation of the sexes: 'Look around here, it's still a macho game in the way women are secondary to rugby. I think there's still an old boys' network operating. I do worry about him [on tour] and what could be happening. I get concerned and know I might not be right. I talk to the priest and people near me. But their comments on rugby behaviour don't often help as they aren't close to rugby, and have stereotypes of rugby players in mind. I think of players on an All Black tour and the talk about their sleeping around, and yet I know he isn't like that.' She noted the differences between the club and representative scenes. 'The rep people (and even more so, the All Blacks) might treat you more equally, but you see club wives and partners more often than rep ones, so there's more cohesion among the club women. I didn't know much about rugby, though, at first. Yesterday I was quite sad when the season was over. Once I got to know positions, and more about the game and what rugby is, I enjoyed it, and now get more out of following [my boyfriend].'

This woman's partner talked of the macho image of players and the tradition of the back seat of the All Blacks' bus being occupied by senior players. As a 'new boy', he sat in the front of the bus. He provided a picture of the touring team, with its endurance of the 'heavies', or boring conversationalists, who become a problem by forcing their attentions on the All Blacks. 'Like some of the women, the heavies just zero in on you and show an interest. It's difficult to get rid of them. Nobody ever has a word with a younger player about how to meet with people like that in a social situation. Sure, you might have a signal and be helped out by a team mate if you're being bothered, but the management seem to assume you know how to engage in small talk.' He described his first game for New Zealand, when he thought of everyone who'd helped him develop his rugby, and who mattered in his life and was important to him. He thought of his girlfriend deliberately, just before running out in his All Black jersey for the first time: 'I'll play this one for her . . .'

Increasing demands

In early All Black tours and home test series the pace of life, demands upon time and examination by the media were markedly less than in the era of professional rugby. However, in the 1990s seasons immediately prior to the introduction of formalised professional rugby, the off-field commitment of All Black players to training and rugby-related activities was high. A survey revealed ten players averaging 6–10 hours' training a week (Monday–Friday) and six spending 11–15 hours. Additionally, in that final year of the amateur era, the time per week spent on non-training rugby activities was 6–10 hours for seven players, 11–15 hours for three players and over 16 hours for another four. Overall, the average time spent on rugby related activities *and* training was some twenty hours.

The All Black coach also faces off-field time commitments. An observer's notebook illustrates this:

> The All Black coach receives a telephone call from a sponsor executive about a player who 'feels he is in a hopeless position at the moment'. He discusses with the executive the need for player security, assistance with the player's financing of a home for his parents and employment security. 'I felt quite devastated by the whole thing. I think now that despite the fact that rugby needs X right now, I want to help him get his life sorted out. If we could get him through to the World Cup that would help him sort out his future.' He moves on to discuss a player who has disclosed league offers and these are weighing on him in test week. 'Those are two things I could have done without, this week.'

A typical week away from test match rugby in the dying days of 'amateurism' saw All Blacks involved in an average of 13–18 hours a week rugby activity, including practice, socialisation associated with rugby and matches. This highlights the concerns raised then by players and certain administrators about the need for greater financial support. Off-field today, in the professional era, different considerations arise. These include the balance of playing commitments and their physical or mental effects, personal life and wellbeing, building a career in a secure off-field environment and, inevitably, optimising off-field marketability.

12

The tradition continues:
a new All Black speaks

*In five years' time . . . I want to be still playing for the All Blacks — I'd
like to be seriously looking at being a number one test player.*
Mark Robinson, 1998

Mark Robinson was selected as one of the new All Blacks in the 1997
touring team for Britain. Coming from a rugby and sporting family, the
North Harbour halfback stands behind a great All Black scrum and on
the threshold of the AD 2000 All Blacks — in the era of the career
professional and the 1999 World Cup. We talked at the Albany Campus
of Massey University, where Mark Robinson is studying sport management and coaching.

*Most All Blacks seem to have had family encouragement in getting involved in
sport when they were young because their parents played sport. Did your parents
play sports?*
Yes, I'll give you some background, starting with my mum's side. Mum's
side was Jenkins, and my grandfather, Ralph, was a professional golfer,
and his dad, my great-granddad, was Alf Jenkins. He's done quite a lot
for wrestling. He was quite short at only 5 foot 2, and all muscle. He was
involved in New Zealand wrestling, coaching, umpiring, New Zealand
roller skating, gymnastics, softball. So Mum's side of the family are really sporty — they have mainly gone into the golf side of things with a
couple of golf professionals in the family.

My father's side, the Robinsons, originated from Horowhenua. My dad,
my two brothers, Uncle Richard and Uncle Warren, played provincial

rugby for Horowhenua. My father captained Horowhenua. Uncle Richard also played for Hawke's Bay. Supposedly Warren and Richard could both have played at a higher level but they weren't in the right area — they made the Junior All Blacks. They played for Manawhenua — a combination of Manawatu and Horowhenua teams. The Robinson heritage in rugby for Horowhenua has been quite prominent. We're very sport orientated.

How many brothers and sisters have you got?
Three brothers — the two younger ones are at school and one is overseas — he is into the shepherd side of things. The two younger brothers are promising players, and both are involved in age grade rep rugby in Northland.

You are now an All Black. How did you get started in representative football?
We left Horowhenua when I was eight. Dad was dairy farming and moved out of that, going for a change into the hospitality business, so we moved to Whangarei. In 1987 I first played rep rugby for primary school. I played Roller Mills in North Auckland in Forms 1 and 2, getting selected for two years, which was really good. I was not picked as halfback but as first-five. I went to Whangarei Boys' High and made the transition to halfback pretty much straightaway. I was extremely tiny until I was about seventeen. About the end of the sixth form or start of the seventh form I started to grow a bit — not much though! It was a size thing really as far as coaches go, I think, that led to them playing me at halfback.

And after Whangarei Boys' High?
Throughout the following seasons I played in representative teams. I went to the Under 21s from school. In 1994 I shifted out of Whangarei and went to the North Shore in North Harbour. I had been getting caught in a circle and wasn't going anywhere — not really doing anything — so I moved. It wasn't necessarily for my rugby that I shifted, it was a lot of other things and I just wanted something different from what I was doing. I got a job with Nike, it was something different and had prospects — rugby wasn't the main issue for me. I had organised to go to a rugby club because I knew someone at the rugby club at North Shore. He knew Dad and me so he asked me to come along. I played for Shore for two years, and after that I moved to East Coast Bays, where I've been for two years. Then I got a call for North Harbour in 1995.

I've played for the New Zealand Colts and went on the tour to Argentina and so that was the first taste of rugby at that international level and that was intense. I gained a lot from Ross Cooper and Lyn Colling as coaches. It was awesome! I think it was because of that when I got back I was made reserve halfback to Ant Strachan for North Harbour, as Boyd Gillespie had a broken ankle. I understand Ant Strachan had a lot to do with my selection. He organised things and virtually got me in the team to stand by for him. I was just a reserve for four or five NPC games until Boyd's ankle came right and he moved back and I just played for the Under 21s after that. In 1996 I moved to East Coast Bays to play senior rugby because I hadn't played senior rugby before then and 1996 was my first year in senior rugby. That led to regular selection for North Harbour. Then I was selected for the New Zealand Barbarians 1996 tour to the UK. That was a real surprise because it was my first year of senior rugby and to be part of a prestigious team and to be involved with All Black players and selectors was awesome.

How did you find out you were going to be a Barbarian? Did someone give you a ring?
Harty came and saw me in the changing rooms after our NPC game against Auckland. I knew that I was in the framework because a couple of people in the Barbarians Club mentioned to me that it could happen and I was just pleased with that. John Hart asked me to be at his press conference and told me I had been selected!

So you were now picked for a significant short tour to Britain with a Barbarians team virtually comprised of All Blacks. That experience would have been a quick learning curve?
Yes. It was a quick introduction into professional rugby I think. All I'd ever known before was amateurism. The biggest impact was in my mind. I didn't get involved too much with the tour. I sort of sat back and did what I was told! But just watching the other players build up for what was basically a test match gave me real insights, for example, how they can just switch on and off — for me that is a big thing. The guys are so relaxed, so easy, so cruisy — and then get them on the match day and they are able to just switch on and be ready to play test match rugby. I think, from what I've been told, that when you're in with the All Blacks its another step up from that. It's going to be another learning curve being away with them.

261

What would be a typical week for you now as a professional rugby player?
An NPC week, with a game on Saturday . . . Sunday generally I do a recovery session — generally a hot bath or hot pools, stretch, I might even go for a run if I can or a swim — it just depends. Monday — training at night with the team. Tuesday I do individual things like ball skills, etc. and then Wednesday is a training night with the team. During the NPC season the team trains together two or three times, and at least three training sessions per week are on my own individual skills. I have to fit in work and study as well. It can be quite hard! I work a full day Monday and a full day Wednesday and sat three Massey University papers at Albany in 1997. The second semester this year has only one day of lectures, on a Thursday, whereas last semester I had lectures on a Tuesday and Thursday and I found that hard working it in with my job.

A typical week during Super 12 is different — we'd get in camp on Wednesday or Tuesday and we'd stay in camp and we'd train Tuesday, Wednesday, Thursday, have a break on Friday, play Saturday, and then go back to our homes for two or three days. Then get back together again, be in camp together training two or three days, as well as individual training. That is quite different from the NPC team, where we only train in the evening because there's a mixture of amateurs, semi-professionals and professionals — a lot of guys working and a lot of guys not able to come just at any time.

How did you find out you were in the All Blacks?
I got a call on Sunday night and was told then, plus I was asked to go to the press conference on Monday. That was a bit of a *déjà vu*, 'I have been here before' sort of thing. The same thing happened the previous year when I made the Barbarians. But hearing my name read out for the All Blacks was a real buzz.

What are your main interests/hobbies outside of rugby, if any?
I am really keen on surf-lifesaving — I try to be available as much as I can but it is getting harder and harder. Tennis is another interest and I play golf as much as possible. I always enjoy swimming and I've always got a lot of pleasure out of athletics but I do not belong to a club as such.

On a big match day, a key match, what do you do for your own preparation?
For a night game the build up is different from an afternoon match. I have breakfast reasonably early around 9.00 a.m. Then I do stretching

to release tension. I would drink at least five or six litres of water during the day — I have lots of water to drink! Relaxing is important and I read a lot. Stretch some more later in the afternoon and then have a late lunch — mainly high-carbohydrate foods, high-protein foods, which you have about four hours before the game. There is also a time in the morning when we go out and have our line-outs, which would happen about eleven o'clock in the morning. At 6.00–6.30 p.m. we'll have a team meeting, then we're off to the game. We get to the ground about one hour before kick-off. I like to have another stretch then and I do all my strapping before I get to the ground so I don't have to worry about that once I'm there. Then, basically for an hour before the game it's just you and the team and that's about it and you just build up from there.

I like to do a warm-up. I like to throw some passes, do some kicks, do some sprints, and then come back in, stretch, warm up and do some physical stuff inside the changing rooms to get my heart rate going. I'll do some more stretching and then go out. That's what I like to do basically.

We have our little spots in the North Harbour dressing room. Some players like to sit in corners but wherever my jersey is, or has been put, I just sit there. I don't put my jersey on until I go out — I always warm-up in my T-shirt and jacket and I don't put my jersey on until it's time to go out. That's probably the only thing I do that is absolute routine, not put my jersey and boots on until I go out, before the game.

When do you think you first started to become conscious of the chance or desire to become an All Black? Has it always been a part of playing rugby — the possibility of the black jersey?
I think that my New Zealand Colts selection was the first time it became a real possibility in the future. I've always aspired to be an All Black, ever since I was about four years old. Even though it was a national age-group jersey I was selected to wear it still had a lot of feeling behind it — you do the haka, listen to the national anthem and to me that was it — it just did it for me! It's pretty emotional stuff you know, and it's the pride of wearing the jersey and playing for your country that does it. And then, when Ross Cooper was selected as an assistant All Black coach, I thought maybe there was a possibility — you know you've always got it in the back of your mind, and I've always tried to look at what's next. It's always hard to make it into an NPC team or the New Zealand Colts a first time and it's even harder to make it again.

What does it mean now that you're in the All Blacks and facing your first tour in the team?

I don't regard myself as an All Black until I've got the jersey on. I've been selected as an All Black but am not yet an All Black. I don't really know what to do as I haven't been in this situation before and I think it's a whole new learning curve. I am well aware of the honour of being an All Black.

Who do you thing has been the biggest influence on your rugby development?

I'm not sure, actually. My biggest one at the beginning was Ant Strachan — a huge influence. He and I did a lot of training together and he provided real support and an example. That was in 1995 when I made the Colts and he made the World Cup touring side and we both trained together and he said, 'Thanks for helping me,' and I said, 'Well thanks for helping me.' We sort of helped each other in both directions, so it was just great. That was Strachany, and he has always been good to me, and technically as well, because he's helped me with passing, working out my kicking, and general play of the game. In 1996 I got in touch with Dave Loveridge. I spent a few days with him and his family in Taranaki before our Colts southern hemisphere tournament. He had a big influence on me at that time. We get on really well and if I've got any problems I just give him a call. I ask for his opinion, or how he thought I played, whether he thought that what I was doing was okay tactically or technically.

Others put a lot of time into me. For example, Brett Hollister, one of my bosses at work this year, has been tremendous. This year we trained a hell of a lot and we'll be training together and although he's my boss we get on really well! He's young and energetic. I'll be training and he'll go out with me and he'll catch, kick, throw the ball and comment to me — he knows about rugby. He's been really great this year helping me. He represented New Zealand in the rowing eight at the Olympics — he was the cox — so he knows what it takes to get to the top, including the mental strength required.

What do you think are the main qualities of a halfback in today's game?

I still believe passing is the main game, kicking is second to that — passing and distribution is the main issue. I think now speed and strength are becoming more important in top level rugby. It's become so much more physical and there is a lot more involved for today's top level halfback around the ruck and maul. If you can make a yard to two though, around the side of a ruck or maul, and get caught, you still place the ball back and know that you made yards, almost like a runner. I mean, that's like you're actually helping the team. There are going to be times when that ball is not perfect and if you can scoot around the side with speed and strength and make a few yards it's a bonus. I just think speed in and around the base of the scrum and getting away from the opposition, creating a gap so you can set someone else up, that's become really important.

You have already experienced a range of rugby captains. What do you see as the main qualities of a captain at the élite level?
The main qualities include leading by example and I think you should be professional. You've got to be able to be at the same level as the players and then step up and be a captain at the same time — similar to a coach in that regard. An All Black or, say, NPC or Super 12 captain, must be able to talk to the players at the same level but then step away and stand out from them. I think leaders I've known — I think you've got to have natural traits for it. You've got to have the charisma, and that rubs off from players, with players just coming up to you and saying, 'We'll do it.' They have got to have that respect for a captain to say things — and play — like that. Ian Jones chews the boys hard, but that's just his style and his high expectations, and I respect him. Sean Fitzpatrick is a natural leader — he leads by example. Buck Shelford is another — they lead from the front and have that little bit of essential distance from the players. Those guys are hard when they have to be. They're straight and hard, they never try to sidetrack or anything, they're just committed to the idea — here's the need, and that's it. No variations. Just get the best out of the players. I think that they talk to you too as an individual within that team commitment.

A coach has got to be knowledgeable about the game with good management skills, which John Hart has. I find him a really approachable person, because I like to talk to the coaches — I like to be able to say to them, 'I did this, I did that, it seemed really good,' and they might say, 'That was good but perhaps you could try this.' As long as the coach is constructive and knowledgeable about the game, they have the basics for good coaching. The players generally know what to do and the coaches have to guide us and organise us — I mean, I'm still learning, but there are other people around me who just about know everything there is to know about their playing positions, say at All Black level, and more than what the coaches might know, especially technically.

What are the biggest demands on a professional rugby player?
I think the most immediate demand would be time. There seem to be so many games and that's a huge demand, especially on families. There just seem to be so many games — trials, Super 12, NPC, the tour, a huge amount. The mental demands are huge. There is pressure — pressure on yourself because of the game, pressure of the media, outside things as well, and the pressure of the game. It just builds up and up, so you've got to find some way to release that. In today's top rugby, players have to learn to get the balance and then, when the time comes, to switch on to the game, play well and forget about the pressures. You have to switch on and switch off — you might have an unneeded distraction in the back of your mind! I think time, the nature of the games, and the mental stress from pressure outside or from the media can impact on a player if you're not careful. Unfortunately, everybody's got an opinion! Every New Zealander is watching — every New Zealander rugby fan has an opinion!

Do you have relaxation exercises that you do for yourself?
Sort of! I use breathing exercises to try and relax properly, visualising, slowing breathing down, and trying to relax my whole body. A close friend helped me as he's a good businessman and rugby administrator, so he helps with financial advice. He got me into t'ai chi but that takes so long to progress through — but I learned the basics of relaxing.

It seems many top sportspeople use music to relax or escape. If you only had a choice of five CDs what would they be, to take away on tour or to the proverbial desert island?
I guess I would want to take some rap music. Cat Stevens is also a favourite. I know he's more of the generation of the coaches and my parents but I like his music! He's good to sing along to as well. Snoop Doggy Dog would be another one to take, and 2 PAC would be the next. Probably Prodigy also. I would like to add something a bit more mellow like Alanis Morrisette. Basically, I like a variety of music.

Where would you want to be in five years, in top level rugby?
I'd still want to be in the New Zealand team. In five years' time I'll be 27

and I want to still be playing for the All Blacks — I'd like to be seriously looking at being a number one test player. If I was not an All Black I think at that age I would maybe look at going overseas. If overseas is still dominant in terms of income and employment, I'd look at going somewhere like Japan, somewhere over there for three years on a playing contract, then come back and still be young enough to be settled in New Zealand with a career. Financially a move like that, seen from the present-day, appears attractive, if you can make it.

What are the main challenges facing 1998 rugby?
Rugby's life is at the grass roots. Clubs and a lot of unions in New Zealand need attention and support. It seems to me that they get neglected, they get left out in a lot of discussions. I think Rob Fisher, as chairman of the NZRFU, wanted to do something about that. He wanted to bring the grass roots through, which is great, but there is a real need out there in the clubs because there's not that much money to go around! I can see some ares being unable to develop top-level players, simply because they don't have the resources to put into coaching. 'Are we going to get money?' is a club's big concern, and how much is needed, and, again, is it going to get filtered down? At the moment we've got the All Blacks, Super 12 and a little bit goes to NPC. I like the soccer structure. With soccer's structure the money starts with the clubs and then it goes up, and clubs think that's where all their money come from. I just think that we can't lose sight of where we came from, and our rugby heritage.

That heritage means, to me, such things as the great All Blacks, the great teams of the past, the Ranfurly Shield. New Zealand rugby has a real heritage in it. That still has a reality for the guys picked for the All Blacks. I know that stuff like that is awesome. In terms of sport finances, are we going to be owned by businesses? We are a commodity now so what's going to happen to us — are we going to get shifted here and there? For example, I still have loyalty to a top team but money is important and helps with securing your future. There's a time where you're going to be seen as, excuse my slang, a mercenary because you're going to forget your loyalty, you're going to forget your background, and you're going to be chasing a dollar. It's difficult to prevent this from happening and you've just got to look after yourself, but a lot of people are still in the amateur loyalty era and they've got to be considered. I still think it's good to have our values.

13

Living with the future: where to now in professional rugby?

You can never trade the mana, the history, the honour of being an All Black.

Colin Meads

All Black rugby in the 1990s is in good heart. Radically reshaped by the final year of the amateur era, the core of the All Black team was maintained by John Hart, who continued and expanded the playing style. Inside the All Blacks, Hart has forged a modern, professional, well-managed organisation. Not so healthy are the lower branches of the hitherto sturdy tree. The NZRFU, in its usual reactive style, has instituted an examination of club rugby and divisional structures two years after the onset of open professionalism. Indeed, there is some evidence that, over all age groups, rugby may no longer hold the greatest numbers of sports participants in New Zealand.

The number of adults playing rugby during the New Zealand year is now some 143,000. Affiliated rugby players, numbering 123,481, indicate a sport barely ahead of golf in terms of members linked to a national association, and which may well be behind that sport in terms of actual participants. In 1988, touch rugby had 24,000 adherents but nine years later it had some 75,000. Despite such challenges of allegiance it is still the All Blacks, almost mystical and sometimes mythical, who provide the poutokomanawa, or mainstay, of New Zealand's sporting house.

Professionalism in rugby has brought its own individual rewards and administrative challenges. What will happen to clubs? All Blacks of diverse generations such as Tori Reid (1930s), Colin Meads (1960s–1970s), and Mark Robinson (1990s) have indicated that they share this concern. To what extent can rugby clubs or provincial teams amalgamate and preserve a regional sport identity? If heroes influence affiliation, what will happen to rural rugby areas where the lure of town life and dollar in hand draws potential rugby stars to the city? There is a need for New Zealand rugby to determine, as suggested by David Kirk, its vision, its essential values and goals. From these come the consequent practicalities of organisation, structures and player involvement. In a land bereft of leadership there is an overdose of management, and the rugby corpus is sometimes drugged by mediocrity in key places. On the council, and in various offices, there are outstanding persons, but the business of rugby and the provincial and national progress of administration are still variable. To some extent this is not surprising as the demands upon small unions are difficult for them to encompass. Some 'practical' research has been carried out in New Zealand rugby with relevant findings for administrators. One of the rare theses on rugby, acclaimed in the academic (and international sport) world, studied the professionalisation and corporatisation of the game in New Zealand and recorded perspectives of provincial union and club administrators. Its author was recruited by the International Olympic Committee, but was never called up by the NZRFU to present his findings or the information he had obtained from clubs and provincial administrators.

Rugby coaching is variable in New Zealand. The lack of a realistic fast-track process for past All Blacks, such as Mike Brewer and John Mitchell, to attain positions in New Zealand coaching needs examining. The appointment of Graham Mourie to coach Wellington is to be commended but the challenge he faces requires clear administrative support. The present NZRFU coaching courses, helpful as they are, do not adequately reflect rugby as a professional sport, nor do they successfully utilise the knowledge of élite rugby coaching that has been gained through All Black coach experience and New Zealand research. One ex-All Black, Greg Kane, for example, has completed a valuable and substantial MBA research study of coaching in the professional era, and a New Zealand doctoral study of élite rugby coaching and captaincy has been utilised by overseas sports bodies but not the NZRFU courses. There are too few opportunities for provincial coaches to come together and share perspectives, needs and coaching methods.

Greg Kane, the 1974 All Black, comes from a rugby background. His 1997 MBA research on developing professional rugby coaches underscores the need for better rugby coaching programmes in New Zealand. 'More needs to be done for training and succession planning, and the implementation of proper human resource practices in relation to coaches,' argues Kane, after a substantial range of interviews and surveys involving top provincial and All Black coaches. He further suggests the importance of developing coaches' management skills. 'There needs to be an implementation of strategies to have quality coaches with broad skills to meet the varied demands of the game's stakeholders.' Despite the efforts of the NZRFU to develop a rugby coaching certificate and its success in producing qualified coaches, Kane found that only one coach in his provincial survey effectively utilised sport science (other than pre-season fitness and nutrition), and that New Zealand rugby coaches needed more linkages with sports scientists and management specialists. Only nine rugby coaches were employed full-time in the professional rugby era of 1997 New Zealand. It is to be hoped that the NZRFU will, at some stage, consider such studies that have actually gone objectively into the real world of club, provincial and All Black coaching and administration. Given that half of Kane's respondents had completed NZRFU–Massey University coaching courses (good news), it is of concern that the courses or unions do not appear to have successfully developed élite rugby coach awareness of coach associations and resources other than NZRFU manuals (bad news). There would seem to be real value in utilising the skills and knowledge of past and present All Black coaches to work more with rising coaches.

In some unions the nation's potential All Blacks have guidance on careers, study, financial investment and life as a professional rugby player. In others these matters are barely touched in depth. The overseas lessons of professional sport have often been ignored. The vision and concerns of John Hart, with the 'All Black product', and his resultant efforts to develop appropriate supports for his professional players, building on the earlier work of Thorburn, Mains, Kevin Roberts and the All Blacks Club, need replication and expansion at all lower levels. When this author surveyed the All Blacks on a range of team leadership and other All Black issues, a heartfelt note was written in response to a question on educational qualifications. It read:

Robin

My greatest regret is that I left school too early. I completed my sixth form year but left before the exams. I wish I had carried on with my studies and would now jump at the chance of further education. I'm lucky to have rugby. I didn't realise then how much I would need education and how much I miss it. I wonder how many others there are?

A burgeoning body of overseas sports organisations and associated researchers have been examining life for players after professional sport. Rugby in New Zealand would gain from their considerations.

Jock Hobbs, a key figure in 1995 WRC negotiations, stated at the time that rugby is owned by New Zealanders. Just two years later an All Black suggested to me that already the game had dispossessed those owners, who are now permitted by a television mogul to watch his depiction of rugby at the time it is played. Politicians who voiced their intentions to have All Black rugby on free-to-air television now watch it on Sky and debate selling off Television One.

Notwithstanding concerns about administration, development and access to rugby, the game is still the centre of New Zealand's sport and achievement. The open and skilled play of the All Blacks, their mana as the nation's sport heroes, and their impact upon both staunch and occasional followers, continues to be high. The coach skilfully relates to the media and the players are still accessible, especially in comparison with certain overseas professional sportsmen.

The image of All Black rugby is well served by its players off-field and, generally, on the field. Violence at the highest level of rugby is rare. International opponents do not associate All Blacks with violence. Aggression? Ah, most definitely. Violence in sport is not new, nor at its most evident in rugby.

Past and present All Blacks note one of the most sustaining qualities of rugby is its ability to cater for men and women of all shapes and sizes. 'The essential character of rugby is that it has the slow guy, the short guy, the leggy fella and the strong man — they all have a role to play.' With recent changes to the game's rules and the demands of fast, mobile play, this quality may be at risk. There are implications here for the game's ongoing appeal, player recruitment, coaching and school rugby.

Women in rugby have achieved greater prominence in recent times. Administered primarily by men, New Zealand women's rugby has been dominant around the world. The marketing of this sport appears to be virtually non-existent, however. An informal survey by the author of a class of sports studies students indicated none had ever read or received information or publicity material on playing women's rugby. In contrast, *Mana* magazine, commercial rugby publications, and Maori newspapers provided more 'shop-windows' publicity on women's rugby than any other outlet — the NZRFU included.

The cultural dimension of All Black rugby — and of the game at all levels in New Zealand — has changed. Representative teams in New Zealand's most populous region, Auckland, are primarily Polynesian. Coaches rarely have training in understanding the background and social milieu of their players, despite the more effective communication and relationships that can result. Administrators too often take the view that 'everyone is treated the same', which usually means 'I will operate with the beliefs and practices of my Pakeha culture and assume that fits Pacific Island and Maori players.' At the best in top rugby, as in wider society, there is understanding of cultural differences. At worst, the same mirror of ignorance is held up in sport as in society. I asked a prominent rugby official why, as so many Pacific Islanders and Maori play top rugby, their numbers were not reflected in high level rugby administration. The reply was, 'Well, we all know those bloody darkies need a white man to lead them.' Whether this be an isolated or representative opinion, it is a racist view that has no place in 1990s New Zealand rugby or in New Zealand sport. Although All Black coaches and captains in the 1990s have generally respected players' cultural differences and made an effort to accept their differing practices and beliefs, all representative rugby needs a closer examination in this dimension. Non-Pakeha All Blacks and provincial players see potential for this understanding and acceptance to be developed further in New Zealand rugby at all levels. David Kirk, past All Black captain and Wellington provincial coach, has noted the need for coaches to have such understanding.

The World Cup is now dominant in international rugby. Colin Meads regards the Cup as a culmination of four years' work, and believes rugby history now follows a four-year cycle. This presents a challenge for administrators in terms of team life, appointments, national competition structures and player contracts. Demands upon players are high in overseas professional team sports, and it can be argued that rugby has not yet adjusted to this and to the 'pay 'em and play 'em' commercialisation of their well-paid rugby commodity. Conversely, excessive demands upon All Blacks through test schedules and in-your-face marketing may develop an element of public immunity to the 'product'. Implicit in administrators' and sponsors' expectations is the intangible and economic value of the famed jersey. To what extent should second-tier players be selected for a test in order to release first-stringers for rest or play in an alternative match?

The future of rugby depends, in part, upon its foundation levels. All Black wives and partners have clear ideas on their wishes for their children's future in playing youth rugby. They were asked, 'If you had a daughter or son playing rugby, what qualities would you want in their (a) coach (b) captain?' Their replies present expectations for those who wield influence over young sporting lives which may, or may not, ultimately lead to the coveted black jersey. The messages, for those who shape future All Black lives, are clear:

'I want an ordinary decent citizen who is capable of setting an example, who is able to look after younger players'; 'First, to enjoy the game, and then to lead, whether it be coach or captain, in a manner that will be remembered by their team in later years'; 'Just enjoy the game, be honest and don't single the boys out'; 'If I had children, I would hope that no daughter of mine played rugby or any other contact sport, but the main quality I would want in a son's rugby coach would be a balanced approach'; 'Man and woman management, playing ability, discipline'; and, 'I would want the coach to be firm, a communicator, and patient, while the captain should have leadership qualities and the respect of players.'

In summary, for those inside the All Blacks the sport is generally in excellent health. The state of team coaching and captaincy illustrates this. For players, the remuneration, prospects of commercial gain and test match selection provide a relatively substantial income, recognition of their skills and a certain security and lifestyle. But difficulties loom in meeting professional sport's demands regarding performance, scheduling, the pressures and rewards of sponsorship, marketing the NZRFU, career-building for players and moving successfully into post-All Black life. Outside the All Blacks, rugby faces particular challenges to its traditional structures, staunchly held beliefs about its appeal to all body types and the grass-roots basis of the game. The 1990s reality of the sport is that club rugby will never be the same, professional circuits are evolving, and a different form of rural, small-town, lower-grade rugby will provide an amateur sport which also serves, as in other codes, to launch rising professional players. In terms of constituent populations, rugby will be represented at the higher level by an increasingly dispro-portionate number of Pacific Island and Maori players relative to the population of the country as a whole.

Colin Meads is succinct on the personal meaning of being an All Black. 'You have to protect the silver fern, the All Black jersey. I would never train in it. You'd swap it with a Welshman, after a test, and train in their national jersey the next day . . . You can never trade the mana, the history, the honour of being an All Black. The pride is not in the money you make, it is in being selected to be an All Black'.

Inside the All Blacks, the era of professional rugby has not yet oblit-erated tradition.

14

The fourth World Cup era: the Hart-felt goal

You still measure yourself against the Blacks.
Rob Andrew, Newcastle, December 1998

The lodestar of the 1999 Rugby World Cup has dominated the four-season cycle of 1996–99. Inside the All Blacks, the ethos of invinciblity, the assumption of territorial, skills and points dominance, has shifted from certainty to contestability. The rugby world in 1999, however, still conjures up images of Black Magic from the Antipodes. In Arlington, Texas, watching a brother refereeing a rugby game the writer was frequently assailed with questions such as 'How will the All Blacks go in the World Cup?' The same enquires had been made of the author when in New South Wales, and when in England in the last months of 1998.

Rob Andrew, the ex-England and Lions fly-half who now efficiently carries out the executive role at Newcastle, was typical of past and present opponents of New Zealand when he stressed their tradition and rugby culture. Over lunch he noted, 'They will be right up there in this 1999 World Cup . . . You still measure yourself against the Blacks.' From the grass-roots game of the Consett Rugby Club lower grade team on a frosty field with five spectators to the England Rugby Football Union's President's table before the Australia–England test match, the mana accorded the All Blacks was so great it was virtually tangible. And all this despite the disastrous record of the five test losses in 1998!

In 1996 and 1997, the new John Hart era of All Black coaching had seen sublime rugby. The All Black coach was perceived by the press as walking on water to retrieve practice balls. The erosion of faith in his third season, 1998, was furthered with each unprecedented All Blacks failure and Hart narrowly survived the vote for his retention. In 1999, the World Cup looms as a test of coaches as much as teams.

The first Hart year, 1996, saw the continued selection of an All Black team that essentially comprised players from the 1995 World Cup and French tour, their international rugby in accord with the 1992 vision outlined in Chapter 5. In that first year of professional rugby, Hart brought a management style of precision and organisational clarity, deployed assistant coaches and espoused the concept of distributed leadership. (Ironically, it would be the lack of shared, forceful and productive leadership that was to be criticised in 1999.)

The media were rapidly brought onside by the astute All Black coach in 1996. Initially Hart intended to have the media liaison primarily undertaken by himself and the manager. The writer recalls personal meetings with Hart early that year, following the new coach's survey of members of the media on All Black–press relations, when Hart, with typical thoroughness, explored the issue of not only having a new media liaison person but possible reactions to a woman being appointed to this position. Also discussed at these meetings were issues of team leadership and the possible successor to Sean Fitzpatrick. Hart, more than two years before Taine Randell's appointment, clearly saw the Otago captain as a leading contender.

The 1996 season was one of adjustment — to the new All Black coach and to the new era of professional rugby. Faced with demanding test schedules, Hart broke the season into individual test match challenges. Despite the gruelling nature of the programme, Fitzpatrick stated that he had few worries about the players as he knew the team's capabilities from 1995. His confidence was fully justified by the results.

The season saw the All Blacks enjoying their rugby and 'doing the damage' in style. Illustrative of the new era, and in marked contrast to the previous four years of NZRFU officialdom (and some would say, obstruction), was the decision to take 36 players in the All Black 'team' to South Africa, to allow a mid-week match respite for the test team.

The All Black scrum consistently achieved its goals and met its own high expectations in 1996, being assisted by a lack of injury to forwards and consistency of selection. Individual players also shot across the firmament. Christian Cullen had been picked by Mains for the 1995 All Black tour of France, but the number of players was restricted by the NZRFU and as a consequence Cullen was omitted. A year later he received his opportunity and spreadeagled opposing backlines like a switchblade slicing through balsa wood. Cullen's four tries against Scotland at Carisbrook in 1996 altered the alchemy of All Black back play. And so it would continue as Cullen glided to rugby kids' folk-hero status, along with Jeff Wilson and Jonah Lomu.

In 1997 the All Blacks continued their superior play. Although the warning signs were flashing at times, there were few commentators looking at the lights when the rugby itself was so dazzling. Team composition remained relatively constant, and players were injury free: against Fiji, in a night test which was won 71–5, with Wilson scoring five tries, the All Black scrum comprised the same eight forwards who had played the ten tests of 1996: Craig Dowd, Sean Fitzpatrick, Olo Brown, Ian Jones, Robin Brooke, Michael Jones, Josh Kronfeld and Zinzan Brooke.

In five of the twelve tests in 1997 Cullen scored four tries, Frank Bunce three, Wilson two and Lomu was not on the field. (In the last five tests of 1995 Lomu had scored seven tries and Bunce three, with the backs scoring 18 of the team's 20 tries.) Although tests against Australia and South Africa were won, the matches hinted at features of the year to come. The 1997 players commented on the 'soft tries' allowed to their opponents — soft tries being those scored by the opposition in the absence of a steely, 'gutsy' or sustained All Black defence. Indeed, at Carisbrook Australia came back from being down 0–36 at half-time to score 24 points to nil in the second half. In Johannesburg, at Ellis Park, Fitzpatrick left the field with knee trouble. The doomsters were writing up the signs, but few were noting the message.

The injury to Fitzpatrick led to the appointment of Justin Marshall as All Black test captain: not one of Hart's best man-management decisions. Marshall rarely synthesized onfield leadership with the drive, durability and decision demanded of an All Black halfback. At Twickenham the country saw their test skipper marched back by a referee penalizing him for arguing his ruling. The unfortunate Marshall's performance underscored the centrality of Fitzpatrick's leadership and mana in this All Black team. The great hooker had played 63 continuous tests, 128 games in his cherished black jersey and 92 tests overall. His number of appearances as an All Black is second only to the legendary Colin Meads, who tallied 133 in an era of less frequent encounters. The linkage of the two players is apt.

Along with the once indomitable Fitzy was the dominant figure of Zinny. Despite Zinzan Brooke's intention to leave All Black rugby he was included in the tour of Britain, where he played his 100th game for New Zealand. Ebullient, talented and as ready with a quip or bet as with a dropkick, the physically gifted No. 8 left a template fitted readily by none. Brooke's departure would also see the team deprived of his experience, onfield panache, motivation and decision-making. With the captain meshed in the engine room it was first Mike Brewer and then Zinny who called the game and initiated onfield options.

Then came 1998.

It has become customary for critics to pinpoint the loss of key players as the cause for the disasters of 1998. To certain players inside the All Blacks, however, there were signs in 1997 that vital organs required transplants in order to prevent the need for life-support systems later. One such player noted to the writer the parallel with the 1991 All Blacks and the 1995 Australians: all three teams carried aging players a season too far. In addition, the 1998 All Blacks suffered an overemphasis on management and meetings, and arguably should have developed long-term planning for leadership, positional succession and the evolution of their playing style. Given the rapidity with which other test countries pick up on any All Black innovation in tactics or pattern of play, the last of these criticisms is too harsh. The factors were many: loss of key players, overmanagement and undercoaching in technical skills and strategies, selection errors, and a lack of physical presence and staying power. The performance of the opposition also improved. 'Unlike great All Black teams, we allowed others to dictate to us, we let the opposition spoil the ball too often,' was how one player saw it. The team in the final two tests of 1998, for the first time in this four-year cycle, had more selected-only-by-Hart players than originally-selected-by-Mains players. The wheel had turned.

Losing Fitzpatrick, Zinzan Brooke and Bunce was a major blow. With more long-term selections, better preparation of successors and a deliberate development of team leadership the impact could have been lessened. Michael Jones and Mark Carter were doubtful prospects for the 1999 World Cup and, despite astute critics noting the need for their replacement, were not supplanted early enough in the Cup cycle by the All Black coaches. It could be argued that Brooke also could have been denied his final tour, as he had no future with the All Blacks beyond those games in Britain. The impression is inescapable, too, that a different handling of Bunce could have led to a more effective midfield transition. In the last five internationals of 1998 against South Africa and

Australia, Cullen scored a solitary try, as did Lomu, but Wilson and the centres went scoreless. The contrast with 1997 and 1995 was dramatic.

Ironically, going into the 1999 season, the All Black selectors made the selection of loose forwards and midfield backs for the World Cup team a priority. These are the positional areas causing most concern to the All Black selectors some months out from the Cup.

Given that Isitolo Maka, in February 1999, met the 3 kilometre fitness run requirement and assuming that his season progresses from that point, then he is the likely No. 8. The challenge is to programme Maka's high-impact force so that he maintains more of a Shelford-like presence onfield for the greater part of the game. Randell may be challenged for his blindside flanker position, but Josh Kronfeld remains undisputed ruler of the openside fiefdom. This World Cup will not see Michael Jones as a first-team contender. The rugby world is a universe of lesser persons with his absence. Jones has swept through international rugby, inside and outside the All Blacks, with a personal grace and fusion of physical and mental gifts that moved, at special moments, beyond excellence to imprint the eye as rugby perfection.

In the midfield the All Black coach has tried a number of players at centre following the rejection of Frank Bunce. The post-Bunce period in 1998 saw four players used in seven tests; there were also four different centre pairings — Walter Little and Mark Mayerhofler (three tests), Eroni Clarke and Mayerhofler (two), Caleb Ralph and Mayerhofler (one), and Scott McLeod and Little (one).

The midfield pairing for the World Cup team may well result from a virtual unknown being brought through with high-intensity development or from the relocation of another backline player. The post-Bunce pairings, examined ruthlessly, do not measure up to the inside and outside centre combinations of Bunce and Little, Mark Taylor and Joe Stanley, or Bill Osborne and Bruce Robertson. The injury to Alama Ieremia has meant this intelligent and hard-hitting player has to use the Super 12 as his proving ground — as do the plethora of emergent young, fleetfooted sevens-into-fifteens fliers. Ralph, Little, and Craig Innes are immediate possibilities for centre, but the odds also favour an outsider such as Reuben Parkinson or Rua Tipoki. In 1998 Parkinson, for example, had 25 tries scored by his wings and fullback. This view of a 'possible bolter' is shared by the great All Black centre, Bruce Robertson. Robertson rates Eroni Clarke as having developed his game so well that selectors know what they will get (though Clarke's early-season injury removes him from contention), Ieremia as strong on defence but needing to enhance his offensive work (in direct contrast to McLeod's abilities), and suggests we 'keep an eye on Jeremy Stanley as inside centre'. He acknowledges the flair of Mayerhofler and Little but states succinctly, 'Jeff Wilson would probably be the best centre, with his skills and vision, but would probably be the best in any back position.'

Backing the midfield, the fullback position may allow flexibility of planning, but if not settled relatively early it might create concern about the time available to fuse the players into a cohesive force for the Cup. Wilson prefers fullback but his play on the wing is outstanding. Placing Wilson at fullback and Cullen at centre raises questions not fully addressed by advocates of such positional changes. The creative surges and missile-like forays of Cullen that were so effective in 1996–97 might cause concern if he were to play at centre: this role requires a player whose moves can be 'read' by his wings and who has both the understanding and ability to run them into position. If Cullen is to be the All Black centre he must be played there with frequency. Radical armchair selectors would play Joeli Vidiri and Wilson on the wings and work intensively with Lomu to develop him as a substitute No. 8 or wing! Tana Umaga has test achievements that justify his place on the immediate replacement list and Roger Randle is also in the frame.

It was Lomu who stalked across the wheatfield of the 1995 World Cup games like a Titan with a scythe. He had responded to the challenge of Mains and Fitzpatrick to get fully fit and had burgeoned in confidence and skills. Suddenly his nephritic syndrome illness, which he may have had for three years, sidelined him in 1997. It would have spelled premature retirement for most athletes. That the big man is back in contention for the 1999 World Cup is indicative of personal qualities that move beyond the desire to play and excel in top rugby.

The inside back pairing offers Justin Marshall, Mark Robinson, and Rhys Duggan and outside half or first five-eight possibilities such as Carlos Spencer, Andrew Mehrtens and Tony Brown. Brown offers reliability and goal kicking ability, but there is doubt whether he has the flair to lift an All Black backline. The Super 12 series will gives us some clues, no doubt. Ofisa Tonu'u appears to have been discarded from the halfback ranks and Marshall has not played at his best since his tendon injury. Despite the record and World Cup experience of Mehrtens it is Spencer who is seen by persons close to the 1999 All Blacks as the forerunner for test selection. It may be that Mehrtens is an example of a player who requires a particular coach–player empathy and approach to enable him to fully achieve. Mehrtens emphasises the importance of personal qualities when he notes the need for a coach to 'give encouragement, be someone that can relax and be one of the boys but not lose respect . . . At times players will rely on him against outsiders . . .'

The tight forwards appear to have only two certainties — Royce Willis and Anton Oliver. Willis and Robin Brooke loom as the likely locks, but Norm Maxwell and Ian Jones are competitive and skilled and there is the possibility of a Reuben Thorne-type of lock-cum-loose-forward (or loose-forward-cum-lock) emerging as Blair Larsen did in the Mains era. Brooke did not play well in 1998: he did not show the application or consistently high achievement expected of a man in the black jersey. However, he has the ability to excel, especially at number two in the lineout.

The front row usually needs test veterans but may not have them for the World Cup. Olo Brown appears to be out of contention with a prolapsed disc. The sometimes underrated Brown, a prop's prop, is a big loss. Though Brown is the very antithesis of verbose, his analytic mind and humour will be missed. His usual team-mate, Craig Dowd, will not step aside lightly. Dowd is now the most experienced active front-rower in the country, and has a commitment that has seen him top the team tackle count in a Hart test; he knows the realities of a short and intensive campaign. Kees Meeuws is a potentially outstanding tighthead prop with the requisite technical skills; he will be integral to the squad. Carl Hoeft has stepped up his Otago performance to reach the international stage. Oliver, the incumbent, is still on a learning curve and needs to improve his lineout throwing — an essential requirement for the 1999 hooker. Norm Hewitt was seen by Kevin Roberts, a NZRFU Board member and rugby columnist, as the first choice Cup hooker. Hewitt has personal challenges to overcome but will be a strong contender.

In the early months of 1999 the All Black captaincy was the focus of commentator debate. Randell did not have the full confidence and support of all his players, despite rugby administration assurances to the contrary, and was not consistently selected at number six, his true position. If Jeff Wilson were captain there would still be a vital forward leader role to be played, and Randell is the logical contender. The research on élite rugby captains indicates quite definitively that a major criterion for an outstanding All Black skipper is his ability to lead from the front, to provide an onfield stimulus through his physical, mental and tactical commitment to pressure, pace and persistence, fused with game-reading acumen. Randell does this with Otago. Randell, in a February 1999 discussion, emphasised the importance of the captain 'being part of the team and setting an example on and off the field'. He has not yet done this to the level he would expect of himself with New Zealand, but clearly has the potential to do so. Whatever the decision on captaincy, there are clear indications that the distributed leadership has not resulted in contenders for captaincy nor has it perceptibly led to some of the veterans shining through. The experienced Mehrtens speaks again: 'The All Black captain needs similar qualities to the coach. He must lead from the front. Sean Fitzpatrick was most remarkable as he was always driving himself . . . he was intent on doing well. He also had the valuable capacity to sit down with the younger guys and play cards and have the piss taken out of him — and not lose any of their respect. He had age and experience and was uncompromising.'

John Hart believes the All Black selectors must pick a World Cup team which is in its ascendancy but also has sufficient test experience to cope with the campaign and its playing demands. In turn, he sees success stimulating sponsor interest and income for New Zealand rugby. This is the professional era. The All Black players' review carried out prior to Hart's reappointment in 1998 emphasised the need for Hart to engage more directly in coaching. He has the astuteness to respond and to refocus, and has special coaching skills which the players value. Given that Hart's predecessor was rated so highly as a technical coach by such experts as Fitzpatrick, Zinzan Brooke and Ian Jones, the role of Peter Sloane in developing the forwards into a technically proficient and integrated force is challenging and critical. Sloane has clear ability and the confidence of players. Both are essential.

Heading into 1999 the All Blacks have an incalculable tradition and unity of self-expectation built up over 95 years. Taine Randell sees 'the All Black tradition and team atmosphere as its greatest strength'. Andrew Mehrtens stresses this dimension of the team. 'It is the unity and togetherness that is the real strength of All Black rugby, and all levels of our rugby. There is an ability to get along with each other, and a positive team spirit. You could take two or three players at random and put them together and they would relate to each other. I think the All Blacks have a culture of equality, while the younger guys still respect the older players. The older guys make it easier to fit in.' It is this team culture that fuses an ethos of tradition with high self-expectation that underpins the strength of those inside the All Blacks. As their predecessors have, Mehrtens and other current players use the word camaraderie to capture the All Black spirit. Inside the All Blacks there are, thankfully for sport perhaps, certain unchanging values.

The World Cup playing style places demands upon coaches to develop clear player understandings of the broad game-plan requirements, knowledge of how to adapt this, and the opportunity for spontaneity. The All Black first-five is clear about his desired style of play. 'I would like to see simplicity and a back-to-basics approach. Rugby,' says Mehrtens in a direct repeat of All Black five-eighth, Fred Allen, 'is basically a simple game. The actual game is still, in 1999, pretty basic. I would be happy with us having a team this year in which the older guys called the shots and the others were head down and arse up!' Given the physical presence of other countries and the proven style of the 1995–97 All Blacks, the team has the players to take the international game up a notch and place a premium on moving the ball, generating individual and cohesive power, and attaining exceptionally high technical proficiency in set pieces. Clearance of the ball, option taking and defensive screens will be critical. The All Black captain, Taine Randell, speaking in February about the World Cup year, expressed his wish for the test focus: 'I would like to see the All Blacks this year get the ball and get going forward.' Supporters approach the 1999 season with optimism rather than the surety of earlier years.

The Rugby Cup year ends for fans with the millennium. It is not the other way round. South Africa are seen by those inside the team as the favoured finalists to oppose the All Blacks. Rugby critics note the Boks' tiredness and the aging bodies of key players. Let the 1995 All Black flyhalf who well remembers the last Cup final, comment: 'The Springboks have now forged a team unity that previously was imposed upon them by their country for the 1995 World Cup. They are single-minded and absolutely committed. I expect them to be in the final.' Australia without John Eales is points down in a test, given his leadership, play, lineout skills and goal kicking. England are still pedestrian but are developing a sense of their own strengths — a key facet of any successful team. And the French? Mon Dieu, quel imprévisibilité! Be it the Boks, the Pommie Pragmatics, or the mercurial French in the final against New Zealand, the 1999 Rugby World Cup will open a new century's surge of debates and discussion, commendations or critiques of those who are, or have been, inside the All Blacks.

Index

Abbott, H.L. (Bunny) 67
Adkins, George 250
Aherne, Fergus 19
Aitken, George 73
Allen, Fred 13, 78, 82, 104, 128, 131–2, 134, 139, 153–6, 158, 161, 163, 172–3, 196, 248
Allen, Mark 201–35 passim
Andrew, Rob 201, 224, 275
Andrews, Alan 75, 171
Archer, Robin 171

Babrow, Louis 168–9
Bachop, Graham 227
Batty, Grant 113
Bayfield, Martin 201
Beaumont, Bill 125
Bedell-Sivright, D.R. 68
Best, Jack 250
Bevan, Vince 172
Blair, Jim 157
Boggs, Eric 82
Botica, Frano 205
Bowen, Dr Mike 12
Bowers, Guy 13
Boyle, Veysey 192
Bracewell, Barry 151
Bradley, Michael 19
Bremner, Mick 177, 180–1
Brewer, Mike 19–54 passim, 101, 112, 141–2, 188, 247, 252, 269, 278
Briscoe, Kevin 140, 181
Brohm, Jean-Marie 81
Brooke, Robin 19–59 passim, 110, 115, 188, 201–44 passim, 277, 281
Brooke, Zinzan 12, 16, 86, 88, 93, 101, 112, 115, 147, 185, 188, 201–44 passim, 247, 277–8, 282
Brown, Olo 19–59 passim, 103, 201–44 passim, 247, 277, 281
Brown, Ross 174–5
Brown, Staff Sergeant Charles 166

Brown, Tony 280
Brownlie, Cyril 74, 129, 190
Brownlie, Maurice 74, 80, 167, 191
Bruiser, see Mike Brewer
Bull, see Mark Allen
Bunce, Frank 19–60 passim, 96–102, 105, 115, 187, 201–41 passim, 256, 277–9
Burmeister, R.D. 181
Burnell, Paul 201
Burrows, Jim 84, 145

Calder, Finlay 198
Campbell, G.F.C. 67
Campbell, Ollie 197
Campese, David 189, 228
Carey, Ron 19
Carling, Will 201, 213
Carter, Mark 153, 278
Caughey, Pat 76, 249
Cavanagh, Vic 113, 153–4, 161, 172–3
Claasen, Johannes 181
Claasen, Wynand 184
Clark, Bill 13, 178–9
Clarke, Allan 194
Clarke, Ben 201, 205, 213
Clarke, Don 174, 176–7, 180–1
Clarke, Eroni 19–58 passim, 279
Clarke, Ian 13, 136, 174, 237
Clarke, Jack 19
Clement, Anthony 201
Cobden, Donald 168
Coker, Troy 228
Colling, Lyn 15–16, 147, 155
Collins, Bill 76, 135, 248
Cooke, Bert 13
Cooke, Geoff 240
Cooksley, Mark 110, 114, 187, 201–25 passim, 247, 251
Cooper, Greg 20
Cooper, Matthew 19–59 passim, 201–40 passim
Cooper, Ross 16, 100, 261, 263

Corner, Merv 76, 249–50
Cottrell, A.I. (Beau) 169
Cranmer, Peter 194
Craven, Danie 163, 169–70, 173, 179, 198–9
Crean, Thomas 67
Crowley, Pat 80
Cullen, Christian 93, 101, 109, 115, 276–7, 279–80
Cunningham, Vincent 19, 51

Dalton, Andy 86, 111, 119–23, 125, 130–1, 138, 142, 149–50, 163
Dalton, Ray 63, 121–2
Daniels, John 194
Davies, Gerald 91
Day, P.W. 167
de Villiers, Dawie 126, 182
Dewar, H. (Norky) 72
Dixon, Maurice 174
Donaldson, Mark 124
Dowd, Craig 12, 201–38 passim, 277, 281
Dowd, Graham 19–57 passim, 187, 201–38 passim
Downing, Albert 72
Dryburgh, Roy 181
du Plessis, Morne 183–4
du Toit Roux, Francois 182
Duff, Bob 176, 178–9
Duffus, Louis 78
Duggan, Rhys 280
Duncan, Jimmy 68–9, 144–5

Edwards, Ray 191
Ellison, Tom 67
Elvidge, Ron 80–1, 128, 139, 154, 172–3
Evans, Ieuan 201
Everest, Dick 155, 175

Fisher, Rob 267
Fitzgibbon, Mick 19
Fitzpatrick, Brian 113
Fitzpatrick, Sean 11–12, 14–15, 17–60 passim, 101, 106, 111, 113–15, 130, 141–2, 152, 177, 187, 201–44 passim, 247, 254, 265, 276–8, 282
Fox, Grant 16, 19–60 passim, 93, 114–15, 147, 152, 157, 159, 201–43 passim, 255
Freethy, A.E. 190
Fright, Bill 175, 178

Furlong, Neville 19

Gadney, Bernard 193–4
Gage, Davy 66, 256
Gallagher, John 86, 115
Gallaher, Dave 67–9, 72, 119, 189–90
Galwey, Mick 19
Geddes, Keith 73
Geffin, Aaron 172–3, 179
Gentles, Tommy 180
Gibbs, J.C. 190
Gibbs, Scott 201, 211
Gifford, Phil 248
Gilbert, Mike 250
Gillespie, Boyd 261
Ginge, see Paul Henderson
Gleeson, Jack 104, 134, 151, 155, 161, 163
Graham, John 82, 131, 220
Grant, Lachie 172
Gray, Bill 174, 176
Gray, Ken 131
Gray, Neil 14, 26, 43–6, 57, 59–60, 115, 203–43 passim
Green, Frank 170–1
Gregan, George 12
Grenside, Bert 192
Griffiths, Alf 73
Griffiths, Jack 13, 171, 250
Grizz, see Alex Wyllie
Guscott, Jeremy 102, 201

Haden, Andy 86, 217–18, 227
Hadley, Bill 13, 74, 76, 137, 193, 248
Halpin, Garrett 19
Hardham, Major William 67
Harrigan, Charlie 71
Hart, George 249–50
Hart, Gus 70
Hart, John 16, 18, 90, 93, 96, 99, 100–2, 104–5, 111, 115, 142, 152–3, 159–60, 183, 248, 255, 261, 265, 268, 270, 275–8, 282
Harvey, Lester 154
Hastings, Gavin 201, 208, 212–13, 240–1
Hegglun, Tris 171
Hemi, Ron 175–7
Henderson, Paul 19–56 passim, 156
Hewitt, Frank 190–1
Hewitt, Norm 106, 281
Hill, Tiny 177–9

Hobbs, Jock 139–40, 156, 271
Hobden, E.D. 66–7
Hoeft, Carl 281
Honiball, Henry 101
Horsley, Ron 82
Howarth, Shane 114
Howe, Brian (Peewee) 179
Howitt, Bob 119
Hunter, Gordon 16, 100

Iceman, see Michael Jones
Ieremia, Alama 106, 187–8, 279–80
Inga, see Va'aiga Tuigamala
Innes, Craig 225, 279

Jarden, Ron 174–5, 179–80
Jenkins, Vivian 199
JK see John Kirwan
Johns, Pat 19
Johnson, Martin 201
Johnson, Peter 162–3, 196
Johnson, Robert 67
Johnstone, Peter 77, 126, 136, 170
Jones, Ian 19–59 passim, 110, 112, 198,
    201–39 passim, 265, 277, 281–2
Jones, Michael 12, 19–57 passim, 86, 98,
    115, 201–43 passim, 277–9
Jones, Peter 174–9
Jones, Robert 201
Joseph, Jamie 201–39 passim

Kamo, see Ian Jones
Kane, Greg 269–70
Karam, Joe 93
Kearns, Phil 197
Kendrew, Douglas 194
Kenny, Paddy 19
Kerr, J.M. 72, 192–3
Kilby, Frank 119, 135–6
Kingan, Jesse 171
Kingston, Terry 19
Kirk, David 86, 114–15, 140–2, 152, 269,
    272
Kirkpatrick, Ian 115
Kirton, Earle 14–16, 25–61 passim, 113,
    142, 147, 156, 247
Kirwan, John 11, 16, 19–60 passim, 86, 115,
    138, 142, 160, 187–8, 201–42 passim,
    247, 254
Knight, Gary 184

Knight, Lindsay 119–20
Koch, Chris 178
Kronfeld, Josh 109, 277, 279

Laidlaw, Chris 92, 158
Lambourn, Artie 170–1
Lamby, see Blair Larsen
Larsen, Blair 19–55 passim, 114, 281
Lawlor, Jack 144
Lawton, Tom 136
Leonard, Jason 201, 207
Leslie, Andy 14, 159, 183, 187
Little, Paul 156
Little, Walter 19–55 passim, 147, 279–80
Loane, Mark 125
Lochore, Brian 17, 35, 64, 69, 86, 90, 105,
    115, 117, 119–22, 124–5, 128, 130–4,
    137–8, 141–3, 149–52, 154, 156, 158–
    9, 161, 163, 182–3, 220
Loe, Richard 112, 114, 188, 247, 252
Lomu, Jonah 11, 90–1, 93, 101, 106, 109,
    115, 197–8, 277, 279–80
Lord, David 85
Louw, Rob 184
Loveridge, Dave 264
Lyster, Pat 170

MacEwan, Nevan 13, 177, 181
Mains, Laurie 12, 14–18, 20–61 passim,
    88, 90–1, 93, 96, 105, 110–11, 113,
    115, 117, 142, 146–7, 152, 156, 158–
    9, 183, 187, 203–45 passim, 255, 270,
    276, 278
Maka, Isitolo 279
Malan, Avril 173, 181
Manchester, Jack 136, 194
Marshall, Justin 106, 109, 277, 280
Marslin, Arthur 176
Maxwell, Norm 281
Mayerhofler, Mark 279–80
Mayhew, Dr John 39, 42–3, 47, 57, 238–9,
    241
McCall, Mark 19
McCallum, Ian 183
McCarthy, Paul 19
McCarthy, Winston 177, 182
McDonald, Alex 145, 155, 172, 182
McDowell, Steve 19–60 passim
McGeechan, Ian 240
McIntosh, Don 81, 176

McKenzie, Craig 13
McKenzie, Norman 170
McLean, Hugh 13, 76, 136, 169
McLean, Jack 171
McLean, Sir Terence (T.P.) 64, 119, 158, 172, 191, 194
McLeod, Scott 279–80
McMillan, Neville 119
McMullen, Frank 181
McNab, Jack 154
McPhail, Neil 77, 124, 134, 155–6, 171
Meads, Colin 11, 35, 82, 86, 115, 123, 131, 141, 156, 159, 182–3, 187–8, 252, 269, 272, 274, 277
Meates, Bill 84
Meeuws, Kees 281
Mehrtens, Andrew 109, 115, 280–3
Meldrum, Brigadier General William 72
Meredith, Vinnie (later Sir Vincent) 155, 248, 250
Mill, Jimmy 74, 167, 191
Milliken, Harold 76, 145
Milne, Ken 201
Mitchell, John 105, 269
Mitchell, N.A. (Brushy) 169
Monkley, Duane 153
Moore, Brian 201
Morkel, P.K. 168
Morris, Dewi 201
Morrison, Tom 145, 176–8
Mostert, Phil 167–8
Mourie, Graham 13, 83, 104, 119–20, 122, 124–6, 130, 134, 138, 143, 148, 155, 163, 269
Mulder, Jaapie 102
Mullen, Karl 80
Muller, Hennie 172
Muller, Brian (Jazz) 248
Mulligan, Andy 131, 133
Munro, Charles John 63
Murdoch, Keith 248
Murphy, Ken 19, 57
Murphy, Noel 34–5

Nathan, Waka 154
Nel, Phil 168
Nepia, George 13, 74–5, 84, 191
Nicholls, Mark 13, 154, 167–8, 192
Nola, George 175
Norrie, D. 120

Obolensky, Alex 194
Ofahengaue, Willie 28
Oliver, Anton 281
Oliver, Charlie 136, 250
Oliver, Frank 125
Osborne, Bill 279
Osborne, Glen 109

Page, Colonel J.R. (Rusty) 170, 249
Palenski, Ron 119, 191
Palmer, Brian 196–7
Parker, A.C. 127, 172
Parkinson, Frank 174
Parkinson, Reuben 279
Pearce, Tom 155, 177
Pene, Arran 19–58 passim, 201–39 passim
Phillips, Jock 92
Pienaar, Theo 73
Pinetree, see Colin Meads
Popplewell, Nick 19, 201, 207
Porter, Cliff 13, 119, 129, 136
Preston, Jon 19–58 passim, 201–43 passim

Rabin, Patrick 226, 240
Ralph, Caleb 279
Randell, Taine 276, 279, 281–3
Randle, Roger 280
Ranfurly, Lord 68
Reid, Ponty 136, 174, 177
Reid, Tori 136, 169, 269
Rewi, see Arran Pene
Richards, Dean 201, 207, 213, 221, 223
Richardson, Jock 73–4, 119, 123, 129, 135, 145, 190
Rigger, see Mark Cooksley
Rigney, Brian 19
Rives, Jean-Pierre 124–5
Roberts, Kevin 255, 270, 281
Robertson, Bruce 183, 279
Robinson, Brian 19
Robinson, Mark 259–67, 269, 280
Rope, Bryce 158
Roper, Alan 196–7
Rosenberg, Wilf 180
Russell, David 93
Russell, Peter 19, 51

Salizzo, Ric 227
Saxton, Charlie 13, 69, 78, 161
Scott, Bob 172–3

Scott-Young, Sam 228
Serfontein, Divan 183–4
Shehadie Sir Nicholas 199
Shelford, Frank 121
Shelford, Wayne 86–7, 108, 111, 115, 119–21, 123–4, 126, 128–33, 135, 138, 140, 142, 148–9, 151–2, 163, 187, 200, 265
Simpson, Johnny 128–9, 154, 173
Skinner, Kevin 13, 123, 140, 172–4, 176–9, 199
Slack, Andrew 162–3, 197
Sloane, Peter 282
Smith, Lee 21
Smith, Steve 19, 57
Spencer, Carlos 280
Stanley, Jeremy 280
Stanley, Joe 115, 248, 279
Staples, Jim 19, 22, 51, 57
Stead, J.W. 69, 190
Steel, Tony 92
Stensness, Lee 201–44 passim
Stewart, J.J. 127, 145, 157–8, 183
Storey family 71–2
Strachan, Ant 19–58 passim, 147, 201–38 passim, 261, 264
Stuart, Bob 137, 176
Stuart, Donald 73
Sullivan, Jack 155, 170–1, 176, 181
Sye, Gary 39, 53, 203, 208, 232, 234, 237

Tanner, Haydn 195
Tauroa, Hiwi 151
Taylor, Mark 279
Teague, Mike 201
Thimbleby, Neil 17
Thomas, J.B.G. 82
Thorburn, Peter 14–16, 26, 30–1, 39, 56, 120, 203–45 passim, 270
Thorne, Graham 92, 124–5, 137, 182
Thornett, John 126
Timu, John 19–60 passim, 201–42 passim
Tindill, Eric 250
Tipoki, Rua 279
Tonks, Eddie 237
Tonu'u, Ofisa 280
Toomey, Marty 36
Tremain, Kel (Bunny) 115, 123, 131, 248

Tuigamala, Va'aiga 19–60 passim, 201–43 passim
Turner, Richard 88
Turtill, H.S. (Jum) 72

Ulyate, Clive 164, 180
Umaga, Tana 280
Underwood, Rory 201, 236
Upham, Charles 72

van der Merwe, Bertus 175
van der Westhuizen, Jacob 167–8
Vidiri, Joeli 280
Vincent, Pat 175–7
Vodanovich, Ivan 157, 182
Voyce, Tom 191

Wallace, Billy 145, 154
Walsh, Pat 177
Warbrick, Joe 66
Ward, Ron 13
Waterman, Alf 13, 75, 129
Watson, Eric 138
Webb, C.S.H. 194
Weller, Sam 78
Wesney, Arthur 170
Whetton, Gary 16, 115, 134, 141, 141–2, 157, 160
Whineray, Wilson 82, 92, 119–22, 124–7, 130–5, 137, 140, 147, 149–50, 159, 163, 180, 181, 220
White, H.L. 'Snow' 199
White, Tiny 174, 178–80
Williams, Bryan 182
Williams, J.P.R. 198
Willis, Royce 281
Wilson, Colin 170
Wilson, Frank 71–2
Wilson, Jeff 93, 106, 277, 280–1
Wilson, Nathaniel Arthur 166–7
Wilson, Stu 202
Winterbottom, Peter 201, 209, 212, 221
Wyllie, Alex 11, 105, 140, 142, 145, 156–7, 159
Wynyard, Jim 250–1
Wynyard, Tabby 66

Young, Dennis 177